His Humble Servant

Sister M. Pascalina Lehnert with Pope John Paul II.
Courtesy of *L'Osservatore Romano*.

His Humble Servant

Sister M. Pascalina Lehnert's Memoirs of Her Years
of Service to Eugenio Pacelli, Pope Pius XII

By Sister M. Pascalina Lehnert

Translated by Susan Johnson

ST. AUGUSTINE'S PRESS
South Bend, Indiana

Translated from the German: Ich durfte ihm dienen:
Erinnerungen an Papst Pius XII by Sr. M. Pascalina Lehnert
Würzburg, 10th edition, 1996
Original translation of U.K. English, edited to U.S. English.
Explanatory footnotes and background material added.

Manufactured in the United States of America

2 3 4 5 6   26 25 24 23 22 21

Library of Congress Cataloging in Publication Data
Pascalina, Sister, 1894–
[Ich durfte ihm dienen. English]
His humble servant: Sister M. Pascalina Lehnert's memoirs of her years of
service to Eugenio Pacelli, Pope Pius XII / by Sister M. Pascalina Lehnert;
translated by Susan Johnson. – 1st [edition].
pages cm
Includes bibliographical references and index.
ISBN 978-1-58731-367-7 (paperbound: alk. paper)
1. Pius XII, Pope, 1876–1958. 2. Popes – Biography. I. Title.
BX1378.P3313 2014
282.092 – dc23   2013042090
[B]

∞ The paper used in this publication meets the minimum requirements of the
American National Standard for Information Sciences – Permanence of Paper for
Printed Materials, ANSI Z39.481984.

ST. AUGUSTINE'S PRESS
www.staugustine.net

Contents

Ad maiorem Dei gloriam

PREFACE

Most of the following reminiscences were already written down in the spring of 1959, that is, just a few months after the death of Pius XII. This was done on the instructions of my Mother Superior, who considered it advisable to set down a record of what I had come to know and could recall about the life of this great Pope in the course of my humble and limited duties in his household. It was clear to me from the start that, compared to a comprehensive biography, this was not enough to justify publication. For this reason, I have hesitated time and again to hand over the manuscript. My hesitation seems to have been proved correct by the fact that in the meantime I have been able to add this or that episode as it was brought to light in, for example, conversations with friends. Nevertheless, I am even now painfully aware of the incompleteness of these reminiscences.

Meanwhile many years have passed. Inquisitiveness has turned its attention to other persons and spheres, while genuine interest has remained, and requests are still received daily for information about the life of this great Pope.

Let this simple portrayal of his life as it presented itself to me be dedicated to those of all creeds and nations who recall Pius XII with pleasure.

Rome, Summer 1982
Sister M. Pascalina Lehnert
Teaching Sisters of the Holy Cross (Menzingen)

TRANSLATOR'S FOREWORD

When this translation was only half completed, news came of the unexpected death on November 13, 1983, of Sister M. Pascalina, who had been so lovingly and patiently awaiting the English version of this final tribute to the man she served for forty years with humble admiration and devotion (cf. the literal translation of the German title *I Was Allowed to Serve Him*). In her correspondence, she expressed her joy that the English version would be able to reach a worldwide readership to which the German version, first published in autumn 1982, could never gain access. This translation was completed in January 1984, but without Sister Pascalina, no one seemed to know how to move the project forward to publication. Finally, thanks to Bruce Fingerhut of St. Augustine's Press and to Sister Hedwig Cichy, Provincial Superior of the Order of the Holy Cross, this English translation commissioned by Sister Pascalina nearly 30 years ago is going to print.

After Pius XII's death, Sister M. Pascalina lived in the suburbs of Rome at the "Casa Pastor Angelicus" belonging to her Order, trying to keep out of the public eye, and suffering enormously at certain vicious attacks made on the memory of Pius XII and even on herself. The present book contains much to disprove these accusations, but anyone who expects a systematic analysis of Pius XII's theology, ecclesiology, social teaching, diplomacy, and political acumen will be disappointed. Its form is narrative, recounting daily life as the "Madre"—as Pius XII called her although she in fact was a simple sister within her Order—experienced it in her capacity as housekeeper, private secretary, and organizer of the international relief service from the Pope's private storerooms. Certainly, theology, diplomacy, and pastoral commitment are all touched on in the book, but what it centers on is the man Eugenio Pacelli.

In accordance with the instruction given by Pope John Paul II regarding the publication of the German text that Sister Pascalina's original manuscript should not be revised in any way, this translation attempts to remain faithful to the style of the German text, which speaks from the heart in its simplicity, sincerity, and boundless admiration. Colloquialisms, repetitions, simple syntax, frequent exclamations, as well as terms and titles of respect and reverence have been retained in English as far as possible so as to retain the flavor of these reminiscences, which were not originally intended for publication. Some Italian phrases and names have been left to provide "local color" where this does not impede understanding, but there are far fewer of these than in the German edition. In the chapters dealing with the Nuncio's time in Germany much of the effect of the direct speech depends on the use of Bavarian and Swiss dialect, an effect that has unfortunately been lost in translation. Another loss is the unavoidable use of "I" and "we" for the German word for "one," wherever a passive was not possible. The German usage was a sign of Sister Pascalina's humility, of trying to keep herself out of the book (which she admitted was one of the most difficult tasks in writing these reminiscences). She constantly emphasizes the humility of Pius XII: this book is proof of her own.

May readers also remember Sister M. Pascalina as they learn more about her saintly "master" in these pages, even though she herself in everything echoed the words of Saint John the Baptist: "He must increase, but I must decrease" (Jn 3:30).

May 1, 2012
Feast of Saint Joseph the Worker
Susan Johnson

PROLOGUE

FROM THE DIARY OF A FIFTEEN-YEAR-OLD

After the death of our Holy Father Pius XII, a number of personal notes were found among the surviving school exercise books and lecture files. They were thoughts written from the heart by the fifteen-year-old schoolboy: precious insights for us into the inner world of a young person who was to become one of our greatest and most revered Popes. Let us now quote a passage from these notes addressed "to myself":

> There is someone who entered life as a good, devout person loving God and religion, but who then, perhaps blinded by vain delusions, began to have doubts. I feel sorry for him, for peace has soon abandoned him: that peace of mind, the firstborn daughter of God, the peace that proceeds solely from the certain knowledge of possessing the truth. This person has Hell in his heart; whereas before he knew only joy, now pain has become his pasture, pain his repose, pain even his hope. With sad eyes he watches those who, kneeling in their churches, send up their devout prayers to God. He watches them and the sweet memory of times past, which may never return, floods into his mind; a recollection of the days when he believed and was united with the happy throng of the faithful, when God filled his heart with ineffable joy . . . and he weeps! The unhappy man! Where will he find solace? Will he turn to his friends? But which of them will lend him wings to soar like an eagle from this miserable earth to the loftiest heights, and rend the evil veil that always and everywhere surrounds him? To that Heaven, for others so serene and beautiful but for him like molten lead, that Heaven he hates? Will he return to prayer, the only solace of mortal man? Alas! For while he attempts to lift up his heart, he is beset by even more violent doubt: "What if God does not exist at all?" But that is too much, that is the culmination of pain;

}1{

the poor man cannot bear it any longer, he struggles for breath, his voice is strangled in his throat, he runs his hands wildly through his hair, closes his eyes . . . Does he then perhaps wish for death, or does he rather wish he had never been born? Dear God, enlighten him!

For the young Eugenio Pacelli, whose faith was the meaning and heart of life, being beset by doubts in this way must have been veritable Hell. Probably only very few people will appreciate the depth of the suffering that comes across in these lines written on August 17, 1891. But the entreaty "Dear God, enlighten him!" was to become—on the loftiest level—an unparalleled act of self-sacrifice for *every* endangered soul. Inspired with love, as Pope he would fight constantly for souls. He would suffer and pray for them, labor selflessly, and help them untiringly to overcome the terrors of World War II, and amid all the dangers of those times, to preserve unharmed or find anew their most precious possession: faith. Moreover, in so doing, he was to strive unfalteringly toward heights that allow us to recognize or at least sense an ultimate, grace-given, human realization and perfection. Has any Pope ever bequeathed to mankind so rich an inheritance as Pius XII, who faced up to all the problems of his time, taking them upon himself so as to shield others from danger as far as it was within his power? "Meek and humble of heart" like his Divine Master, he drew during his lifetime countless people into the light of the Catholic Church in an epoch of false doctrines carried to the degree of madness. To those who are searching, he still continues to give an answer to the urgent questions of their hearts and times. Again and again, one hears of people who, overwhelmed by grace while occupying themselves with him, have embraced the Cross, never to let go of it again.

Admittedly, the most beautiful aspects of this unique personality are bound to remain a secret forever. Nor should I dare to write down these few brief reminiscences of the time I was allowed to spend close to the Holy Father Pius XII if obedience did not require it of me. I am infinitely grateful for the gift of these long and yet so short forty years in which I had the privilege to see and speak to a truly great person and prelate day in and day out. May God grant that my poor, inadequate words will at least not detract too much from the wonderful spectacle I was permitted to witness!

CHAPTER ONE

AN ENVOY OF PEACE TO THE WORLD

March 1918! As a young nun I was endeavoring to teach a crowd of girls in a little Swabian village—among other things—the skills of sewing and needlework. In the few months since the beginning of school, the children's enthusiasm had increased so much that there was an outcry of regret when a telegram arrived from the Provincial House summoning me to Altötting. I told the children confidently, "Tomorrow, Tuesday, there's no school, but I'm sure to be back on Wednesday." That "Wednesday" never came, since I was instructed to go to the nunciature in Munich as a temporary help for two months and this "temporary help" never ended.

His Excellency the Nuncio was not at home when we two sisters entered the house—he had just been called away to Rome—and we tried to accustom ourselves to our new task. At the beginning it was not easy to satisfy the two Monsignors: the Auditor, Monsignor Schioppa; and the Secretary. However, with my twenty-three-year-old's cheerfulness this did not trouble me particularly. The big old house was in need of a thorough cleaning, and the sister in charge of the cooking had to get used to the Italian cuisine too.[1]

After about a week the Nuncio returned from Rome. What should I say about this first meeting? Involuntarily one hesitated a moment before taking the slender hand to kiss the ring. It went without saying that one knelt before such a person, not because Eugenio Pacelli was in any way authoritarian—nothing is more ridiculous than to maintain that he was—but because he simply inspired respect. Never had we come across such majestic kindness.

---

1   According to the Order's Archives, the following sisters served in Munich during the years 1917–1925: Sister Pascalina Lehnert, Sister Bonifatia Walle, Sister Johanna Kolb, Sister Antonia Reichenberger, Sister Theodosia Weber, and Sister Hilaria Wagner.

A few friendly words in not quite perfect German were the first greeting the Nuncio addressed to us two sisters.

The daily routine brought a great deal of work, and in order to fulfill what everyone expected of us, we got up very early and went to Mass at the nearby church of St. Boniface. However, it was not long before the Nuncio asked why we did not stay in the house, where there were three Masses every morning. So the next morning—it was a Sunday—we attended the Nuncio's Holy Mass for the first time. This was a wonderful experience and one to be repeated again and again during the next forty years.

His very appearance in the house's simple chapel already lent everything a note of solemnity. His genuflection, which bore such glorious witness to his faith; the way he made the sign of the cross, dignified and yet humble; his preparations; his putting on of the vestments for Mass with every syllable of the accompanying prayers audible; and then the Holy Mass itself. It was moving and convincing in such a new way that one knew with infinite joy that there could be no other truth—even if one did not think it in words but simply felt that everything about it was utterly genuine. After this first occasion, I did not miss a single opportunity in all the forty years and more to attend his Holy Masses.

Moreover, I was not the only one to take this impression away with me. At the Catholic Congress in Munich, where the then-Archbishop, Michael von Faulhaber, delivered an address, the Nuncio celebrated a Pontifical Mass on August 27, 1922. Immediately after the celebration, the Archbishop came to see me at the nunciature and said, "I have just attended the most moving Mass in my life. Only a saint can celebrate like that!" My reply was, "It's the same experience every day, Your Excellency!"

What struck me about His Excellency Eugenio Pacelli from the very beginning was his precision everywhere and in everything: punctual at Mass, punctual at work and at audiences, punctual for meals, punctual for walks. How greatly this lightened the work even though it did not always make life easy for those working with him. Despite all his high-minded consideration in his dealings with the secretaries, the Nuncio wished for precision and strict adherence to schedules from them too. He was full of understanding for anyone who did not find the work so easy, but time-wasting and idleness were repugnant to him.

One of Eugenio Pacelli's longstanding collaborators (Father Leiber) always said whenever he saw a superficial or half-hearted piece of work,

"It would do him good to have to spend a few months working with the Nuncio. He'd soon mend his ways!"

The Nuncio had already acquired a good knowledge of German in Rome, but he had only read the language, never spoken it. During his first few months in Munich he had very little time to spare, but then he began all the more conscientiously to take regular German lessons. And the schedule was kept to exactly. Day by day, there was more progress to be seen. Neither of us sisters understood a word of Italian and so he was forced to talk to us in German, enjoining upon us that we were to correct him at once if he made a mistake.

It sometimes happened that the German secretary was not in the house when the Nuncio was working on a letter or document, the exact content of which he was not quite sure about. On such occasions, he would ask and not rest until he had received a completely satisfactory and exhaustive answer. It was not long before it was said at the Foreign Office that the Nuncio wrote the best and clearest German.

Despite all his eagerness to learn pure and precise German, he liked to repeat particularly novel Bavarian dialect expressions, which sounded really delightful on his lips and which he never forgot again. To the delight of the pilgrims and others present, even as Pope he was still able, when the occasion arose, to use one of these expressions learned right at the beginning of his stay in Bavaria. With his indefatigable industry and his excellent memory, the Nuncio soon acquired a complete command of German so that, toward the end of the war, he was able to conduct extremely difficult negotiations in it. But how well he made use of his time! Even then, he did not waste a minute of the day right until late in the night.

World War I was still raging. As early as 1917, on the instructions of Benedict XV, the Nuncio had already gone to the German headquarters in Kreuznach—but how disappointed he had returned. There had been no lack of friendliness, but despite all his efforts the Nuncio had failed to achieve what he wanted, namely to persuade the Kaiser to enter into peace negotiations. A deaf ear was turned to all his proposals and he was forced to regard his mission as a total failure.

Thinking back today on that time, when we Germans still all believed that our weapons would be victorious and the Nuncio was deeply sorry that the chance had been missed to save what there was to save, it occurs to me over and over again how clearly he foresaw what was to come. Once, as he traced the course of the Rhine with his finger on a map, he said sadly, "No doubt that will be lost as well." I did not want to believe it, but here too, he was to be proved right.

Now the Nuncio tried to bring relief and help to the prisoners of war. Pope Benedict XV, whose heart was moved by the distress of these poor people, sent railway trucks full of provisions of all kinds. How long it had been in these difficult years since people had seen all these things—tinned meat and milk, but also masses of woolen underwear. Bearing these gifts, the Nuncio went into the prison camps. The mere announcement of his visit was a comfort to the prisoners, for now everyone became friendly, from the Commandant down to the last soldier. The barracks were repaired, blankets were put on the plank beds, and the infirmary received medicaments and bandages. The prisoners also were given new clothes. And then the Nuncio himself really came to them! He was accompanied by the Commandant and officers in full dress uniform. On reaching the prisoners, the Nuncio as quick as lightning removed himself from his escort and was among the prisoners, addressing a friendly word to each of them in their beloved mother tongue. To all he brought the greetings and blessing of the Holy Father; he gave consolation, strengthened their trust in God's help, and willingly undertook to carry out small errands. This was not only with the Italians; it was the same with French, English, Russian and Polish prisoners. On returning from such visits, His Excellency joyfully recounted his experiences there, which were uplifting and brought happiness to both him and the prisoners. Hundreds of letters testify to the gratitude and joy of the poor prisoners, whose hearts the Nuncio's goodness had taken by storm. From the nunciature contact was maintained with the prisoners and help given as far as was possible. How many relatives could be sent news, how much real distress alleviated!

Many years later I chanced to meet a man in Rome who described to me with visible pleasure the Nuncio's visit to the prison camp. This man had been among the Italian prisoners and his greatest sorrow was that he had no news whatever of his wife and children. The Nuncio had made it possible for him to send a letter. Soon afterwards, a reply came back from his family, again via the nunciature. Many of his comrades had done the same, he said, and from then on their imprisonment had been only half as difficult to bear.

In those difficult times, it was not easy for the sister in charge of the cooking to get hold of food that agreed with the Nuncio's sensitive stomach, especially since he did not allow any exceptions to be made for him. Gradually, however, ways and means were found to get things in from outside. Thus the stomach trouble, undoubtedly caused in part by the completely different diet, gradually subsided. But to the Nuncio such things were mere trifles, for he lived exclusively for his noble task and left no stone unturned to help the nation to whom the Holy Father had sent him. The distress was not restricted to the prison camps; it was everywhere. Even those who still possessed money could not buy anything with it. There was nothing to be had, neither food nor clothing. Thus word soon spread when another goods wagon arrived from the Vatican.

How many people went in and out of the nunciature in those days! Just one small episode: people knew exactly when the Nuncio left the house for his walk and a little old lady wanted to wait and catch him to see if there was anything to be had for her. She stood at the corner of the house, but not well enough concealed, so the Nuncio saw her just as he was about to leave. He went up to her and asked if there was anything he could do for her. Somewhat embarrassed, she confessed that she had been waiting for him to leave the house in order to ask for something. The Nuncio accompanied her into the house and waited until her two bags had been filled to the brim, sharing the good woman's happiness with her. "So, now I want to help you carry it home," he said. "No, no," came the energetic reply, "I'll do that myself. I'd die for shame if Your Excellency carried my bags for me." And she waited until the Nuncio had left the house accompanied by her professions of gratitude before setting off home with her burden. To us she said, "However much we may need all this, the loveliest thing is that I had a chance to experience the Nuncio in all his immense kindness of heart."

It came as the Nuncio had prophesied: the sad collapse of Germany, the armistice, and the revolution.

His Excellency suffered a severe attack of influenza and his doctor advised sending the patient to his clinic. One day we sisters were about to go out to see how the Nuncio was, when we came up against two men trying to force their way into the nunciature. At first we resisted, but the door was pushed open and an insolent voice shouted for the Nuncio's car to be handed over. I told him that His Excellency was not at home, that the secretaries had also gone out and that we did not have the right to hand over something that did not belong to us. In the meantime, the servant had rushed to the scene, and numb with terror, tried to pull me away, whispering, "Can't you see the revolvers in the hands of those...?" I had never in my life seen a revolver, so I remained quite calm and explained to the intruders that we could not do what they wanted and anyway did not have the key to the garage. Now they turned to the servant, who was so terrified he could hardly speak, and pushed him in front of them to open the garage for them. At that moment, the front door bell rang and I rushed to open the door. There in front of me stood the Nuncio. At the sight of him, the two Spartacists were as if paralyzed. His Excellency quickly grasped the situation, declared calmly that both the house and his person were extra-territorial, and called upon the men, who were still standing in front of him as if stunned, to leave the house immediately. Shaking off the spell, they shouted insolently, their revolvers against the Nuncio's chest, that they would not leave without the car. In the meantime, I had managed to make a telephone call. The Revolutionary Government had let His Excellency know several days before that if the nunciature was in any danger, a telephone call to them would bring immediate help. However, to my horror the answer was, "If the car is not handed over at once, I'll line the whole lot up against the wall!" I hurried to inform the Nuncio and whispered to him what had been said to me on the telephone. He gave the order for the garage to be opened. However, a few days before he had given instructions for the car to be immobilized, so the men were unable to make it budge from the spot. A passing car was then stopped, our car attached to it and towed to a garage.

This all happened in just under an hour, but what this hour held in the way of upset and terror only those know who lived through it.

Two hours later our chauffeur brought the car back safely to our garage since the Spartacists had suddenly been in a great hurry to get away and had dropped everything.

The Nuncio was later threatened a second time and ordered to leave the nunciature and the country. But when he stated quite firmly and categorically that he would never leave his post, the men went away again. Soon these turbulent days passed and the Nuncio could devote all his energies to alleviating the distress of the postwar period, consoling, helping, supporting all in word and deed. His noble goodness was renowned everywhere and no one turned to him for help in vain during these terrible times. There was a lot to do since inquiries about prisoners and missing persons flooded in, in their thousands, alongside the petitions. Thanks to His Excellency's precise planning and utilization of his time, everything was duly dealt with: prayer and work had their rightful places. The evening rosary together in the private chapel was never missed and we were always uplifted by the concentrated composure of the master of the house. All the same, nothing ever escaped his notice. Once, for example, he asked me after the rosary if I had heard how the other sister pronounced "Kir*che*" (Church) like "Kir*sche*" (cherry) in the Creed. For a long time after that, I had to pull myself together so as not to laugh about the "Holy Catholic Cherry" when we were supposed to be praying. In other cases as well, His Excellency noticed immediately if we pronounced something incorrectly or unclearly and corrected us at once.

The Nuncio was never unfriendly or moody. His invariable cheerfulness infected everyone around him with happiness. He could join in the laughter when some prank had gone off well and spurred us on to gaiety. He never took a well-meant joke amiss. He could not understand how anyone could be offended at being the target of a witty idea. But if he noticed—and he was distinctly gifted with insight into people's natures—that someone could not take a joke, however well it was meant, he would say, "You were born on the wrong planet," but carefully avoided hurting such a person's feelings, an act of consideration he made it the duty of others to practice too. Thus despite all the work, worry, and troubles, the old house in the Brienner Strasse was filled with a pleasant atmosphere felt by everyone. Archbishop von Faulhaber, who came regularly to confer with the Nuncio, often said to me, "How good you have it at the nunciature!"

Whenever His Excellency had something to celebrate, everyone shared his happiness with him. One such occasion was the silver jubilee of his ordination in 1924. It was to be celebrated quietly with the members of the household, but the great love and respect the Nuncio enjoyed brought young and old to delight him with presents great and small. We had secretly festooned the large drawing room since we knew that His Excellency seldom went into it and would not be surprised if he found it locked. And lo, it was not too large for all the tables and furniture in it to be richly laden with the gifts that love brought to this celebration: hand-embroidered Eucharistic vestments, the finest albs, surplices, altar linen, chalices, hand-painted altar cards, miters, and above all a large number of very valuable books, which even then were the Nuncio's greatest joy.

CHAPTER TWO

HAPPY TIMES AT "STELLA MARIS"
AND IN MUNICH

Unfortunately, the Nuncio's health had suffered a great deal in the recent past, so Archbishop von Faulhaber advised him to do as his doctor said and allow himself a change of air and relaxation. He said he knew of a very nice house on Lake Constance where he himself had stayed while visiting internment camps in Switzerland. To my great surprise, it was a house belonging to our order in Switzerland and so I had the honor of accompanying His Excellency and staying there too. But if Archbishop von Faulhaber thought that the Nuncio really would rest and recuperate there, he was mistaken. All the reports for Rome, all important pieces of work were now dealt with at "Stella Maris" in Rorschach, which His Excellency became very fond of right from his very first stay there. Here, as at home, he worked all day long. Nothing disturbed him. When French lessons began with their constant repetitions of "en, in, on, un" in the classrooms over his study, I asked whether he could work with this in the background, but he was so engrossed in what he was doing that he did not hear anything at all. Nevertheless, when the weather was good and he walked up and down in front of the house, reading or studying, it often happened that he said afterwards, "The lesson went badly today; the children didn't pay attention." One can imagine how this spurred the children on, for they were never sure whether the Nuncio might be listening to them. It was altogether a happy event for young and old at the lovely house on Lake Constance when he stayed there. In letters to their parents, the children painted a colorful picture of the eminent visitor and people came not just on account of the children but also in order to be allowed to greet the important guest. How lovely the celebrations at the Institute were with His Excellency present! What a joy it was to act in a play in front of him, to recite a poem, to be allowed to display little skills! And when the Nuncio even visited the school, the delight of the little ones knew no bounds.

People tried in all sorts of ways to meet him and be allowed to shake his hand and kiss his ring, to snatch a smile or a word from him. The children knew exactly when and where he was to be seen; they were soon familiar with his habits down to the last detail. Even though it was in fact forbidden to linger in the visitors' corridor, they invented all kinds of excuses to stage a "chance" meeting; but it was not uncommon for them also to admit openly something like, "I knew that I'd meet Your Excellency now, so I came this way." It was the tiniest ones who were his favorites, and they were also always the most artful. They regularly went to bed earlier than the other children and so, if they were clever about it, they bumped into the Nuncio just as he was going to dinner. The sister overlooked these little tricks since these encounters were to her advantage too. When the little band came rushing up to him, he would ask the teacher whether the children had been good and worked hard. Then he would look closely at each little forehead, and the children were firmly convinced that he could read it, for he told them what they had done wrong and where they ought to do better, etc. Sometimes a child would hide and not be there because she had a guilty conscience. But that did not help. There was nothing for it but to come, and in the end the child was glad to have done so because His Excellency was always so kind and understanding that she went to bed contented and full of joy. What things came to light at this evening "parade"! The children admitted things they had concealed from the sister: the copied work, the broken glass, the neighbor's apron torn in anger, the little task left undone because of wanting to go on playing—all the little sins of the day came out here because His Excellency could have read them on their foreheads anyway! But there was also a pretty little picture for good behavior, a kind word for a little sacrifice, an award for particularly good work, chocolate because all of them were very good children, and again and again, the kind smile and finally the "Good-Night Blessing"—a rich reward and supreme bliss for the children.

When His Excellency was in the house and celebrated the Conventual Mass, every single child was there in the chapel, even on sleeping-in days. And there were no longer any excuses for staying away from the evening rosary. How the children were uplifted by the deep devotion with which the Nuncio celebrated Mass and prayed the rosary! And even if at first they went only because "he" was there, they themselves said later that they had come to love praying so dearly because he had led them so convincingly in prayer. Many years later a former pupil of Stella Maris wrote to me, "The fact that I have never foundered in my faith, have upheld my ideals in a non-religious environment, and still do so in my family, passing them onto my children—this I owe to the wonderful example set to us by Nuncio Pacelli at Stella Maris when I was still a child."

Every afternoon the Nuncio went for the walk that was absolutely essential for his health. As with every other hour, he made good use of this time, whether he went alone or in company. The Spiritual Director, who often accompanied him, said that special preparation was necessary to be knowledgeable enough and to be able to answer questions about the events of the day or other happenings. Yet in spite of this, the beauties of nature did not escape his notice. He delighted in the magnificent flowers, the babbling stream, the nimble squirrel, the peaceful cows, the bright butterflies, and did not fail to notice the little cowherds watching over their cattle. With one of these boys he spoke especially frequently.

"Little boy, what are you doing there all the time with your cows?" asked the Nuncio.

"But, Curate, you can see! Or are you so daft that you don't understand?" came the reply in broad, familiar Swiss German. "I'm looking after the cows to make sure they don't run off or go over to the neighbor's. They do that sometimes, you know; and then there's a slap on the bottom, a real spanking!"

Another time: "Hansli, why have you got that baby carriage with you today?"

"Well, you see, Curate, my mother's gone into the village and Gretel isn't back from school yet, so I just had to bring it along with me!"

"What's in there then, a girl or a boy?"

"What a silly question. It's a baby, what else?"

"Look, Hansli, I've brought you some chocolate. You can share it with the baby."

"How silly you are. As if it could eat stuff like that! It's better if I keep it all. Bring me something again, Curate! Bye!" The Nuncio's companion was doubled over with laughter and had to translate every word afterwards for His Excellency, whose knowledge of Swiss German turned out not to be perfect after all.

Another time the little boy's sister was looking after the cows. "So, where's Hansli today?" asked the Nuncio.

"To begin with he's called Sepp, and anyway I can watch cows just as well as he can. And you, have you ever watched cows?"

"No, never," said the Nuncio.

"How about that! But perhaps you can do my homework for me?" And the Nuncio was handed the book. There were a few sums for him to do.

"Right, that's done; but now you'll have to copy them out again or the teacher will see from the writing that you didn't do them."

"Of course I will. I'm not so stupid that I'll get myself caught."

"Now tell Hansli . . ."

"He's called Sepp!"

". . . All right, tell Sepp that I'm going away again now."

"What a pity, you can't even watch cows and you could have done my homework for me now and then!"

There would be so much to tell, incidents so delightful that even today I cannot help laughing when I think of them. And even years later, His Holiness Pius XII would still laugh when these charming episodes were mentioned.

In the first years of his pontificate, the Holy Father Pius XII sometimes deliberated whether there would be any possibility of returning to his beloved Stella Maris for a few weeks of quiet work there. Unfortunately, the "contras" again and again outweighed the "pros" and so it remained an unfulfilled dream. But the lovely house on Lake Constance can boast for all time of having been for many years a well-loved, modest, yet very cozy vacation home for this eminent prelate. Many hundreds of children will cherish lifelong memories of a man who was to them pastor, confessor, and a particularly shining example of piety and absolutely faithful fulfillment of duty. Yet it was not only the children who loved him. He was constantly at the service of the other occupants of the house too.

Let one example suffice. One day a nun asked to be allowed to speak to the Nuncio. A few days later, I met her and she admitted, "I cannot say how happy I am. I was able to pour out my heart and the Nuncio did not interrupt me once. He just listened in silence, his eyes lowered; and when I had finished, he remained silent for a while before answering the questions I had asked. Finally he looked at me and said, 'Dear Sister, isn't your suffering partly caused by the fact that you are thinking only of yourself instead of HIM to whom you have perpetually consecrated your life?' And again there was a silence while the eyes of the Nuncio seemed to be reading the depths of my soul. Then he stood up, extended his hand with a friendly smile, blessed me and said, 'Courage, dear Sister, seek HIM to whom your whole being belongs and your life as a religious will—even in suffering, sickness and distress—be pure joy!?" Never shall I forget the radiant face of this sister, whom I often met after that and who always assured me how happy she had been since this conversation with the Nuncio.

When I saw Stella Maris again after an absence of twenty-five years, it seemed as if time had passed it by. The simple study had remained the same. At that same desk, His Excellency and His Eminence had sat working hour after hour. There still stood the prie-dieu at which he used to recite his Breviary, when he did not do so in the chapel or out of doors. There, the modest bedroom! Even the chapel had remained just as it was twenty-five years before, beautiful and inviting one to prayer. The same big prie-dieu was still there! Reverently one knelt down, hardly able to believe that the person who had used it so often should no longer be among the living. But his spirit is still tangibly present, and the dear sisters, so many of whom had known him personally, say time and again that they turn to him with their problems and always receive help. Of the many children educated there who like to keep returning to the "Stella," there is not one who does not remember and talk about the beautiful times when as Nuncio—and later as Cardinal—he had stayed there.

The recent death of one of the dear sisters recalled a little episode from those times to my memory. The sister's duties consisted mainly in humble, simple household tasks, and the many children in the house often tried her patience sorely. Nevertheless, she was always cheerful and happy; and even if she did sometimes threaten one of the little imps with a broom, the children never took it badly since she was also the one who showed them with endless patience how to keep cupboards and drawers tidy. She always knew too how to ward off the teachers' reprimands or scoldings, and this was something the little ones certainly noticed. One day it was raining, and the children came home from their walk with dirty shoes. The sister was quickly at hand with rags and pails of water. Just then, the Cardinal came by and she wanted to disappear; but he was quicker than she was. He took the hand holding the dirty rags, and said, "There is nothing. Sister, that escapes the notice of HIM whom you serve, and one day in eternity you will see that humble actions perhaps count for more in the eyes of God than conspicuous ones."

"But, Your Eminence," said the sister, "now you've dirtied your hands."

"That doesn't matter. They can be washed," he said and was gone. The sister told us of this incident afterwards, adding, "The Cardinal does not make a scrap of difference between a domestic sister and himself!"

From Rorschach His Excellency—later His Eminence—always visited the motherhouse in Menzingen. Here too, the children and sisters looked forward to his coming all year long. A Pontifical Mass in the beautiful church, a visit to the school, a "recital" where the children tried to offer their best, especially in singing and music, which they knew the eminent guest to be particularly fond of—all these brought a really festive atmosphere to the house. It went without saying that they were not allowed to make a lot of noise at night because His Eminence worked very late and was also a light sleeper. However, this was recompensed by a day off school, a nice excursion, or whatever else can gladden a child's heart.

Naturally the days there—there were not many of them—were always used to the full so that on the way there the Cardinal's companion (the then-Monsignor Spellman) had the car stop in the last little village before Menzingen in order to bid a formal "farewell" to His Eminence, knowing that its residents would never set eyes on him during his days at the motherhouse. A heartfelt laugh was the Cardinal's reply to his faithful friend and companion.

The Holy Father Pius XII retained Menzingen in loving memory. It was he who, at the request of very many sisters, wished work to begin on preparing the beatification proceedings for the foundress of the Institute of the Teaching Sisters of the Holy Cross ("Menzingen Sisters"), Mother Maria Bernarda Heimgartner. He promoted the work as much as he could. The Holy Father knew the life of Mother Bernarda very well and wished the new seminary being built at Menzingen to bear her name. He even considered attending the consecration of this seminary in October 1958 and was sorry to see that for a number of reasons he would have to forego this.

God called the Holy Father to Himself before that festive day.

In the nunciature in Munich, the servant fell ill and the Nuncio asked the Abbot at Scheyern to send "temporary help" for a short time. So it was that our good Brother Andreas came to the nunciature.[1] This "temporary help" did not turn out to be quite the forty years that it did for me, but all the same a good few years. How fond we all grew of Brother Andreas and how much cause for laughter he gave the Nuncio! He was always cheerful and good-humored, never taking anything to heart. Punctual as a good monk should be, he found favor right from the very beginning with the man who was precision personified. "But," he said in the broadest Bavarian, "you'll have to put up with the way I speak, Your Excellency. I'll never learn Prussian in my old age!" For him proper German was "Prussian." His appearance was a little ridiculous on account of his large, bluish nose, but his behavior and manners were nothing of the sort. He received visitors politely and obligingly in his own way although he was a man of few words. "You see, Excellency," he used to say, "it's better if I keep quiet. You understand my way of talking, but with those people I have to repeat every word three times!" When he served at Mass, it was very dignified and beautiful, and when I once told him so, he said, "Just look at Excellency there. He celebrates like a saint, so there's nothing else to do but concentrate too."

Breakfast used to be laid out ready on the table, and the Nuncio would serve himself so as not to lose any time. However, he sometimes told me that towards the end of it, he often saw Brother Andreas's bluish nose poking through the velvet curtain that separated the dining room from the ante-room. Brother wanted to be there, preferring to drink his coffee cold rather than to miss the moment when he would have a chance to wish his master good morning, to ask him how he had slept, and who would be coming for audiences that day.

When a particularly large number of visitors were expected, he would say something like, "What do you think, couldn't we tell the people it's enough now—the Nuncio is worn out?" Depending on how the morning went, he greeted His Excellency at lunch with "All those people! I wanted to send them away but Sister wouldn't let me." Or "Excellency, folk have been a bit more decent today." Once Archbishop von Faulhaber came unannounced and a little late. Although Brother Andreas liked the Archbishop because he could speak "German," i.e. Bavarian, with him, he said indignantly, "Are you picking up bad manners too, now, and coming late? I hope

1   Brother Andreas Stadler, OSB, served at the nunciature from 1922–1925.

it won't happen again." He told me this at once, adding, "I gave the Archbishop a piece of my mind." While we were still standing together, the bell rang, a sign that the visitor was leaving again quickly. Brother Andreas gave him a further lesson, saying, "Thank God you're being reasonable and going again quickly; people can't go killing our good Excellency with nothing but visits."

Even to ministers and diplomats Brother Andreas made no bones about speaking his mind and there were delightful scenes. However, neither His Excellency nor the visitors took ill of the guileless brother.

How his inexhaustible humor added spice to His Excellency's meals!

"I've already eaten, Excellency, so that I can stay with you. I think you eat a bit more when I'm here. You know, Sister isn't at all pleased when you send so much back."

"What is it today, Brother?" asked the Nuncio.

"That's roast veal—good stuff too—and those are potatoes and that's kohlrabi."

The Nuncio, repeating the word in the dialect form used by Brother Andreas, said "*Koirabi*. What's that then?"

"Oh, it's good feed for pigs."

"What did you say, Brother?" came the reply from His Excellency. The brother, noticing his stupidity, said quickly in great embarrassment, "And for all other animals too!"

"Brother Andreas, what do you think about asking Father Paulus (the farm manager at Scheyern Abbey, about whom Brother Andreas talked a lot to the Nuncio) for an ox since we have such a big garden and all that grass? It would certainly have enough to eat there."

"But, Excellency, an ox doesn't eat just grass; it would lose all its strength."

"Sister could make something else for it, and if there isn't enough grass, you could take it into the English Gardens. There's so much grass there." (Brother Andreas had repeatedly told the Nuncio that he felt it was a pity about all the grass in the English Gardens, which would be so good for all the animals in Scheyern.)

At that, Brother Andreas was at his wits' end. "No, Excellency, you don't understand. It gets into stock-breeding and that's something you have to grow up in!"

"Brother Andreas, I've thought about it a lot, and I want to enter the

Abbey at Scheyern. What do you say to that?" Over and over, the good brother used to tell the Nuncio what things were like in Scheyern and what he'd experienced in his long monastic life there. For him the Abbey was Heaven on earth. Now His Excellency wanted to see how he would react to his suggestion. But the reply that came was not what he would have expected.

"Don't do it, Excellency, that's not for you."

"But why not, Brother? Look at all the people who keep coming, and all the work I have. I'd be better off in a monastery."

"Yes, but what would they do with you? Hearing confessions and preaching aren't easy. And, you know, you'd have to sit way down at the far end of the table. I could make you meals, of course, but it's no good making exceptions all the time in a monastery. You've got to start right at the bottom when you come. Take my advice, Excellency. Don't do it."

"But, Brother, I'm an Archbishop. That's higher than the Abbot, so I'd go right to the top end."

"Put that out of your head, Excellency. There's none of that in monasteries. You can't get around starting at the bottom even if you've been something important before."

But His Excellency did not relent and said he wanted to give going into a monastery a try. And so Brother Andreas came to me because he and the Nuncio had agreed that he should prepare a request for admission for the Abbot at Scheyern. I was supposed to correct it, but naturally I chose not to change a word of this delightful piece of prose and passed it on to the Nuncio just as it was. When he came across it in later years, even as Pope, he could laugh heartily about it and say what good times they were when Brother Andreas cheered and entertained him at meals.

Brother Andreas was attached to his master heart and soul. If the Nuncio had to travel to Berlin, which often occurred toward the end of his stay in Munich—His Excellency was also Nuncio in Berlin—the good brother would stand in the doorway long after the car had left, saying all the time to himself, "Go, but be sure to come back soon!" If the Nuncio stayed away for more than two or three days, Brother Andreas could hardly stand it anymore. "Sister, what do you think; nothing will have happened to him, will it? Can't you find out?" So it was then that we hit upon the idea of preparing the Nuncio a pre-addressed postcard so that he only had to write a greeting on it. When one of these cards arrived, the brother's happiness was complete. "Sister, look what I've got!" The radiant face and the eyes moist with tears bore testimony to his bliss.

"But, Brother Andreas," I said, "I've been at the nunciature so long, and I've never gotten a card."

"Well, you know, Sister, Excellency is very fond of me; but so am I of him."

At that time Monsignor von Preysing—the later Cardinal of Berlin—was Archbishop von Faulhaber's secretary and sometimes would accompany the Nuncio to Berlin. He had the gift of mimicking people so perfectly that you could see the person in question in front of you in the way he walked and carried himself, in the words and voice he used. The Nuncio was often amazed at this and laughed too. I just have to think of how he mimicked Archbishop von Faulhaber and had him off to a T, or Brother Andreas, or so many other people. We once asked him to mimic the Nuncio too, but to our great surprise he said he couldn't. "But why not?" we wanted to know. "His Excellency has something about him that just can't be copied . . ." was his reply!

But now the time came for the final move to Berlin. "Excellency, I don't fit in with those Prussians at all and I'm getting on in years too. It'll be better if I go home to my monastery. It's been hard enough with my language here, you know. And in Berlin not a soul would understand me. But I'll pray every day and I won't forget you. You can count on that!"

"But Brother Andreas," said the Nuncio, "we can't manage without you."

"You'll see, Your Excellency. It'll be all right without me, and the sisters will take good care of you and write and let me know how you're doing. They've already promised."

Never a celebration or day with special memories passed without bringing us a greeting from Brother Andreas, and his letters were just as simple, charming, and cheerful as he always was himself. He never failed to receive a reply from his master, who was very happy to be remembered and often laughed heartily. Brother Andreas lived a good few years longer and his death at the age of eighty-three sincerely grieved His Eminence Pacelli, who in the meantime had become Cardinal Secretary of State in Rome.

CHAPTER THREE

FAREWELL TO MUNICH

AND THE MOVE TO BERLIN

During his years in Munich, the Nuncio had become very fond of both the city and the Bavarian people, to whom he had given the best years of his life and work and done inestimable good. He knew the magnificent Bavarian churches and cathedrals. He often visited the national shrine of Our Lady in Altötting, always also honoring the mission house of the Sisters of the Holy Cross with his presence. He knew Bavaria's famous castles and also once saw the Passion Play at Oberammergau. He knew its universities and other educational establishments, its seminaries, its charitable and social institutions. He had experienced Bavaria in wartime, during the revolution, and in time of peace. And Munich knew its Nuncio too. He attracted attention without wanting to or even noticing it. His tall figure, his spiritualized, noble features were everywhere a source of amazement. Those who knew him were glad to meet him; those who did not know him involuntarily turned and gazed after him. His outward appearance alone inspired respect and admiration. But what won him the hearts of everyone he had dealings with was, despite his rank and refinement, his genuine modesty and true humility. One Cardinal—Tardini—was asked much later why it was that he intoned the *"Magnificat"* at Pius XII's deathbed when the Holy Father had breathed his last. His reply was, "Because the *Magnificat* is the song of humility, and I have never met a more humble person in my whole life."

It was also the Nuncio Pacelli who first brought the nunciature and the holder of this office to the people in Germany. What did we know before about the nunciature? We learned a bit about it at school, but it was through this Nuncio that it really came to mean anything to us. What a splendid and universally admired greatness he was later to give to the papacy!

Now came the time for him to leave the city of which, despite work and worry, he had grown so fond. For several years His Excellency had been Nuncio in both Munich and Berlin, but now he was to move to Berlin. On July 14, 1925, a festive farewell worthy of the departing Nuncio was arranged for him in the banqueting hall at the Odeon in Munich. Not only the elite, but the simple people too, wanted to be with him in this hour. Cardinal von Faulhaber, the President of Bavaria, and the Lord Mayor of Munich extended their warmest thanks to the Nuncio! How much he had done for Bavaria! The depth and refinement of His Excellency's address impressed everyone profoundly. How sad everyone was at his departure!

The Nuncio had an auditor and a secretary with him. During those first years in Berlin Monsignor Ludwig Kaas, the well-known leader of the Center Party, and Father Robert Leiber, S.J., already came to see him frequently. The German bishops had proposed the former as a negotiator with both the Bishops' Conference and the Government—for example, in Concordat matters. Father Leiber was released from other duties by his Provincial for the same function. Both of them remained with Nuncio Pacelli later when he was Cardinal Secretary of State and even Pope, rendering him invaluable services. Pius XII had a most cordial relationship with them and obviously esteemed both highly.

Monsignor Kaas sometimes also accompanied the Nuncio—later the Cardinal—on vacation in Rorschach, where his effervescent sense of humor never ceased to lend a cheerful note to the rather busy days. His witty jokes made it possible to glean a little cheer from even the most difficult problems and sometimes there was hearty laughter with the Nuncio at mealtimes. Monsignor Kaas was most ingenious and was happy when, on days when the work piled up, he managed to relax the atmosphere with his inexhaustible good humor and saw happy faces surrounding him. Since the Nuncio/Cardinal was always working on vacation too, this cheerfulness, along with the clever ideas Monsignor Kaas always had for making at least the hour's walk and the half hour over meals relaxing, was of enormous value.

After a serious stomach operation he had to undergo, Monsignor Kaas's so exquisite sense of humor no longer seemed to be as light-hearted as before. However, what I always admired in him was the fact that in spite of all the secular duties he had to fulfill his manner was truly priestly, always giving time and attention immediately to any question on religious matters, in which he must have been very well versed. The fact that this prelate was first and foremost a priest was clear to everyone else in the house too, and I more than once heard Pius XII himself say how highly he valued precisely this aspect of him.

Aptitude, far-sightedness and a very good understanding of the situation made Monsignor Kaas an excellent adviser and invaluable help. His swift grasp of things, the speed and accuracy with which he worked, as well as his excellent judgment were of great service to the Nuncio, the Cardinal and the Holy Father, so that again and again I heard the highest praise for him from the lips of Pius XII. It was to him that Monsignor Kaas confided that his health was not as good as he allowed others to believe.

Monsignor Kaas knew very well that the Holy Father was particularly fond of him and he always assured me how profoundly happy this knowledge made him. Reverence, sincere love, and absolute loyalty united Monsignor Kaas and the Holy Father up to the former's death. How much the Holy Father regretted the quick, almost sudden death of this splendid person was seen best by those who were always around him. On every conceivable occasion, Pius XII remembered him and spoke of him with great gratitude.

As far as Father Leiber is concerned, I have come across a few notes written down during the time in Berlin. "He is a born monarch, Pacelli," I heard Father Leiber say. He had just left the Nuncio's study after a longish consultation and uttered these words in amazement, confirmed as he was in his own character. This was between 1926 and 1929, the years in which the Prussian Concordat was being negotiated and there were fierce, tough battles to be fought. The Nuncio was well aware of his aide's abilities. He had in him an expert helper, who, working in the background as was his own wish—and in keeping with his character—added to the nunciature library and brought in specialist literature from the Library of State. With an alert eye and feel for current events, he tried to offer valuable advice and many a reliable interpretation based on his extensive knowledge of history, especially ecclesiastical history. He was concerned about everything that had to do with the work of the Nuncio in Berlin and it constantly occupied his mind. On these matters, he was soberly frank and communicative with the Nuncio and those working with him. He and the Nuncio were united, and will be so for all eternity, by a pure, strong love of the Church, which gave their lives their shape and orientation. It was a strong, steadily burning flame, which melted away everything personal. In this love for the

Church, they knew themselves to be in agreement and stood by each other with firm, manly loyalty. They knew they could count on each other. Different work rhythms, work piling up from other quarters, debilitating asthma, the torturing awareness of lengthy pieces of unfinished work, all these led to tensions, which, however, a profound goodness and a good-humored smile on the part of the superior helped to overcome. Rare were the days in the Rauch Strasse when there was no laughter. And to this, Father Leiber was also glad to make his short, natural contribution "*in statu viatoris.*" For example, he liked to relate the howler made by a German bishop when he was addressing the young men studying at the Collegium Germanicum in Rome: "My dear young friends, I congratulate you on being allowed to sun yourselves in the shade of the Holy See." He was quite sure that the Nuncio would never forget this delightful dictum and, in fact, it really was often heard at the nunciature. He also liked to quote from a necrology: "*Abscisso uno pede, altero migravit ad Dominum*" (With one foot cut off, he departed on the other to the Lord). Then he himself would rush off to catch up on the minutes wasted in chatting.

Just as Father Leiber, in conscious, disciplined fulfillment of his vows as a Jesuit, served the representative of the Holy Father with knowledge, circumspection, and integrity, so he also received in return the rich gratitude and trust of the Nuncio. The latter appraised his work, requested expert reports from him, asked his opinion—"*Che le pare?*"—used the material he prepared and the information he procured, and entrusted him with difficult and responsible tasks. And what collaborator does not appreciate an honorable citation and the growing inner closeness and the strengthening of community born of sharing a burden? He was thanked with a simple, immutable trust on the part of the Nuncio, who asked his advice with generous openness and matter-of-fact humility not only on official matters. A comment of Father Leiber's after a lengthy discussion would indicate with what inner joy and what sensitive, respectful affection he could respond to the trust shown him by the superior he so admired, which in turn fueled his devotion to Holy Church.

That is how it was a long time ago, and in thirty years nothing changed in the faithful, selfless commitment of Father Leiber. How well Pius XII knew this and how highly he esteemed Father Leiber, I was able to see and experience at close quarters. Later he was extremely busy as a professor at the Gregorian University, but even then the Holy Father repeatedly sought opportunities to show him that he continued to enjoy his total trust and affection. How often Pius XII himself descended the stairs to Father Leiber's study on the floor below to show him a piece of work or to ask his advice and opinion, how often I heard him say how much he valued these. But from Father Leiber too, I frequently heard how happy the Holy Father's trust made him.

Sadly, Father Leiber's asthma, which he had contracted as a medical orderly in the war, grew worse and worse. Pius XII inquired everywhere whether there were any courses of treatment that could help him. Father Leiber had to subject himself to a great number of treatments, however expensive they were, but unfortunately none of them helped. He suffered repeated attacks and we often witnessed how Pius XII helped him as caringly as one would stand by a suffering brother. And when subsequently—certainly to a great extent as a result of his illness—some kind of tension arose or, as Father Leiber said to me himself, his temper got the better of him, the Holy Father always overlooked it and repaid it with unvarying charity and kindness. Father Leiber was well aware of this and assured me of it over and over again.

In Father Leiber, Pius XII valued not only the extremely able scholar and faithful, devoted worker, but above all the excellent religious.

Between two so gifted, able and intelligent men as Monsignor Kaas and Father Leiber there could now and again be friction, too. Since I got on well with both, I soon learned the reason for it. Both of them, knowing that they were each other's equals, could not get over the other's opinion or work being valued more highly than his own. In such cases, it was not difficult for the Holy Father to smooth things over again. However, if the difference of opinion resulted from personal disagreement on intellectual or political questions, it was not easy to settle the matter. Yet, again and again, I witnessed the edifying reconciliation between the two and sometimes heard them laugh heartily about their difference of opinion, which turned out not to be one after all, or about the different interpretation that could indeed be put on the matter. If it did happen, which was very rare, that the Holy Father noticed that something was wrong between the two of them, he then found a way to restore peace with such subtle skill that they were both amazed that they had not thought of it themselves.

I saw very clearly that not only the Holy Father but also Father Leiber suffered as a result of the sudden, unexpected death of Monsignor Kaas.

Berlin! I have many happy memories of this city and of the house that I myself was allowed to choose, renovate, and furnish comfortably. It was not easy to find something suitable for a nunciature, but I succeeded in the end and the master of the house liked it from his very first look around it. Far away from the bustle of the great city, lying quiet and beautiful near the Tiergarten Park, which was well suited for afternoon walks, it was an unpretentious, simple house in accordance with the Nuncio's taste. Today this house with its beautiful garden is a pile of rubble, and I think back wistfully to our time there and to the dear people who helped to provide the representative of the Holy Father with a comfortable place to live.[1]

The task awaiting the Nuncio in Berlin—where he arrived on August 18, 1925—was no easy one. We had decorated the house festively to receive him and were happy that its master could now move in. It was only later that we learned of the official welcome at the train station. On arrival at his new home, the first thing the Nuncio did was to celebrate Mass, thus giving the great Protestant city one more tabernacle. United with HIM in the tabernacle, we happily set to work. His Excellency grew fond of Berlin too, just as he had loved Munich.

We had all been at pains to provide the Nuncio not only with a pleasant workplace but also with a hospitable home. The fact that we had succeeded was testified to by his deep gratitude after his first tour around the house. He never said a lot, but his eyes and his gestures told more than words could have done.

It is questionable whether it would have been possible to establish a nunciature in the Protestant metropolis of Berlin without the labors of this very person. His indefatigable peace efforts, his untiring work for prisoners and the needy, and his dedicated exertions for reconstruction after the terrible World War, had won him the respect of the German nation irrespective of denomination. What the 1929 Prussian Concordat cost the Nuncio is known only to God and to the man through whose extraordinary diplomatic skill and selfless work it was brought about. After the solemn signing of the Concordat, the whole household sang a *Te Deum* in the nunciature chapel because in all things the master of the house gave the glory first to God.

---

1   The following sisters worked with Sister Pascalina over the years in Berlin (1925–30): Sister Hilaria Wagner, Sister Theodosia Weber, Sister Maria Berchmans Schoch, Sister Friedberta Epple, and Sister Edgar Hettich

This quiet sanctuary also saw many a baptism, many a confirmation, and a large number of conversions. On the anniversary of the Pope's coronation and on other festive occasions the whole of the diplomatic corps present in Berlin, along with ministers and high officials, were to be seen gathered in the park-girt house on the Rauch Strasse.

Apart from swimming, there was one sport that His Excellency had loved in his young days in Rome: riding. Through a fortunate coincidence, he was able—though only rarely—to roam through the extensive forests in Eberswalde on a magnificent horse. His pronounced sense of duty and responsibility imposed restraints on him even when he could certainly have taken more time off. However, requests that he permit himself this relaxation more frequently, since it was extremely good for his health, were in vain.

I remember well His Excellency telling me once on his return from a ride in Eberswalde how there was nothing he had enjoyed more by way of relaxation as a young man than riding and swimming. If his studies and time allowed, he would go to the sea in the afternoon, hire a boat, and set off for the open sea. Then he would leave the boat and swim for an hour or more with nothing but sky and waves above and in front of him. These hours were for him the most beautiful contemplations of the greatness and majesty of God. He was often laughed at by the other boys, who could not understand what he did alone so long, but that did not trouble him. Although his mother sometimes worried when he stayed out so long, she was consoled when he told her how glorious it was to float on the waves, gazing at the deep blue sky or to test his strength against the sea when it was rough.

He had also welcomed it when a relative who had magnificent horses invited him out for a ride. Since he rode much better than his uncle, he was mostly alone there too and was always greeted at the end of his gallop with "Where did you get to again, you rascal?"

It was in Berlin too that he was given a piece of sports equipment, an electric horse that made all the motions of a galloping horse. He used it about ten times at most as Secretary of State and Pope, not because he did not like it but simply because he did not have the time. I remember Nuncio Pacelli clearly in riding dress, which suited him extremely well. It would have been nice to take a photograph of him wearing it, but he did not allow this since he always hated being photographed. Even as Pope he avoided it wherever possible and it was only when one of his closest collaborators convinced him that it was part of his ministry to fulfill the request of people who wanted a picture of him that he tried to resign himself to this necessary evil, as he called it. However, we often heard him sigh, "Oh, all these photographs!" Whereas previously people had resented his constant avoidance of photographers, later, when he resigned himself to patiently suffering the glare of flashlights and floodlights, there was no lack of voices accusing him of vanity. He was so taken up with the duties of his office that there was no room left for vanity. A quite characteristic indication of his critical attitude towards himself seems to me to come to light in a school essay written by the thirteen-year-old Eugenio Pacelli entitled "*Il mio ritratto*" (A portrait of myself):

> Since I am to paint a physical and mental portrait of myself, I shall attempt at least not to leave anything out that I discover in myself, be it good or bad, and to describe myself as I really am. Everyone will find it easy to tell whether what I say is true.
>
> I am thirteen years old, and as anyone can presumably see, neither particularly tall nor particularly small for my age. I am slim built, my skin is brown, my face a little pale, my hair is chestnut and fine, my eyes black, my nose is somewhat hooked. About my chest I do not want to say more than that it is, to tell the truth, not very broad. Finally, I have a pair of rather thin, long legs and two feet of no small dimensions. From all this it is easy to understand that physically I am a mediocre young man.
>
> Now let us move on to the mental side! Nature has equipped me with adequate gifts, so with a little good will I succeed in doing a lot of things. I enjoy coming to school and love learning, for I see that everything I can do now will be of use to me later. My parents and my dear teacher are extremely good to me and I try to repay their loving endeavors as well as I can. I should certainly be a liar if I said that I deserved their love; no, for I cannot find enough good qualities in myself to be worthy of it, nor do I flatter myself that I possess these, either; everything is to be ascribed to their goodness. Indeed, the little good that may be in me I owe solely to God, who has given me such wise betters, and to those who try with their instruction to instill true virtue into my nature. I have been foolish not always to have made use of their wise advice!
>
> With respect to my inclinations, I can say that I am sometimes

inspired by the sacred muses, and also feel in me a strong propensity for the Classics, delighting especially in the study of the Latin language. Since I am a passionate music-lover, I enjoy playing some musical instrument or other in my leisure hours and particularly during the holidays.

In character, I am somewhat impatient and fiery, but I feel it my duty to temper this through education. It consoles me on the other hand to see that I harbor an instinctive magnanimity in my heart, and in the same way as I cannot bear contradiction, I also easily forgive those who offend me. For the rest, I hope that age and reflection will serve to make the pernicious shortcomings I see in myself disappear.

It seems to me that with this I have told the truth.

Throughout his life, Eugenio Pacelli was simply incapable of dissembling or pretending to be something he was not. However, the youthful sobriety expressed in this charming essay was later to gain in profundity and develop into genuine humility.

As a young *minutantus* at the Papal Secretariat of State, Eugenio Pacelli had engaged in a great deal of pastoral work alongside his main duties. Several educational institutions in Rome had him as a confessor and religious instruction teacher. He held lectures on asceticism and liturgy, regularly gave the Eucharistic Benediction in the evenings, and made use of every minute for priestly activities. He once asked Pope Pius X to give an audience for one of these institutions, where approximately two hundred young people were being educated and trained. The children welcomed the Holy Father joyfully and Don Eugenio Pacelli presented the teaching staff and their Mother Superior to him. The otherwise so affable Pope frowned, looked the Mother Superior up and down from head to foot and said, "*Sone pazze queste Suore* (Have these sisters lost their heads) to choose such a young Superior?" Don Eugenio told His Holiness that she might be young in years but certainly not inferior to any sister in experience and pedagogic qualities. Recovering from her initial shock, the Mother Superior—a Spaniard called Madre Mercedes—said simply, "Your Holiness can show me no greater favor than to remove me from this office," the expression on her face requesting this favor more than her words.

This reconciled Pius X and it was a really lovely audience that made the children happy. His comment, meant only for the Mother Superior, had been made in front of the children, who did not keep something like this to themselves. Parents, brothers and sisters, aunts and uncles were told and soon half of Rome knew about it. Nevertheless, it in no way damaged the excellent reputation of this teacher. Many years later this sister passed through the Eternal City—she had long since left Rome and the house in question—and was granted an audience with Pius XII in Castel Gandolfo. Afterwards she came out radiant and said with profound happiness to her companion, "I found Pius XII just as simple, modest, and humble as Don Eugenio was so many years ago."

Nuncio Pacelli was keenly interested in ecclesiastical and social life in Germany. He never missed a Catholic Congress; he visited hospitals, children's homes, seminaries, schools, and places of work of all kinds. He was present everywhere that Catholic life pulsated, and the towns of Paderborn, Breslau, Hannover, Hamburg, Frankfurt, Trier, Mainz, Magdeburg, Dortmund, Fulda, Speyer, Stuttgart, Dresden, Freiburg, Rottenburg, and many others can be happy today that they lodged Eugenio Pacelli, whom history will one day count among the greatest Popes.

The impression of the Nuncio's address in Berlin-Tegel at the "Congress of Witness" ("*Bekennertag*") of the Mark-Brandenburg Catholics in August 1926 recorded by Carl Sonnenschein in his *Großstadtnotizen* (Metropolitan Notes) seems extremely significant to me:

> The great event was Pacelli's speech. How he stood there! The Roman figure! The flowing purple vestments! The gloved right hand! The chiseled head! . . . He was in Paderborn a month ago. Tegel seems like a different world to him . . . Over there the Borsig empire![2] Storm clouds of the giant industry of the last century! . . . The Nuncio speaks of the secular culture whose gigantic growth should not be allowed to enslave us. Room must be left for the world of the supernatural. The struggle seems to him to resemble the attitude of Christianity of old. In Ancient Rome . . . That is how he greets Tegel and Berlin. That is how, from the viewpoint of the

2   Johann Friedrich Borsig was a nineteenth-century industrialist manufacturing machines and railway engines. Carl Sonnenschein, a priest committed to social and pastoral work in big cities, saw the problems of the urban proletariat working in such factories.-TRANS.

Nazarene, who is the ultimate answer for every culture, he blesses this city of raging, stamping, too-powerful work. The city of factory chimneys. In his hands, the swaying, gleaming monstrance is raised above the kneeling crowd . . .

Everyone must have felt that, in Nuncio Pacelli, not only an official representative of the Church had come to them but above all an apostle inflamed with divine love and truth, constantly struggling for their souls against the growing dominion of irreligion and despair by awakening and strengthening the best and noblest forces in them. In an address at the Basilica of St. Matthias in Trier in September 1927, on the occasion of the 800th jubilee of the rediscovery of the relics of St. Matthias, he called to the faithful assembled there:

> Matthias was called to fill the gap left by the treachery of another. From the first moment of his calling, the fulfillment of this task was the object of every act of his will, every sinew of his heart. "To be faithful where others had turned faithless"—that was the theme running through all his apostolic work and endeavor and resounding in the heroic final chord of his martyrdom. His body rests here in your midst. Rejoice at this honor. But do not forget the sacred obligations that his presence incessantly preaches to you . . .

With what enthusiasm His Excellency told us about the impressions he had brought back with him from his visit to the mines! What a sincere interest he took in the lot of the miners! How happy he was when a collier told him spontaneously that he loved his work and that he had a wife and children at home, who were waiting joyfully for him every evening in his little home, which they made cozy and beautiful for him! "If only I could procure the same satisfaction, the same happiness for everyone!" exclaimed the Nuncio, to whom "the frugal, joyless solace-hungry existence of the worker" (cf. his address at the 1927 Catholic Congress in Dortmund) had been a burning problem since his youth.

It went without saying that the Nuncio spoke at every important congress. Everywhere his speech was *the* event. Let these extracts from the words he addressed to the Berlin Foreign Press Association at their annual dinner in March 1928 serve here as an example:

If history did not illustrate it hundredfold, our own experience forces us to recognize that the fate and development of peoples are governed first and foremost and deeply by the intellectual trends and moral views alive in them . . . But to evaluate the intellectual trends, to channel the healthy and constructive ones into the body of the nation and to erect a dam against the poisonous and pernicious ones, this is what the Press is pre-eminently called to do. Frequently it is less a mirror of public opinion than creator of public opinion . . . In the newspaper palaces of the modern world greater power is perhaps concentrated than many a royal throne has called its own. The Press does not merely mirror opinions and conditions, it can analyze them critically, approve and accept them, or reject and condemn them. It can sit in judgment, establishing right and wrong to such a degree and with such effect that the official authority of the State can hardly prevail against it. It can maintain a neutral stance regarding error and moral decay, it can even glorify them, but it can also denounce them and speak out manfully for the oppressed, for the helpless, for those whose consciences are being violated . . . It can be a brightly burning torch of truth, but also a glowing, wavering will-o'-the-wisp. It is capable of guiding the peoples along the steep, high paths to moral advancement, but also of paving the way for decline, even downfall. In the forefront of the enormous problems, whose successful solution depends on the single-minded work of the Press, is the intellectual battle for peace, for the laying of its foundations and its development, for the warding-off of dangers threatening it . . . The spiritual front of peoples fighting the suppression of justice and the scourge of war will not be able to close ranks until the day when, without prejudicing the safeguarding of legitimate patriotic interests, the call for peace resounds with one powerful voice from the columns of the world's Press. In this struggle, morally far superior to the glorification of war, lies the lofty task of worldwide education to be fulfilled by our time . . .

The Nuncio was well known as a good speaker, but few knew what these speeches cost him! They were always prepared in the greatest detail, with neither effort, nor time, nor labor spared. He sacrificed many a night to their preparation, resting only when he had put the finishing touch to them and had everything just as he wanted it, down to the last detail. His excellent memory then would help him to know the content completely by heart when he came to deliver the speech. Memorizing them came more easily because he wrote the speeches by hand. He said that only in this way could he remember every letter and even mentally turn over the pages as he spoke.

I remember well—it was back in Munich—how a young curate told the Nuncio that he had not found time to prepare his Sunday sermon and would have to rely on the Holy Spirit this time. His Excellency replied very sternly and seriously, "If you have not prepared your sermon, don't go into the pulpit, either. That would be tempting God! Naturally the Holy Spirit helps, but only when we have done our share first. Anyway, the sermon isn't until tomorrow, you still have the whole evening before you. Sacrifice a few hours of the night, God's word is worth it!" So saying, he left the nonplussed priest standing. The next morning he went to the church himself in order to hear the sermon. The priest afterwards told me that he had worked on it until two in the morning—after such a lesson there was nothing else he could do—but that he had almost sweated blood when he saw His Excellency in the church.

His Excellency spent four years in Berlin. He had become a byword to the Berliners. He was part of every great celebration and won every heart with his refined, high-minded modesty. Everywhere he showed himself to be a convincing priest and prelate who was nevertheless so humanly close to all, whether at banquets given by the Government or at big receptions of the diplomatic corps, or especially at Church festivals. He was just the same in the peace of his own house. Here, in his simple everyday cassock His Excellency was just as dignified as he was in full array in public.

He did not fail to notice the flower decorating his table or the small token intended to embellish his simple meal, not even the cat that had crept in and fawned at his feet. He would carefully carry back the ladybug so that nothing should happen to it. He loved animals, apart from flies, for which he felt a particular dislike. He took pleasure in small family celebrations and added to their enjoyment by both his presence and his kind words. How uplifting every Christmas Eve was! After the nocturnal Masses, which His Excellency usually celebrated one after the other and which introduced us completely into the mystery of the feast, the big double doors leading into the drawing room adjoining the chapel would be opened and we would follow His Excellency to the bright Christmas tree, where we sang together the old, yet ever new carol "Silent night, holy night." Then he was led to the table on which the presents for him lay. With unsurpassable kindness, he marveled at the little gifts thought up to delight him. Then he went to the tables with the presents for the rest of the household. How he could share in their joy and happiness when they were handed their gifts! The love with which the master of the house himself distributed them enhanced their value a hundredfold. After this delightful gathering, the Nuncio would withdraw while we had something to eat. He could not understand how anyone could eat anything else apart from breakfast, lunch, and dinner, but he was happy when others did so. He never left without asking, "Have you prepared something nice?"

In Berlin, our requests now and again still managed to persuade His Excellency to join the secretaries and us in a game of Halma or something else when he returned from his walk on Sundays. He very seldom allowed himself this diversion. However, if he did stay to the end of the game, he was certain to be the winner because he always played with such concentration.

He was full of sympathy if anyone was afflicted with suffering or illness. He would pay tribute to the gardener when his flowers and vegetables were doing well; he did not fail to notice the work done by the sisters in the house and kitchen. In his understanding, kind, benevolent, refined manner he gave everyone the feeling of being at home and yet never fell into familiarity. He radiated nobility and dignity, a certain something that called for reserve. A friend who later accompanied him on vacation to Rorschach as Secretary of State once said, "He is a true friend to you; he puts his complete trust in you and makes being together as cordial as it possibly could be—and yet there is still a certain something, an inviolable distance that you can't put a name to." (Cardinal Spellman) And had not Monsignor von Preysing—as already mentioned—found back in Munich that "the Nuncio has something about him that just can't be copied"?

Perhaps the little boy who once spoke to the Nuncio in the Tiergarten Park in Berlin wanted to express a similar feeling in his childlike way. His Excellency told us how, when he was on the last part of his walk along the Tiergarten Strasse, reading as usual, a boy he had often seen at the corner of a house waved to him. This time the boy came up close, looked him up and down, and asked, "Who are you? You're so different from other people, you're so tall, so refined, and have such beautiful eyes! Are you perhaps—God?"

One of the winters we spent in Berlin was exceptionally cold. The temperature fell to -31°F (-35°C). No one was out in the streets who was not forced to be. A workman whom the Nuncio had often met on his walks asked him why he did not stay at home in such bitterly cold weather. The Nuncio told him that he did not take his walk for pleasure but for his health because he could not work otherwise. "But that doesn't matter," the man replied. "Just do nothing for a change! You've got enough to eat and no one will reproach you for it!"

"You're quite right," was the answer, "but then I won't have done my duty, and that's something God certainly sees!"

"I went away shaking my head," the old man told me later (he lived nearby). "I couldn't get the Nuncio's words out of my head. These days, I do my duty to God and my family; I've seen that you live much happier that way."

Several weeks later an old woman came to the nunciature and told me what her husband had told me before, adding, "Shortly after we were married my husband got into bad company. He was good before, but he got more and more dissatisfied and treated me and the children badly. Since he spoke to the Nuncio, he's found his way back to God and his family and our relationship is as good as it was at the beginning of our marriage. I had to tell you this so that you'd thank His Excellency."

At that time Father von Galen (later Cardinal von Galen) was parish priest at St. Matthias in Berlin. He often came to see the Nuncio since the two of them got on very well. On Holy Saturday, he would always come to congratulate me on my name day although he knew that I did not celebrate it at Easter. He said simply, "Pasqua means Easter, so . . ."

Once the Nuncio was just coming down the stairs, reading matter in hand, on his way out. After they had greeted each other cordially, Count von Galen said, "But, Your Excellency, leave your work at home and enjoy this first sunny day of spring!"

The reply: "I can't afford to, I'd have to become the parish priest of St. Matthias first and have his humility not to mind getting stuck in the middle of a sermon!" (That actually had happened to Count van Galen, who always envied the Nuncio his good memory.) Hearty laughter from both, a handshake—and the Nuncio was gone.

That day Count von Galen was particularly talkative. When the hour was over and His Excellency returned to the house, he quickly hid behind the door so as not to be seen. However, he said to me, "What's to become of our Nuncio? He is conscientiousness and punctuality personified. It's more than anyone can stand!"

When Pope Pius XII created Clemens von Galen a Cardinal, His Eminence came to me and reminded me of our conversation at the nunciature in Berlin. I had almost forgotten it. "You see, I was right! He was always something special: especially pious, especially conscientious, especially good. He must have forgotten all my bad qualities, otherwise he wouldn't have made me a Cardinal."

I told His Eminence that I would come to his titular church when he took possession of it. "Aha," he replied, "I'll have to study my speech, otherwise it'll be the same as in Berlin, I'll get stuck and you'll tell the Holy Father!"

There would be so many lovely, uplifting things to tell about the years Nuncio Pacelli spent in Germany, blessed years full of grace and fruitfulness, for which our country can never be grateful enough! God alone knows the work, the sacrifices, the goodness he offered us, all of which did not end when he left the country. On the contrary! From now on, having ascended to the highest level, he was to do much more for the country to which he had dedicated completely thirteen of his best years.

CHAPTER FOUR

CARDINAL SECRETARY OF STATE

As had been his habit since his Munich days, Nuncio Pacelli now left Berlin for a month each year to work quietly at "Stella Maris" in Rorschach. It was here that the news reached him of his being recalled to Rome and created Cardinal. "And yet I've told my brother so often to prevent the Holy Father from doing this," His Excellency exclaimed as he held the telegram in his hand (this brother was particularly close to Pius XI and worked with him a great deal). How much Nuncio Pacelli would have liked to engage in pastoral work! Even as a young priest this was his ideal and he often talked about it, hoping that when his mission as Nuncio was over, he would be given a diocese, so as to be able to satisfy his heart's desire and dedicate himself to the care of souls. Nevertheless, he understood that he could not resist this summons and returned to Berlin quickly to put everything in order and to prepare for his departure.

One development preyed heavily on the Nuncio's mind when he left Germany: the steady rise of National Socialism. How well he saw through Hitler even then! He constantly drew attention to the terrible danger threatening the German people. No one would believe him and people of all stations and classes told the Nuncio on his departure what hope they placed in Hitler: hope for the rise to greatness of the German nation. The fact that the Nuncio did not agree with them on this point was something they could not grasp. I once asked the Nuncio whether Hitler did not after all have some good aspects too, and could help the German people to their feet as Mussolini had once done for Italy. His Excellency shook his head, saying, "I'd have to be greatly mistaken if this were to end well. This man is utterly possessed with himself. Anything that does not serve his interests he rejects; what he says and writes bears the stamp of egoism; he stops at nothing, trampling down anything in his way—I simply cannot understand how so many of even the best people in Germany fail to see this or at least to learn a lesson from what he says and writes. Which of them has even read his hair-raising book *Mein Kampf?* . . ." When one of these one-time supporters of Hitler later came to Rome, he said to me, "What dreadful misery, what terrible degradation and shame would have been spared us and the whole world if we had listened to Nuncio Pacelli back then!"

Although bidding farewell to Munich had been hard enough, then at least the Nuncio was staying in the country. This time, however, he was leaving Germany for good, the country that had for so long been home to him. Hence, the last few days in Berlin were shrouded in genuine sorrow. The last Holy Mass! It was always a profound experience for us, but this time we were all moved to tears, and the final blessing was at the same time a farewell blessing to Germany. The day of the journey itself was filled to the last minute with work. Meanwhile the nunciature was beleaguered by people of all stations in life throughout the afternoon. That evening, music struck up. The house was flooded in light. Thousands of people carrying torches had turned up to accompany the Nuncio to the train. The open car passed through an immense crowd lining the streets on both sides. It was a triumphal procession of love and loyalty, a glowing profession of faith by Berlin's Catholics. It could not conceivably have been more impressive and moving. We sisters also went to the railway station and shared with the thousands there the overwhelming display of veneration presented to the representative of the Holy Father.

In the royal audience hall, the representatives of the government and the diplomatic corps gathered with many other persons of rank to bid the Nuncio farewell. One could hardly take in all the manifestations of enthusiasm and sincere gratitude shown to the departing Nuncio by people of all stations, young and old, great and small. Even when he was already inside the railway carriage, the boldest still did not want to give up. They vied with each other in chasing the moving train until it began to get really dangerous. We remained standing at the station as if spellbound, scarcely able to believe that the man who had meant so much to the Berliners throughout the years of his work there had left forever. As we were leaving the station, several ladies and gentlemen came up to us and said, "We're not Catholics, but there are a lot of others like us here to see off such a noble person, for it's not only the Catholics who are losing a great deal with his departure. We are, too."

It was already late when we sisters returned to the nunciature from the station. All the way home no one had uttered a word and when we entered the house that was so dear to us, it suddenly seemed unfamiliar. We did not feel like eating anything that evening. The senior official at the nunciature took over the running of the daily business and we sisters stayed on until others came to replace us.

Later I read in the Protestant German periodical *Deutsche Evangelische Korrespondenz* the following lines, which reflect the great esteem in which the Nuncio was held in German Protestant circles:

> He has represented the Roman Church in Germany with dignity, energy and skill. He has undoubtedly won victories for it with tenacious patience, making wise use of every opportunity, never giving up hope, never letting himself be pushed: the Bavarian and Prussian Concordats, for example. Many who had direct or indirect dealings with him, who felt the effect of his work, will breathe an inward sigh of relief to see him go. However, even that does honor to this perhaps most skillful diplomat of the Curia, for he far outstripped them all—there is surely no question about this—in the art of statesmanship and ecclesiastical politics. For the departing Nuncio and future Cardinal, indeed even possible Pope, the years spent in Germany will not have been in vain.

The German bishops had actually planned to present the departing Nuncio, now Cardinal Secretary of State, with a pectoral cross and chain and a ring. However, a friend of Pacelli's told Cardinal Bertram that he would be more pleased if they furnished a study for him. Cardinal Bertram took up this suggestion most gladly and I was allowed to show him what we had chosen. "But we ought not to give him the cupboards empty," Cardinal Bertram said. "I know what a bookworm Pacelli is. Now you find out what books he needs and we'll fill the shelves as well as we can." The reply from Rome was soon there and all the books that were available were bought. Affixed to the desk was a small silver plaque engraved with the names of the donors—the German bishops. Even today, this handsome furniture with its valuable German carving still stands in the Pope's study, because Pius XII bequeathed all his personal belongings to the Holy See.

The bedroom, dining room, smoking room, study, and even kitchen furniture we were allowed to choose and prepare for dispatch to Rome. There—as Cardinal Bertram put it—Secretary of State Pacelli was to have a lasting reminder of the country to which his work had brought so many blessings and where his memory remains shining and great forever.

Now we sisters had completed our task in Berlin. The goods wagons with the furniture and books were on their way to Rome. Soon we too were called to the Eternal City. I was allowed to go first to prepare Cardinal Pacelli's new home for him. I left gladly, but full of apprehension for I did not understand a word of Italian. Everything was strange to me in Rome too, for at that time the Teaching Sisters of the Holy Cross did not yet have a house in the Eternal City.

During the first few months His Eminence Pacelli stayed at his brother's house. How happy I was to be able to go there in the evenings and speak a little German. During the day, I was in the Cardinal's apartments, which were full of workmen whose language I did not know. However, it was not long before I could make myself understood well enough not to impair the work to be done.

How uplifted I was by the truly Christian spirit reigning in the Pacelli household, by the refinement and tastefulness, by the fine and yet so unpretentious behavior of all who lived there! The soul of the household was the master of the house, the Marchese Francesco Pacelli, a nobleman of deep piety, perhaps a little harder and more severe than his brother. Unfortunately, he had lost his wife, whom he so dearly loved, early. The Nuncio had been still in Munich at the time, and I remember well that he had great sympathy for this loss. The four sons were still very young then, but their conscientious, wise father succeeded in bringing them up excellently. The eldest, Carlo, had married not long before we moved to Rome and his dear young wife was the lady of the house. Giuseppe, the second eldest, had been a novice with the Jesuits and given cause for the highest hopes, but he had recently been snatched away from his father by death. The two youngest boys, Marcantonio and Giulio, were still students.

The Cardinal lived in a small flat, which he had occupied before he was sent to Germany: a study, a bedroom, and the chapel, where the family gathered every morning for Holy Mass and every evening to pray the rosary together. Now their brother and uncle was restored to them for a short while. They were all happy about this and relished having him in their midst again even though it was only for the brief hours of prayer and at mealtimes. When I was plagued with homesickness at the beginning of my time in Rome, I could understand very well what this high-minded family—Don Eugenio's mother was still alive, too—must have felt when Pope Benedict XV sent Nuncio Pacelli to Germany.

Living as I did with German sisters, I was unfortunately unable to learn Italian as quickly as I needed to. Hence, I was glad to accept the invitation of a sister of the Cardinal's to go and stay with her. This sister was to be the only one of all his brothers and sisters to outlive the Holy Father Pius XII. In her family too, I found most refined sentiments, nobleness of heart and deep piety. Donna Betinna's brother-in-law, Monsignor Rossignani, lived in apartments adjoining hers and so I had Holy Mass in the house every morning here, too. During the day I helped with the preparation of the apartments for the Secretary of State, which were being renovated after being vacated by Cardinal Gasparri. In the evenings communication with the Rossignani family had to be all in Italian, which helped me a great deal and I was soon able to understand and speak as much of the language as I needed to. As soon as the work on the apartments for the Cardinal was completed, he remained in the Vatican, and once the other two sisters had arrived, the three of us were again allowed to serve him.[1]

How pleased His Eminence was with his "German" home! How much he liked the solid, beautiful furniture! He had not seen any of it before, knowing only that the German bishops wanted to give him the furniture for his study as a farewell gift. It was only now that he saw that, together with dear friends, they had provided everything else, too. His greatest joy was all the books. He was filled with happiness to see that, in addition to his own books, a further valuable collection had been obtained for him, which would be of such great use to him in solving the problems of the universal Church. The delight with which he picked up one book after another and leafed through it infected us all.

All these furnishings were to serve not only the Secretary of State for nine years but also the Supreme Pontiff for a further twenty.

Cardinal Secretary of State! We had a chance to see at close quarters what this office means. And His Eminence fulfilled his task completely. All his time belonged to God and his new office. As was formerly the case at the nunciatures in Munich and Berlin—if possible even more so—his iron will to work was to make full use of every minute in order to do

---

1   Sister Friedberta Epple and Sister Ewaldis Pfanner. In 1958 Sister Maria Konrada Grabmair would be the final sister sent from the motherhouse to Rome.

justice to everything he regarded as his duty. Cardinal Pacelli was excellently prepared for his new office. He had served more than a few years as a *minutantus* in the Secretariat of State and had gathered rich experiences during his thirteen years as Nuncio in Germany. Not least of all, he was eager to continue to learn everywhere and everything through private study. All of this now profited him greatly.

How beautiful the early mornings were with Holy Mass! For this, the Cardinal always had enough time. It was an hour he never allowed to be shortened, however much pressing work was waiting for him. And his "day" ended at 2 a.m.! Thus it had been in the nunciatures, thus it remained until after Pius XII's second serious illness, at the age of almost eighty, when he was ordered by his doctor to stop at midnight at least.

For Cardinal Pacelli his new duties were really a return to work in the Vatican that had already been familiar to him for years. His time in Germany had enriched his experience and knowledge; he had come to know the country and its religious-political problems down to the last detail. All this knowledge was more than useful to him in his new office, which was concerned with the problems of the Church throughout the world. And Pius XI relied on his Secretary of State, entrusting him with more and more tasks because he saw the masterly way in which his "right hand" accomplished them. His Eminence now saw buried forever his heartfelt wish to be able to undertake pastoral work, but he brushed this aside with admirable matter-of-factness.

Weary and toil-worn, Cardinal Gasparri had handed his office back to the Holy Father. Now he was happy to see his pupil and friend as his successor. Cardinal Pacelli worked quietly away as the "shadow of the Holy Father." His time in office was a time abounding in political tensions. Nevertheless, his boundless trust in God and his untiring love of work performed miracles and confirmed the Holy Father more and more in his conviction that he had made the best choice. Pius XI valued his Secretary of State, whose workload increased accordingly. It was only through extremely precise planning and utilization of every minute that it was possible to cope with all this work. What a good thing it was that Eugenio Pacelli had accustomed himself from an early age to a strict work discipline.

In the first few years, Pius XI wanted to take his Secretary of State with him to Castel Gandolfo, but His Eminence asked the Holy Father to permit him to stay in the Vatican since both of them could not be away at the same time. Moreover, the Cardinal feared that otherwise he would not be allowed to go to work quietly for a month in the peace of "Stella Maris" in the autumn.

Pius XI loved his summer residence and stayed there for several months each year. The good air, slightly less heat than in Rome, more tranquility, and simply being in the attractive landscape of these surroundings, did him good since his health was not the best, either. However, he continued to work there as in the Vatican and so at Castel Gandolfo the audience with the Secretary of State was scheduled for 9 a.m. just as it was in Rome. At least five minutes beforehand the Cardinal would be waiting in the antechamber. Now it once happened that the Master of the Chamber was late. When no one had yet appeared after ten minutes, the Cardinal without hesitation knocked on the study door himself and heard the Pope's deep voice answer from within. He entered and said that since he had not wanted to keep His Holiness waiting, he had come himself. A look of displeasure crossed Pius XI's face but then the audience began and since it lasted particularly long that day, the Cardinal had almost forgotten the incident by the end of it. When it was over and he was about to rise, the Holy Father told him to stay and rang for the Master of the Chamber. A storm of remonstrance now rained down upon the latter—as he himself told me later—so that he never again came late when the Secretary of State had an audience.

It was a great joy for His Eminence to be able to participate in pastoral work through preaching and lecturing even though very little time remained for this. Here too everything was done with great precision and the Villa Borghese, where he took his daily walk, could confirm how well he used this hour of walking in order to be able to proclaim the word of God.

For beatifications and canonizations, he was called upon to deliver the panegyric and he always regretted that he was unable to accept every request to do so. What solemnity his appearance and his splendid sermons lent the ceremonies! For the Cardinal too overburdened with work though he was, these occasions were a most profound experience and sheer joy since, as he said, he was allowed once again to engage in pastoral activity.

Part of the annual month spent at Rorschach was used to work on sermons that he had already agreed to deliver. But every day he also received mail and telephone calls from the Vatican keeping him up to date on everything. Nearing the end of his vacation the message would always come:

"The Holy Father asks whether you will be returning soon!" Yet although he always worked at Rorschach, the Cardinal really needed this relaxation. How soon would come a time when he could no longer allow himself any recreation at all.

Pius XI was in the habit of making use of the Cardinal's name day or some other special date to pay tribute to him and show him his gratitude. So it came about that His Eminence would return from the audience with a small gift. Once again it was June 2, his name day. Full of curiosity I waited for lunchtime to come to see what the Holy Father had given his Secretary of State. Since His Eminence did not say anything himself, I asked how the audience had gone.

"Why?" came the surprised reply.

"It's your name day today!"

"Oh, I see," he said, still lost in thought. "The Holy Father forgot that today. It's a good thing he did; the audience was very long anyway."

Nevertheless, I was most disappointed. As always, His Eminence went to the Villa Borghese to walk after taking a short noonday rest. Hardly had he left than the telephone rang. "The Holy Father asks the Cardinal to come to him," the voice said.

"His Eminence has gone out," I replied, "but as soon as he comes home, he'll be given the message."

"You see," I said to the Cardinal on his return, "the Holy Father has remembered!"

But he answered simply, "Do you really believe that the Holy Father hasn't anything more important to think about?"

When he finally came back from the Holy Father after a long time, he had a small parcel in his hand but said nothing at all. Now I could not bear it any longer and asked whether the Holy Father had congratulated him, to which the Cardinal replied that he had. It was only somewhat later that I learned that His Eminence, alluding to the events of recent days—it was the time of the quarrel with Mussolini—had asked the Holy Father whether he had not yet regretted making him Secretary of State. To this Pius XI had replied, "I consider it the greatest blessing in my life to have you at my side. If the Pope were to die today, tomorrow there would be another, for the Church lives on. However, if Cardinal Pacelli were to die, that would be a much greater misfortune, for there is only one of him. I pray every day that God is growing another in some seminary, but up to now there is only one in the world." Then he handed the Cardinal the parcel, saying, "This is my congratulation for you! It would be an infinite blessing for the Holy Church . . .!" The gift was a miniature portraying Our Savior handing over the keys to St. Peter!—Thus spoke Pius XI, of whom everyone around him knew that he seldom expressed praise and never paid a compliment.

We sisters saw the Holy Father Pius XI at functions in St. Peter's, on special occasions or at audiences. In the Holy Year of 1933 so many pilgrims came that the *"baciamano"* ("hand-kissing" —kissing the papal ring as a sign of respect) often went on into the night. At such times, we very often saw the Holy Father walking down the corridor outside the Secretary of State's apartments. One Sunday morning I was returning alone from St. Peter's, going as usual through the *Sala Ducale* to the loggia. No one had stopped me, which was usually the case if the Holy Father was anywhere in the vicinity. Opening the door, I suddenly found myself standing face to face with His Holiness. I knelt down in alarm. The Holy Father blessed me and walked on, talking to the Monsignor accompanying him. Then he turned and came back towards me, this time alone. I remained on my knees. He offered me his ring to kiss and said with great kindness, "*Sia molto attenta e sorvegli bene il mio carissimo Cardinale . . .*" (Be very attentive and take good care of my dearest Cardinal.) The rest of what he said I did not understand in my agitation. Then he blessed me again, laid his hand on my head, and walked on. Several more times we three sisters had the good fortune to be allowed to speak to the Holy Father. On every occasion, he bade us take good care of his Secretary of State. It was clear to see that he was most concerned that he should retain the Cardinal at his side in good health.

Since Pius XI knew what an exceptionally good influence Cardinal Pacelli had on others, he appointed him Papal Legate to the Eucharistic Congress in Buenos Aires in the autumn of 1934. The news of this was received with enormous rejoicing, as it was a very rare occurrence for a Secretary of State to undertake such a mission. Even during the journey there, he was able to undertake pastoral work. His remaining time was taken up with the preparation and formulation of the speeches and addresses he was to deliver during the congress. What a triumph these days in the Argentinian capital were for the Eucharistic Savior! The Legate inquired assiduously whether every circle was included, whether the same fervor, the same enthusiasm prevailed everywhere! How overjoyed he was to see the vast queues of penitents and communicants! When he saw the enormous crowds at the ceremonies, there was always just one question on his lips: Had they all paid homage to the Lord in the Sacred Eucharist yet? When he was informed that people had been keeping watch in front of his house all night so as to be the first to see him and receive his blessing in the morning, this saddened him greatly. "But I am here for Our Lord in the tabernacle and for His glorification!" However, he was consoled on being told that the people simply wanted to see the envoy of the Holy Father.

It did not suit him at all that he had to be accompanied by security officers even on his walks and so he thought up a stratagem. The house where he was living had a back exit through the garden. Dressed as a simple priest, he went out alone and unnoticed, not knowing where he was going. He was not at all familiar with the city and thus strayed into a quarter of not particularly good repute. How he was recognized he did not know. In a flash, the news spread through the streets: The Papal Legate is here among us! He spoke kindly to the people thronging around him, answered their questions, dispensed greetings and blessings on all sides, and inquired whether they had all received the Holy Sacraments yet. When the security officers, who had waited in vain for the Legate at the main entrance, discovered that he had gone out alone, they searched the whole city for him. When they finally came across him, the Cardinal had gathered a crowd of people around him and was engaged in warm conversation with them. But who could have resisted this compelling kindness and simplicity! How proud this poor quarter was to have been visited by the Legate!

At the time, everyone spoke of the importance and overwhelming success of this congress. This was, certainly not least of all, thanks to the Legate, who was the soul of everything and left no stone unturned to increase the triumph of our Eucharistic Lord and extend the kingdom of Christ the King.

Pius XI had ordered a triduum of prayer and sacrifice to mark the end of the special Holy Year commemorating the Crucifixion of our Savior. The three days were to begin on April 18, 1935 in Lourdes and preparations were in full swing there. Once again, the Holy Father was asked to send a legate and once again, Pius XI chose Cardinal Pacelli. Hardly had His Eminence been commissioned with this task than his brother, Francesco Pacelli, who had been ill for some time, died suddenly and unexpectedly. Thus the Cardinal was not even able to pay his last respects to his brother, with whom he was united in profound love and who had rendered the Church such great services. Not only the Cardinal mourned him deeply; Pius XI also took his death sorely to heart. "Fetch yourself—and us too—strength and solace from Our Lady of Lourdes!" were the Holy Father's parting words to the Cardinal.

Francesco Pacelli: how well I remember my last visit to him in the Via Boezio! He had contracted his serious heart complaint in the service of the Church, and the admirable way in which he bore it had to be seen to be fully appreciated. Near the end, he was no longer able to do much work. Nevertheless, I found him at his desk, and in the course of our conversation, I noticed that he had no illusions about his condition although he was still in the prime of life. "I have tried to serve my God, Holy Church, and my family as well as I could. Now I leave it to Him to protect and care for my loved ones, and I trust that God will be a merciful and gracious judge to me," were his words of farewell to me.

The triduum in Lourdes will certainly remain an unforgettable experience for all who had the good fortune to be present. The Legate's drive there was, in itself, a triumphal procession, and the storm of prayer at the grotto at Massabielle is sure to have called down abundant blessings upon the whole of mankind. The climax of the celebrations was the Legate's final sermon, which was both an eloquent testimony to his heartfelt love of Our Lady and a warm tribute to the humble little Bernadette:

> The Immaculate Virgin, the Queen of Peace comes down to earth in this lost corner of the Pyrenees. She comes to Bernadette, makes her a confidante, her collaborator, a tool of her motherly tenderness and the merciful omnipotence of her Son to restore the world in Christ through a new and incomparable extension of Redemption, to set free—no longer only the homeland[2] but, with it, the whole world—free from a slavery that is just as oppressive and humiliating as subjugation by a foreign power: the slavery of the sick and tyrannical flesh, of the impotent and arrogant mind, of the empty and skeptical heart.
>
> With what weapons, great God, and with what a command! She, the poor little daughter of the Soubirous, is to cry out to this

2   This and other allusions in the extract refer to the comparison with St. Joan of Arc, which is a key point in the sermon as a whole.-TRANS.

frivolous or godless world, this vain and sensual world: Prayer, penance, penance, penance!

Hush, oh Bernadette, hush! We have understood. In this cry of penance, penance, penance there echoes another: the Cross, the Cross, the Cross! You are the messenger of Mary and of Christ, who taught us that anyone who does not take up his cross and follow Him is not worthy of Him. You too will bear your cross: the Immaculate Virgin, who is no stranger to sorrow, did not promise you joy in this mean world. Your life too will be a path strewn with pain, with every suffering of body, mind and heart. Like the shepherdess from Domrémy, you too, since you hear the voice of Heaven calling you, will have your martyrdom; you too, shepherdess of Lourdes, will find your way into the history of France, into the history of the world, into the history of the Church, into the history of Redemption, into the eternal splendor of Heaven; you will enter there never to leave again . . .

Even if the Cardinal was only away for a short time, the Holy Father nevertheless missed him greatly. I remember His Eminence saying after the first audience on his return from Lourdes, "I don't think that the Holy Father will let me go away again now. He was so glad that I'm back!"

The death of the Marchese Francesco Pacelli had left the post of *Consigliere Generale della Citta del Vaticano* vacant. One day the Cardinal came back from his audience with Pius XI and was very taciturn at his meal, hardly touching his food.

"Aren't you well, Your Eminence?" I inquired.

"Yes, I'm well," he replied, "but the Holy Father wants my nephew Carlo to succeed my brother Francesco as General Councillor of the Vatican City, and none of my arguments could dissuade him."

"But, Your Eminence, that's something nice, why aren't you happy about it?"

"You don't understand anything at all! Carlo is too young for the post. People will say he's getting the job just because he's my nephew."

"Is that something wrong, Your Eminence? In any case, Pius XI knows Carlo very well. He certainly wouldn't give him the post if he didn't know he deserved it and was capable of fulfilling what it requires of him."

But then came a further rebuff. Shortly afterwards the front doorbell rang. Carlo, who had just come from an audience with the Holy Father, was standing at the door. When he attempted to inform his uncle of his appointment, he fared no better than I had. The Cardinal feared quite rightly that *L'Osservatore Romano* would break the news of Carlo Pacelli's appointment as General Councillor that very same evening. For this reason, he requested another audience, which was immediately granted, in order—if possible—to get the decision reversed. However, he received no more than the friendly but firm reply that it was the Pope and not Cardinal Pacelli who made the appointment.

Later too, during the almost twenty-year pontificate of His Eminence Pacelli as Pope Pius XII, his talented and industrious nephews were repeatedly forced to reject honorable and lucrative posts because they knew that the Holy Father did not wish any kind of prominence for them. Representations were very frequently made to him on this account, saying that he was harming his family in this way, but he was never to be persuaded to give his consent, and without it none of his nephews would ever have dared to accept a post.

One example in particular has remained in my memory. One of his nephews was offered an honorable post, which was not at all conspicuous, and he would very much have liked to accept it. Pius XII was requested from various quarters to make an exception in this case and allow his nephew to accept the appointment. The Holy Father said that he would think about it and there were hopes that this time the answer would not be negative, since Monsignor Tardini had asked especially for a positive one. But two days later, the answer came. "I have thought and prayed about it and believe that you ought to forego it." When Pius XII was asked why he was against it, he said, "There are certain to be a large number of other people waiting for this nice post who would have all kinds of things to say not only against my nephew but also against the Pope if he took it. I am very sorry, but here I can avoid gossip—even though at the expense of my family. There are so many things where my actions are governed by duty and where I cannot and may not remain silent."

September 1936! The Holy Father Pius XI had promised the International Congress of Journalists an audience at which he usually honored them with an address. A few days before it was to take place, he told his Secretary of State that he had not yet found time to prepare his speech and asked the Cardinal to speak instead of him. His Eminence was somewhat dismayed as there were only a few days left for him to prepare himself for it. On September 25, in the presence of the Holy Father, Cardinal Pacelli addressed the assembled company from all over the world in seven different languages without a script. People present reported afterwards how Pius XI had listened to his Secretary of State, deeply moved and with glowing eyes and then personally expressed his warn and sincere thanks to his "*veramente carissime e mai tanto caro come ora Cardinale Segretario di Stato*" (truly dearest Cardinal Secretary of State, never so dear as now). Everyone else was also deeply moved and it seemed that the applause that broke out would never end. We who had stayed at home and knew the other side of the coin—how little time the Cardinal had been left for preparation—asked him on his return how it had gone. "Oh, all right," he said, "I hope it was of benefit to the souls of the large audience!" Later, when the Cardinal came back from his audience, we learned of Pius XI's great delight, of how he had been quite moved when he received him and had called his speech a "*pentecostale*" (a miracle of Pentecost).

What again and again spurred His Eminence on to the most devoted and indefatigable work and fulfillment of duty was not least of all the unqualified trust and great affection Pius XI showed him. The Holy Father made no secret of his attitude but showed it openly to cardinals, bishops and other visitors. It was not uncommon for this or that person to confirm to us how very attached Pius XI was to his Secretary of State, how much he valued and cared for him. Is it then surprising that the Pope now permitted him to go to America in 1936?

Cardinal Pacelli's achievements during his time in the United States were a source of wonder. As a young priest, he had already been offered a professorship at the Catholic University of America in Washington but had been unable to accept it because Pope Pius X did not allow him to do so. The Cardinal wanted to become acquainted with and study America, the religious situation there, the dioceses, the bishops, the churches and seminaries, the schools and hospitals. He traveled through the vast country by land, water, and air. He consulted with cardinals and bishops, brought his words and example into seminaries, monasteries and convents. He did not rest until he had familiarized himself with everything so well that he could report on the situation of the Church in America to the Holy Father. The universities counted themselves lucky to be able to award him an honorary doctorate, and President Roosevelt, who invited the Cardinal to dine at Hyde Park, felt most kindly towards him from that time on.

Later one of the President's successors was to write the following words on the death of Pius XII: "A light has gone out. The world has become a poorer place." And another great statesman, Winston Churchill, is reported to have said after an audience with Pius XII that he had just met the greatest man then living on earth.

On returning home after these fruitful weeks in America, the Cardinal gave a joyful account of his experience. This time Pius XI presented him at an audience with a picture of himself with the words written on it: "*Pius PP XI. Carissimo Cardinali suo Transatlantico Panamericano Eugenio Pacelli feliciter redeunti. 14.XI.36*" (Pius PP XI To his dearest Transatlantic, Pan-American Cardinal Eugenio Pacelli on his happy return.)

And America now counted herself lucky to have become acquainted with the Cardinal whose reputation had already spread everywhere. Even though such missions were strenuous and demanded many a sacrifice, they nevertheless offered the Cardinal a welcome change from his difficult office as Secretary of State, to which he devoted himself heart and soul. Above all, these missions were in accordance with his urge to engage in pastoral activities, his ideal from the very beginning.

The situation in Germany, especially as regards religion, was becoming more and more intolerable and so Pius XI decided on an encyclical. He was well aware that no one was more familiar with conditions there than his Secretary of State and so the Holy Father delegated the work to him. As with everything that Cardinal Pacelli did, first precise inquiries were made. Nothing must be overlooked, nothing omitted. How the situation was given balanced consideration and studied! Since Cardinal von Faulhaber happened to be in Rome at the time, the Secretary of State asked him to visit, and I well remember the two of them going through the whole work once again in the Cardinal's private apartments before the draft was submitted to the Holy Father. The fateful developments in Germany had already caused Cardinal Pacelli great suffering over all the years in which he was forced to see what Hitler was trying to do with the people he personally had come to know, love and cherish so much in his long years among them. Then in March 1937 the encyclical *Mit brennender Sorge* ("Cum ardenti cura") not only hit Germany like a bombshell—no, it hit the whole world, unmasking as it did the terrible situation.

The degree to which Hitler and his followers took the encyclical personally was proved by the unbounded fury with which this historic document was received and reacted to. God be praised, the Supreme Pontiff had a man at his side whom Hitler could not accuse of not understanding Germany and the Germans.

Pius XI was an ardent admirer of St. Therese of the Child Jesus of Lisieux. When the basilica built in her honor was to be dedicated, he wished to be represented at least by a legate since he could not go to Lisieux personally. Once again, his choice fell on his Secretary of State. It was in July 1937. His Eminence was surprised but said that he would go gladly and do whatever he was able.

As had been the case two years earlier at the triduum at Lourdes, this time too, the French Government welcomed the Papal Legate with a most honorable and dignified reception. Here again, according to eyewitness reports, it was the Legate himself who impressed everyone with his dignity, his modest nobility, and his truly priestly manner.

The dedication of the basilica unleashed the most wonderful enthusiasm. There were said to be almost 400,000 people gathered in Lisieux. From midnight onwards, there were continual Masses and distribution of Holy Communion. The knowledge of this was the Legate's greatest joy.

After the dedication of the new house of God, the Legate addressed the assembled masses. He had warm words of praise for the humble, loving little saint, who yearned for nothing in the world but for Love to be loved and to awaken apostles who would hasten through the world in her place in order to bring full glory to the Lover of her soul. The Cardinal called her a tabernacle in which the flame of divine love glowed. However, he also called her a bride of the Cross, who scattered roses for others but for herself chose thorns in order to prove her love to her God. Interrupted by thunderous applause again and again, the Legate concluded his hymn in praise of St. Therese of Lisieux, who was so much in keeping with his own simple, childlike and yet noble soul. A sacred stir of deep emotion went through the vast crowd when the voice of the Holy Father, trembling with fatherly love, then spoke from the radio: "Our beloved son and Papal Legate represents us personally in your midst. He speaks in Our name! In his fear of God and eloquence he is Our interpreter . . ."

However, the Legate's task was not yet over. On his return to Paris, he celebrated a Pontifical Mass in Notre Dame and preached on France's mission. All Paris sat up and took notice. At this pulpit, the country's greatest orators had stood; the man now proclaiming the word of God from it was their equal. He also possessed the courage to remind his audience, with heart and soul aglow, of their Christian past and to show them what was once France's greatness. The homage and rejoicing of the French nation accompanied the Papal Legate on his way back to Rome.

On his return to Rome His Eminence was struck by the fact that the Holy Father did not look well. "I shan't go away again anymore; I don't think it does the Holy Father good," he said.

The Secretary of State was also Archpriest of St. Peter's and had to celebrate or assist at the Pontifical Mass there on feast days. On one such day, the Holy Father called for him, but the Cardinal was still in St. Peter's. Consequently, a monsignor went to tell him that the Holy Father was expecting him. The Cardinal went directly to the audience, still in full array. "How nice you look, Cardinal," the Holy Father greeted him (so the Monsignor told me). "How well the '*calda*,' pluvial and tiara will suit you one day if the *cappa magna* already looks so fitting on you!" (Pius XI called the Pope's flowing white robe, the *falda*, a "*calda*"[3] because he was rather small and corpulent, which made him perspire a great deal in all the papal apparel.) The Cardinal, Monsignor said, turned as scarlet as his cloak, but the Holy Father merely said with a smile, "Cardinal, that too is a gift of God, to be able to be such a fine ambassador as you are!"

Cardinal Pacelli loved his office as Archpriest of St. Peter's dearly. Consequently, he attached great importance to everything being exemplary and dignified, especially in St. Peter's, which, after all, so many pilgrims visited from all over the world. How he welcomed it later as Pope when an association of priests was formed to promote greater spirituality and dignity in the celebration of the Liturgy and to take on the responsibility for training boys to serve at Holy Mass in the way that the sanctity of the Divine Sacrifice demanded. He did everything to keep this enthusiasm alive, thanked the founder most sincerely, praised the boys at a public audience, and expressed the hope that soon all the basilicas in Rome would rejoice in such a good institution.

What struck me immediately about St. Peter's, which I grew very fond of, was the fact that there was no altar there to St. Joseph, my baptismal patron. All the same, on March 19 I noticed that a beautiful carpet of grass

3   *"Calda"* means "warm".-TRANS.

and flowers led from the main entrance of the basilica into a chapel next to the Pietà. I saw that the chapel contained a splendid painting of St. Joseph and that the altar was beautifully decorated with flowers and candles. However, this chapel had the disadvantage of being open only for the feast day and otherwise shut off by artistically wrought iron bars during the rest of the year. I simply did not think this right for the patron saint of Holy Church. I told the Archpriest of St. Peter's this and asked him to do St. Joseph the honor of being able to be venerated throughout the year by all the people visiting this, the largest church in Christendom.

He may be Archpriest of St. Peter's, he replied, but in such matters it was first and foremost the Holy Father who gave the orders. Nevertheless, the matter continued to prey on my mind and soon I had finally decided. I would write to the Holy Father and tell him what was preoccupying my heart. And so I wrote and asked for one of the many altars in St. Peter's to be turned into one dedicated to St. Joseph. The patron of Holy Church would be certain to reward the Holy Father for this, sure to stand by him in his difficult office and, above all, would beg special blessings for him in view of all the responsibility he bore, etc. Yet how could this letter really get into the hands of the Holy Father? The easiest way would have been to ask the Secretary of State to take it with him to his audience—but I imagined him telling me to mind my own business and not to go bothering the Holy Father or some such rebuff! Well, I did know someone who I could be sure would put the letter on the Holy Father's desk. But how should I sign it? If it were to be successful, the letter would certainly be passed on to the Archpriest, and what then? I did not want to sign it with a false name and so, after much to-ing and fro-ing, decided to reverse my own name, which I then did. Naturally, I was full of suspense waiting to see when and if a reply would come. And lo, on returning from his audience about ten days later the Secretary of State called, "Madre, come here a minute, you've written to the Holy Father!"

"*Me?*"

"Don't be silly, I know your style!"

"And what's the answer? Is there going to be an altar in St. Peter's—a really worthy one—and in a nice position so that St. Joseph can be venerated by all the pilgrims, and—. . . ?"

"And now stop it and don't make a hundred stipulations on top of everything else."

"Yes, Your Eminence, forgive me, please, but don't forget anything I requested."

"And you must remember that it will take a long time before everything is finished and wait patiently."

A great deal of patience was indeed needed and—in spite of being forbidden to do so—I often kept coming to beg, "When is it finally going to be finished?" But it was finished—and although I could not really take to the mosaic at first and told St. Joseph straight away that he should be careful not to drop the Child Jesus, it was nevertheless there and a better position could not have been found for it, either! The tabernacle was then also moved to this altar. What more could I ask for? No one entering St. Peter's can overlook St. Joseph, and I go there so often to say: "Remember, my dear St. Joseph, that it was my doing that you are here. You know my needs; please help me and all those who trustingly bring their cares to you here."

Cardinal Pacelli was most interested in the excavations under St. Peter's and, even at that time, he would have liked to have seen them continued. He said himself that archeology had always appealed to him very much indeed. Even as a student and then as a young priest he had spent many a free hour in the catacombs making a detailed study of them. He knew the catacombs of St. Callistus so well that he could find his way around them excellently without a guide. Small wonder that—shortly after having ascended the Throne of St. Peter—he immediately threw himself heart and soul into promoting the excavations at the grave of St. Peter. He was perfectly aware of the enormous technical, archeological, and topographical difficulties involved in such an undertaking but they did not frighten him. In his enthusiasm, he did not by any means balk at the extremely difficult and dangerous work. Though always overburdened with work and worry, he took the time to listen to the scholars and workmen toiling indefatigably down there, to spur them on, to pay tribute to them, and to express his gratitude. How happy he was to be able to announce the extremely valuable results of the excavations in December 1950.

Several important gaps had remained, however, so in 1952 a new phase of investigations began. The lion's share of the work fell to Professor Margherita Guarducci of the University of Rome, a specialist in epigraphy and classical antiquity, whose strictly academic training and method Pius XII esteemed highly. The Professor avidly studied the inscriptions that came to light on the walls near the grave of St. Peter and was the first to succeed in deciphering them. This unearthed a wonderful side of Christian spirituality containing, among other things, numerous acclamations of the victories of Christ, St. Peter and the Blessed Virgin Mary. The Holy Father lived almost long enough to see the conclusion of this work and was very happy about it. After his death, Professor Guarducci closed the last remaining gap when she identified the relics of St. Peter. After the most stringent studies, analyses and checks in collaboration with other scholars, the results were officially recognized by Pope Paul VI on June 26, 1968. The Pope ordered the relics to be restored to the place where Constantine the Great had put them sixteen centuries earlier after having removed them from their original earth grave. Pius XII must certainly have rejoiced in Heaven over the conclusion of this great work, which he had begun and so avidly promoted.

Pope Pius XI's health was not the best any more. Hence the Secretary of State's audiences became longer and longer. The Cardinal said how much he thanked God that the Pontiff's trust in him was so unqualified that, even when the Holy Father could not work anymore himself, nothing had to suffer on account of this. No one ever learned who was really doing the work since the Cardinal worked for his exalted master with loving loyalty in the shadows and seclusion.

One thing that Pius XI had retained was his healthy sleep! The Cardinal often said how happy he was for him, knowing himself full well what insomnia was. Pius XI willingly admitted that right from the start he had accustomed himself to leaving all his worries and all thoughts of work behind him in his study before entering his bedroom, so sleep came immediately without anything to disturb him. "If only I could learn that from the Holy Father," His Eminence would often say, since for him every serious worry meant a sleepless night.

Pius XI usually stayed a very long time at his summer residence at Castel Gandolfo. Consequently, the Secretary of State always had to go out there for audiences, and since the Holy Father feared that the Cardinal would lose a lot of time in traveling, he advised him to sleep during the journey. "Does Your Holiness sleep in broad daylight?" His Eminence asked, "I'm never bored! On the outward journey I look through everything again so that no time is lost during the audience and on the way back I plan a schedule for the work I've received, so never a minute is wasted."

All that the Cardinal knew of Castel Gandolfo was the way from the elevator to the Holy Father's apartments, the rooms he had to pass through and the Pope's study. It was only when he was himself Pope and went to Castel Gandolfo that he became acquainted with the summer residence.

His Eminence had thought that his journey to Lisieux would be the last of his foreign missions. However, when a legate was requested for the Eucharistic Congress in Budapest in May 1938, he was chosen again. The Holy Father wanted his Secretary of State to be known everywhere because he was convinced that no one could represent him better than Cardinal Pacelli would.

The Pope's ambassador was received with regal honors in the land of St. Stephen. The eminent visitor was to reside in the former royal palace. The country had done its utmost to make the congress as successful as possible. Nevertheless, here again, it was the Papal Legate himself who lent the celebrations an unusual splendor with his outstanding personality. Participants had gathered from all over the world to pay homage to the Eucharistic Savior and to increase His glory. In seven languages the Legate praised God's love, which gives itself to mankind in order to bestow eternal happiness.

An unforgettable experience was the wonderful procession of ships on the Danube by night at which the Legate, surrounded by cardinals and bishops, crossed the river holding on high the golden monstrance containing the white Host. The Legate's last major speech pointed out the terrible tragedy of the way in which the godless seek to combat and enslave the Church. He called upon the people to take note of the admonitions of the Supreme Pontiff and to follow them. Did the Papal Legate perhaps foresee the gloomy future?

> The Lord's disciples, who could not tear their eyes away from the sight of their transfigured Master returning to the Father and from the cloud lying between Him and those He loved, are recalled to earthly reality through the mouths of angels and reminded of the duties awaiting them below. *"Quid statis aspicientes in coelum?"* (Why do you stand gazing into Heaven?) A similar call is repeated in this hour . . . *"Eritis mihi testes."* (You will be my witnesses.) Here at the steps of the altar, within the sacred sphere of the Eucharist, we have once more become joyfully conscious of the *"magnum pietatis sacramentum"* (mystery most divine): the community with Christ and the mutual community in Christ as

undeserved grace, as an inestimable inheritance, as a binding law of life. What could become of the world, of mankind, if the insights springing from such an experience—if the decisions springing from such insights—extended to all the faithful; and if they furthermore made their way to all the places where, from a material or spiritual point of view, the shape of people's lives, both individually and collectively, is influenced and determined! Whoever seeks the ultimate and most profound causes of the inward and outward distress afflicting humanity today with ever quickening pulses, with ever stormier temperature curves and with ever more oppressive symptoms; whoever undertakes this task cannot but recognize or at least suspect that at the deepest and gravest source of this unparalleled crisis there lies a malnutrition of the soul, a spiritual anemia, a longstanding moral infection. It is fermenting and festering in a thousand open and hidden forms, for which the genuine cure with any prospect of being lasting is not to be found in the books of human wisdom and science. If we do not succeed in combining truthfulness and love in a manner appropriate to modern man; in leading mankind back to the living waters from which more pious ages drank; in allowing man both as an individual and as a social being to find his way back to accepting the religious foundations of his being; in giving him a firm moral stand in the manifold relationships in his life, the adherence to which is not watched over merely by human statutes and external force but rather by the majesty of God's law—if we do not succeed in this, then the further slide down the precipitous slope, the process of inner poisoning of the individual and social sphere will continue unchecked.

Where, beloved brethren, is there in the history of mankind a time comparable to our own in the greatness of the tasks confronting it, in its disagreement over the courses to be taken, in its conflicting attitudes and convictions, in the obstinate passion permeating the aggressive conflicts that have already broken out or are imminently brewing? To overcome or even simply diminish to any considerable degree these gigantic, almost demonic contrasts on the earthly level and with earthly means is a Sisyphean task, for whose idealism one may show respect but whose failure is inevitable. And the more palpable the ultimate inability of external power factors to overcome the plight of our times becomes, the more the fronts harden, the more tragic the Babel becomes between man and man, between interest and interest, between nation and nation, between state and state, and the remoter the peace for which, in the final analysis, everyone and everything yearns. The Church is not called to take sides in purely earthly matters and expediencies between the various systems and methods that might be considered suitable to overcome the problems of the present plight. Her service of truth, her worldwide apostolate of love, preclude any one-sided partisanship that would narrow the scope and impair the flexibility of her mission . . .

The Church knows herself to be free from narrowness and prejudice, free from a lack of understanding for new goals and necessities called for by the times. She does not mistrust the new simply because of its newness. She does not cling to the old simply because of its oldness. In her total vision, every age and every people has its providential place in the tremendous plan of creation and redemption devised by the Eternal . . . Christ the Lord, before whom we stand in homage here, is sent to all ages, including our own. If many an intellectual spokesman of today—continuing and intensifying previous errors—seeks to establish individual and collective happiness without Christ or even against Christ, then the hour of "*eritis mihi testes*" has come. Then it is the sacred duty of those who stand by Christ and see in HIM God's final word to humanity to throw themselves into opposing such false developments and defending the cause of "*instaurare omnia in Christo*" (restoring all things in Christ) with dauntless courage and love . . .

This world congress has been dedicated to the Eucharist, the "*vinculum amoris*" (bond of love) . . . Let us carry the message of this "*vinculum amoris*" out into the world, a world that is torn apart, spiritually divided, bleeding in fighting between brother and brother, and possibly facing new outbreaks of fraternal strife and hatred . . . Inspired by the spirit of Christ, impelled by His love, seeking HIM, and seeking nothing but HIM and His glory and the spread of His kingdom and the salvation of our brothers and sisters, whether within or without the Church, we love this our time despite all its dangers and afflictions. We love it precisely because of these dangers and the difficulty of the tasks it poses us, prepared to offer that total, unqualified, selfless commitment without which nothing great and decisive can take place . . .!

On his return to Rome His Eminence saw immediately that the Holy Father was in urgent need of a rest. More than ever he did all that was humanly possible to ease the burden of work for his exalted master. Nevertheless, he never did anything that was not completely in accordance with the Holy Father's plans. For his part, Pius XI made sure that His Eminence was informed of everything, never missing a chance to say, "That is something you must know too, Cardinal. It would be good if you take note of this—it may be of use to you when you're in my place one day . . ."

"It was almost too much for me today," the Cardinal once said on returning from an audience, "all the time the Holy Father kept pointing out what I'd have to do when he was no longer alive . . . and I said, 'Your Holiness, that is the one point where Your Holiness can no longer give the orders.' And Pius XI replied, 'Yes, you're right, but I'll tell HIM who does give them: the Holy Spirit!'"

Even though the Holy Father's strength was failing visibly, he nevertheless remained in complete command of his mental faculties, which he made use of to the last. If the Pope was ever too unwell to work, he knew that it was quite safe to leave anything that could not be put off to his Secretary of State, since the Cardinal never diverged even a hair's breadth from the will of his exalted superior.

It was during the last months before the death of Pius XI. The Holy Father had summoned the German Cardinals to Rome for important deliberations. He received them together with his Secretary of State in his private apartments because his health would not allow him to go down to the official rooms on the floor below. After the more than two-hour audience, Cardinal von Faulhaber came to me. He said that after the end of the deliberations the Holy Father, laying his hand on the Secretary of State's arm, had said with great emotion that for the past two years he had been Pope in name alone for all the work had lain in the hands of his Secretary of State. At this point, Cardinal von Faulhaber said Cardinal Pacelli had interrupted Pius XI, "*Ma Padre Santo, Padre Santo . . .*" (My Holy Father, Holy Father . . .)

But the Holy Father had continued, "Let me speak. I know that no one has ever learned how you sacrifice yourself, but you"—he turned to the German cardinals—"shall know what a debt we owe to our Secretary of State. Remember this when I am gone!" The Holy Father had had tears in his eyes, Cardinal von Faulhaber concluded, and all of us with him.

Cardinal Pacelli's last Christmas as Secretary of State came. He usually celebrated the three Holy Masses one after another, beginning at midnight. His relatives were allowed to be present at them. His poor relatives! Even then, they were given truly little of his time, seeing the Cardinal as they did a mere twice a year, on his name day and on Christmas Eve! I once said to His Eminence, "I wouldn't for the life of me like to be your sister. Those poor relatives are never allowed to see you."

But he simply smiled, "One day, when I have more time . . ." After the Holy Masses, we sisters prepared a small celebration. His Eminence spoke to all the guests and shared their delight at the little gifts spread out for them. But then he retired while we sisters served a light snack for the relatives.

The fact that the Cardinal saw his family so seldom does not mean that he was not fond of them. On the contrary! He suffered with them if one of them was ill; he asked assiduously after them; he shared their joys and sorrows without seeing them. How often he reminded us before Holy Mass in the morning that it was the name day of one of his loved ones so that we should be sure not to forget to pray for whoever it was. After Mass, I had to telephone at once to pass on his congratulations and to say that he had remembered them especially in his prayers.

Even as Cardinal, he never invited his family for meals. As Secretary of State he often had to attend official lunches and dinners but he did so only when it was absolutely necessary. This was not merely on account of his very sensitive stomach; the main reason was that he regarded it as a great loss of time to have to sit at the table so long. Half an hour was sufficient for him. Even this brief period was used for more than just eating since he set the time in such a way that he could listen to the current news or to an English or French lesson on the radio to further his own education.

With us sisters, he spoke only German at home, to be sure not to get out of practice. Occasionally, when someone spoke Italian by mistake, he would reply in German immediately. How very useful his good command of various languages was to the Secretary of State! It was not only in speaking at audiences and with diplomats from all over the world that he mastered these languages, he was also able to compile extremely difficult written reports of a canonistic and diplomatic nature in them. For this accomplishment too, Pope Pius XI, who also distinguished himself by his extensive knowledge but was not so well trained in languages, repeatedly admired the Cardinal with the joy of a father over his son's gifts. For a full nine years, Cardinal Pacelli had held the office of Secretary of State and served the Holy Father as his closest and most faithful collaborator. "I have," the Cardinal himself said, "known every thought of Pius XI concerning the government of the Church because he has trusted me implicitly. However, in these nine years I have never said yes to the Holy Father when I thought no, and never no when I thought yes." I remember clearly the Cardinal being called to the Holy Father one evening. Several hours went by and it was long past the time for dinner when he entered the apartments looking very pale. When he came to the table he said, almost as if to himself, "I couldn't do otherwise. I had to tell the Holy Father that I couldn't go along with him in this matter, that it was something he'd have to do without his Secretary of State. 'The responsibility lies with Your Holiness, but I cannot act otherwise.'"

The absolute candor between Pius XI and Cardinal Pacelli probably contributed decisively to the harmonious cooperation between two men who were basically so different in their natures.

Unfortunately, Pius XI's strength was failing visibly. Work and audiences had to be reduced to a minimum. Nevertheless, neither he nor those around him believed that he would die so quickly.

With a supreme effort of will, the Holy Father was working on an address for the whole of the Italian episcopate. His far-sightedness and perhaps already a vision of another world told him that the most terrible catastrophe was threatening the world. With all the strength that he could muster, he wanted to banish the specter of this gloomy future. On February 11, the anniversary of his coronation, he intended the world to sit up and take note again. But the Holy Father would not see that day. On February 8, his condition had become very critical. The Cardinal was exceedingly concerned. When a fever set in during the night, it was clear that human help would avail nothing. Fully conscious, the Holy Father received the Last Sacraments and prepared himself for death. There was still a slight hope when His Eminence returned from visiting the dangerously ill Pope late that evening. However, all hope was shattered when the telephone rang at 1 a.m. The Cardinal, who was working as usual at that time, went up immediately. We sisters, fearing that this call in the middle of the night could mean only the worst, went to the chapel. It was about 6 a.m. before His Eminence returned and told us that the Holy Father had returned his soul to his Maker.

How this great Pope was mourned throughout the world, not least of all by his faithful Secretary of State, Cardinal Pacelli! As the Cardinal prepared to offer up Holy Mass for the deceased Pontiff, his pain was clearly visible. He himself and all present wept. When the Cardinal walked past the elevator on the way back to his apartments after the Mass was over, he said, "Exactly nine years ago today I entered this elevator for the first time to go to my first audience with the Holy Father as his Secretary of State!"

The world had loved and revered the great Pope Pius XI. This was testified to by the thousands who filed past his coffin. The Cardinal kept saying, "He deserved it, he really deserved it!" Only those who were permitted to be near him at home, in solitude, really saw the amount of suffering this loss caused His Eminence.

People have asked again and again how two so completely disparate personalities as Pius XI and his Secretary of State could get on with each other so well. Once I plucked up the courage to ask the Cardinal personally, to which he replied, "Pius XI is a great and saintly Pope. Where human understanding and personal insight tend to diverge there is always the knowledge of the Pope's divine mission. How often I have sympathized with the Pope that he always has to decide and does not have such an easy task as I have. If I'm not sure about something and wish to give it thorough consideration first, I can always make the excuse that I have to present it to the highest authority. This the Holy Father cannot do. The whole weight of responsibility rests on his shoulders. How could anyone expect me not to lighten the burden of office for him as well as I am able?"

CHAPTER FIVE

PASTOR ANGELICUS

Cardinal Pacelli was now no longer Secretary of State but instead Camerlengo of the Holy Roman Church. How hard this office of Chamberlain was for a man who had been really sincerely attached to Pius XI. When the deceased Pope was carried into the Sistine Chapel, Cardinal Pacelli was the first following his coffin. It was clear to see what this cost him.

We at home did not see much of the Cardinal's work as Camerlengo since he had immediately instructed us to pack everything and clear the whole apartment. He himself used every spare minute to order all his papers and documents and label them, so as to be able to send them to the Secretariat of State clearly and systematically organized down to the last detail. The whole apartment was full of boxes and cases as the Cardinal wanted to leave the Vatican immediately after the Conclave. How happy he was on returning from his duties as Camerlengo to find new boxes and cases packed and ready. In order to spur us on he held out the prospect of soon returning to "Stella Maris" and being able to relax.

"Are your passports in order?" he asked one morning. "But, Your Eminence, there's time for that later," we protested. "No, no! Mine's all ready"—His Eminence had already had a visa for Switzerland stamped in it—"it's better not to have to wait when it's time to leave." So there was nothing for it but to get our passports ready too.

During the Conclave, we were allowed to stay in the Cardinal's apartments, as they became *"Cella no. 13."* "What a blessing to be allowed to be alone and not forced to waste time with a lot of talking!" the Cardinal said when he learned of this decision.

Work in abundance was added to his activities as Camerlengo. Telegrams and letters of condolence were delivered in basketfuls. At least the replies to the important personages of the world had to be dealt with personally. In the meantime all the shutters of the large and small windows overlooking St. Peter's Square had to be securely locked. It was prohibited to open any of them on pain of excommunication. This did not inconvenience us since all these rooms were already empty and all the books and other objects safely packed in boxes and cases. These rooms now merely served His Eminence as a way through to the Sistine Chapel.

How happy the Cardinal was to be able to return to his apartments on March 1, 1939 after completing his work as Camerlengo and to eat and sleep there even though everything was bare and empty. There was many a merry moment when we looked for something and then realized that it was in vain because the object in question was long since stowed away in a box. All the same, His Eminence was content that everything was already packed and that—once the Conclave was over—only the furniture that belonged to him personally would have to be carried away. This last evening before the day of the election was just the same as any other. For us the day ended with the rosary together, whereas the Cardinal continued to pray and work on into the early hours.

Early on March 2, we all waited in the anteroom outside the chapel to congratulate His Eminence on his birthday. He never liked being congratulated and that day he said with a friendly gesture simply, "Pray, pray that everything will go well!"

Holy Mass followed—here it seemed as if nothing could oppress the Cardinal as he drew God down upon the earth. After breakfast, he went into the Sistine Chapel as he had previously gone to his audience with the Holy Father.

We in "Cella no. 13" knew, heard, and saw nothing of the crowds in St. Peter's square since all the shutters and windows were bolted. In addition, it was forbidden to go down to the square. Anyway, a lot still remained to be done since His Eminence wanted to see the last boxes and cases packed and ready when he came home. The birthday cake with its sixty-three candles had to be ready too, even though he never touched it.

And His Eminence came home after the first scrutiny, calm and composed as ever. Although in our inquisitiveness we should have liked to ask questions, we remained silent in the face of the earnestness and gravity that lay upon him. "Now everything is ready apart from this last box, which can certainly wait until tomorrow, can't it, Your Eminence?" I ventured to say. "And in any case we're all very tired."

"No, no," came the calm, clear reply, "don't put anything off. We'll all relax together when everything's over!" I was disappointed, but I could tell at once from the Cardinal's eyes that he had seen through me.

When the time came for his walk, the Cardinal was ready punctually to go out. "Today I'll have to walk round and round in the Cortile di S. Damaso, there's nothing else for it," he said as he left the apartments, breviary in hand. Exactly an hour later His Eminence came back to prepare to go to the Sistine Chapel. Everything was as always: calm, considered, equable, without any sign of agitation.

It was about 5:30 in the afternoon. We were all completely occupied with clearing up and packing when a prolonged shouting and clapping reached our ears from St. Peter's Square. But none of us would have dared to go to a window and no one came to tell us anything. So we waited—until the door of the large study opened. On the threshold stood the so familiar tall, slim figure—now clad in white—flanked by the Master of Ceremonies and other prelates, who, however, withdrew immediately. It was no longer Cardinal Pacelli, it was Pope Pius XII coming home after the first *adoratio* in the Sistine Chapel.

Who could ever forget such a moment! Weeping, we three sisters knelt and kissed the hand of the Holy Father for the first time. The Holy Father had moist eyes too. Looking down at himself, he said simply, "Look how they've dressed me up . . .!" We were lost for words—there simply are none in certain situations—and there was not much time as the prelates were already returning to fetch the Holy Father back for the next *adoratio*.

Soon dear relatives and friends came to offer the Holy Father their congratulations. We could all hardly speak, our voices simply failed us. Nor were the tears to be restrained. It was impossible to tell whether it was pain or joy that filled our hearts.

The Holy Father was exceedingly benevolent to everyone he found in his apartments on his return. But now his pale face betrayed great tiredness. When he was finally able to extricate himself, he sank into a chair and covered his face for minutes with both hands. We hurriedly unpacked everything again that was necessary but we were all too agitated to do anything properly. When Cardinal von Faulhaber stood in the doorway asking for me, I saw that he was not faring any better, "Madre," he said simply, unashamed of the tears streaming down his face, "I'll come back again when we can both speak." And he closed the door behind him.

The whole of St. Peter's Square was still full of jubilant crowds. It was only now that someone had the idea of opening the shutters and looking down on the surging sea of people over whom the new Pontiff had shortly before spoken his words of blessing for the first time. It seemed as if the people could not tear themselves away from the place where they had heard the joyful news. Again and again they shouted: "*Viva il Papa, viva Pio XII. Viva, viva il Papa romano di Roma!*"

The Romans in particular were overjoyed to see a Roman on the Throne of St. Peter after such a long time!

It was now time to be thinking of a light evening meal. Today the Holy Father did not have to change for dinner as, for the time being, he had only one cassock (and that did not fit him at all). The rejoicing in St. Peter's Square could be heard right up into the dining room. After the meal, which Pius XII hardly touched, we went into the chapel for the rosary just as on any other evening. The only one among us who was able to pray with uninterrupted calm and composure was the Holy Father. The rest of us kept faltering because we could not go on praying through our tears. Then, for the first time, Pius XII gave us as Holy Father the evening blessing that he had given us for nine years as Cardinal Pacelli. For us the day was over; for the Holy Father this day, like every other, probably did not end until two in the morning, by which time we already had a good few hours' sleep behind us.

The third of March! "Holy Mass as usual," had been said the day before and so everything was ready as always at 7:30 a.m. The Holy Father appeared punctually. We sisters had the joy of attending his first Holy Mass as Pope. That morning the simple chapel of the former Secretary of State seemed to me like a wonderful cathedral in which the Vicar of Christ was offering up his first papal sacrifice to the Eternal Father in order to receive strength from HIM who had laid such an unutterably heavy burden on his shoulders. This quiet morning hour was the same as usual and yet different—his thanksgiving, too, went on and on.

Then the daily round of work with its demands and duties awaited the Holy Father again. Now that the condolences were finished with, the congratulations began. They arrived in their thousands. The Pope could not lose a minute in order to be able to read and look through at least the most important ones. The telegrams and letters arrived in basket loads, often three times a day. The replies had to be approved or corrected, there were audiences to be granted, people from the Secretariat of State to be received—mountains of work piled up. In addition, the most important of the documents lying stowed away in their boxes had to be fetched out again and put back where they belonged. "That at least I could have spared myself," the Holy Father said when he arrived late and exhausted for lunch. "And you too," he added when he saw us bending over half-empty packing cases to extract the most essential items.

Cardinal Pacelli had always felt sorry for Pius XI because he was forced to take his walks in the Vatican Gardens. "I wouldn't want that," he would often say. "The whole place seems like a cemetery to me. And having to walk round and round in circles—no, I couldn't do that!" Thus it was that when Pius XII returned from his first walk, I asked sympathetically how it had been.

"Oh, the same as usual," came the friendly reply.

"The same as usual?" I asked in astonishment.

Then he remembered and said, "Well, it has to be—if only that were the most unpleasant thing!" This is how it always was. He passed over everything that concerned him personally, however much it was contrary to his taste, in a matter-of-fact way and dismissed it as if it did not even exist. All that counted for him was God, souls, his duty, his work, his office. He himself never mattered. Later the Holy Father became quite fond of the Vatican Gardens—there was nowhere else and he had to take his walks.

This first day was clear and bright but not warm. The tailor had not yet brought the new clothes, which now all had to be white. We had already taken the black ones out of the cupboards. "Where's my warm coat?" the Holy Father asked.

"The tailor hasn't brought it yet."

"Then give me the black one."

"But, Your Holiness, you can't wear black anymore!"

"Do you think I'm going to catch a cold because of that? Allow people the pleasure of having something to talk about." And the Holy Father went out into the garden with a black coat over his white cassock. Before twenty minutes had passed, the telephone rang. "What have you done?"

"Didn't you see that . . .?"

And again; "For Heaven's sake, be careful . . ."

Now we thought of the Holy Father's words: "Allow people the pleasure . . ." But the nicest incident was one that happened to the Holy Father himself. He told me that there had been a man working behind a hedge who had kept staring at him between the leaves. Finally he had come out, knelt down and said, "I couldn't believe it was you, Your Holiness—a Pope is dressed in white, not black and white, but you probably don't know that yet." Pius XII had replied with a laugh that he would take note of it.

In the meantime, we had more or less set the house in order again. The boxes and packing cases had disappeared from the rooms and corridors by the time the day of his coronation approached. Already his first speech on March 4 had made the world sit up and take note. From now on, he would continually amaze everyone with his divinely inspired wisdom and his clear thinking in every field of religious and social life. For everyone he was to find the right words to encourage them and spur them on. He was to speak to members of all professions: to men of science, business, and politics; as well as to workers, farmers, and artisans. All were to feel that they were understood.

The Holy Father had been told that he could not move into the papal private apartments until they had been renovated. Pius XI had already stressed to Cardinal Pacelli that his successor would have to have the apartments thoroughly renovated. Pius wanted to see for himself whether this was necessary and went up to the papal apartments with two gentlemen. We too were allowed to enter the rooms for the first time. This inspection moved the Holy Father deeply. Everything was already completely empty; the low windows in the spacious rooms lent them an oppressive air so that I thought this was the reason why the Holy Father was downcast. Then we heard him say, "Only recently it was here that Pius XI used to receive me . . ." and on entering the bedroom, "This is where he lay on that unforgettable night . . ." With moist eyes he walked back to the exit, taking no further notice of the other rooms. Here we really understood for the first time how much suffering Pius XI's death must have caused the Holy Father and how close he had been to him.

It was not until the following day that the Holy Father asked, "What's going to happen about the apartments upstairs?"

"What Your Holiness orders," was the reply. He then instructed the architect to do what was necessary in the apartments but to keep everything simple, without any luxury. That was so exactly like Pius XII. For himself he never had any wishes, anything was good enough. In spite of his appreciation of beauty and refinement, everything had to be modest and simple for him personally.

The day of his coronation came—March 12. It was a day full of sunshine, a really festive day. We had already attended Holy Mass early since the Holy Father was not, of course, celebrating at home. On our return, we found him in the private chapel. He looked very pale and strained. How must he have felt that morning? Even the celebration of the anniversary of his coronation in later years was something he could never warm to and he often said that he would abolish it if only he could. He had no objection to a Holy Mass, a canonization or beatification or to other such functions in St. Peter's and the Sistine Chapel, but the coronation celebrations, centered as they were so completely on the person of the Pope, were simply too much for his modesty. Every year it was a great sacrifice to him to submit to these anniversary celebrations and several days before they took place we would hear him say, "Now the coronation day is approaching again, I really could be spared that!"

One year I asked Monsignor Tardini as he was leaving after an audience shortly before this anniversary, "Your Excellency, isn't there anything you can do? The Holy Father really wants to abolish the coronation celebrations."

But Monsignor Tardini became quite indignant. "It is not befitting to drop them and we who are close to him should do our utmost to convince him of this."

However, when the Holy Father was seriously ill on the anniversary of his coronation in 1954, he was really happy that the celebrations could not take place, and in his last year—1958—it suited him very well that the sad court case against Bishop Pietro Fiordelli of Prato offered him an opportunity to cancel them.

On this day, though, the Holy Father had to submit to the ceremony, his own coronation, whether he wanted to or not. It was a festive day as dazzling and noble as could possibly be imagined. "Holy Father, just look at St. Peter's Square!" we called enthusiastically. He came to the window so as not to disappoint us but turned away again quickly. The square was filled with a vast, surging crowd, a fabulous display of color with the uniforms and picturesque costumes. Here the elegant lady in her festive gown, there the simple peasant. Young and old, rich and poor—they had all come to pay homage to the Vicar of Christ, who today was to receive the three-tiered crown, the papal tiara. And above all the pomp and splendor there was a never-ending roar of jubilation. *"Viva, viva, viva! Viva il Papa Pio XII, il*

Papa romano di Roma!" (Long live Pope Pius XII, the Roman Pope of Rome!)

And then St. Peter's Basilica! It had decked itself with every adornment it possessed and now it was a riot of dazzling light kindling the fire of its rich gold decorations in all their beauty. It was filled to the last seat. A surging and rustling went through the vast crowd, who had been waiting patiently for hours for the man they had all known, loved, and admired for years, who today was to receive the highest dignity possible on earth. After the Holy Father had left his private apartments to be vested in the Sala dei Paramenti, we too set off for St. Peter's. We had the privilege of being able to watch the ceremony from the Loggia San Longino, where we had had our secluded places ever since we first came to Rome. Can there be anything more beautiful on this earth? Surely no one who had the joy of being present at *this* coronation ceremony will ever be able to forget how impressive it was!

Already the silver trumpets were announcing the approach of the object of everyone's longing! Immense jubilation broke out but subsided again slowly as the first homage was paid to Pius XII in the atrium by the Chapter of St. Peter's, whose Archpriest he had long been.

Now he was carried over the threshold of the basilica on the *sedia gestatoria* (portable papal throne). How often he had received Pius XI, to whom he was attached heart and soul, here as Archpriest, and today of all days he must have remembered Pius XI constantly prophesying this day to him. "*Tu es Petrus*," the choir sang out exultantly. A storm of applause broke out and the jubilation and singing swelled so loud that it seemed that it would collapse the mighty basilica.

The long procession moved off. The Crown Prince and Princess of Italy were at the head of row upon row of delegates who had hastened to the ceremony from over fifty countries. Princes, noblemen, ambassadors, all the world's dignitaries—every nation paid homage to the Pope! All were enraptured as they witnessed the dignity and beauty of this grandiose spectacle.

Finally came the Holy Father himself. In the white interwoven with gold of the long pluvial his ascetic figure seemed even slimmer and the bejeweled miter made his finely chiseled face look even paler. His slender, beautiful hands blessed and waved to right and left. On the right hand raised in blessing glittered the Fisherman's Ring. All eyes were upon the

Holy Father and all the thunderous applause was for him, Christ's representative here on earth.

Again the glorious *"Tu es Petrus"* rang out, this time with such strength and beauty that the ovations subsided a little.

Then the Holy Father began the Coronation Mass. Anyone who had for years enjoyed the privilege of being present when he celebrated Holy Mass could see even here amidst all the splendor and outward pomp simply the priest completely absorbed in the Holy Mass and fully conscious of the sanctity of the act he was performing. With what fervor he prayed the *Confiteor* and intoned the Creed! What inner ardor lay in the *Sursum corda* and Preface. Every syllable was audible of the sacred words of the Consecration. Then came the *"Pater noster."* I shall never forget his *"Fiat voluntas tua."* (I have often heard him sing it since then but, I believe, never so movingly as on that day.)

The sublime Mass was ended. Again storms of never-ending applause broke out. Everyone was in a hurry to go out on to St. Peter's Square in order to watch the coronation. The thousands who had been unable to get into the basilica had waited patiently in the square. Now all eyes were fixed on the specially decorated loggia where the Holy Father's throne had been erected.

We sisters went home to prepare lunch for the Holy Father, but when the Italian military band started to play the papal anthem, we went to a window—from which we could look over to the loggia. Indescribable rejoicing announced the appearance of Pius XII. It even drowned the significant words of the coronation rite: "Receive the tiara adorned with three crowns and know that you are the father of princes and kings, ruler of the earth, and earthly vicar of Our Savior Jesus Christ, to whom be honor and glory forever." Then the antiphon *"Corona aurea super caput eius"* was sung with joyful exultation. Then the Holy Father stretched out his arms as if he wanted to embrace the whole world, and the airwaves bore the blessing *"Urbi et Orbi"* to all mankind. For a long time Pius XII stayed on the loggia waving to the jubilant crowds. Had Rome, I wonder, ever witnessed such sincere participation, such a celebration?

The Holy Father had returned to his private apartments and was certainly very tired. Soon afterwards—it was already very late—he came to lunch. Now the Holy Father, who shortly before had been surrounded by the jubilation of the world, was enveloped in silence. He would be lonely now for almost twenty years despite all the great festivals and celebrations that were to interweave this grace-filled pontificate.

The moment of loneliness that must surely come for every Pope, I could not help thinking as I served him while he ate in silence, was already there and from it there is no escape. The Pope must hold out at his post whether he likes solitude or not. I knew from fourteen years of experience that Pius XII was by nature a cheerful person with a trait of seriousness, good-humored and open-minded, always believing in the good in man. The long and difficult years of his pontificate did not perhaps allow this light-hearted side of his character to be seen outwardly but I think that they helped him to achieve his joyful and total oneness with God!

The Holy Father was so silent that we did not dare to congratulate him. Chance had it that his dear little birds performed an especially lovely concert for him while he was eating that day, so that he finally rose from his silent meal and opened their cage. Flying on to the table, chairs and other pieces of furniture, the chirpy little songsters kept him company a little until he carried them back to their cage before leaving the dining room.

Even on the day of his coronation, his siesta lasted only half an hour. It was already time to go out into the garden. When he returned from his walk, the Holy Father had shed some of the burden of the day. At last we sisters could congratulate him and tell him how beautiful the ceremony had been. He was happy simply because we were.

Early that afternoon Cardinal von Faulhaber came to me and asked, "Do you remember the first Holy Mass celebrated by the young Nuncio Pacelli that I attended back in Munich at the Catholic Congress? At the coronation ceremony today I saw the same unforgettable picture: a saint celebrating Holy Mass. He is certain to be one of our great Popes, but I also know that we have a saint of a Pope!"

Standing by the door were baskets full of telegrams, sacks full of letters. Even on the day of his coronation, the Holy Father did not leave the work lying but applied himself to it as on any other day. The lists for audiences to receive the foreign missions still had to be drawn up and then he worked on until late at night—or rather, early in the morning.

The mountains of mail proved the enormous interest shown by the whole world in the election and coronation of Pius XII as the supreme pastor of the Church. That must have made him happy although he was almost struck dumb with modesty when he was addressed as "Holy Father."

It now became apparent that the whole world knew the Holy Father. Every country called him "our Pope" since he had traveled almost the whole world. Even though he was almost crushed under the weight of work, he still could not help laughing heartily when he was shown letters from simple people congratulating him on an office that would allow him to enjoy life and not have to work as much as when he was still in Germany and having to keep concluding concordats. A simple peasant wrote: "Holy Father, we all congratulate you most heartily. We are glad that you in particular have become Pope and now we know why the Pope is addressed as 'DU.'[1] That is something you only say to someone you really like a lot and you are someone the whole world loves dearly." An old lady wrote: "Holy Father, I am already very old, over ninety, but I have always asked God not to let me die before I had the opportunity to venerate you as the Vicar of Christ for I was always sure that you would be Pope one day. Now I shall be happy to die since my prayer has been heard."

It was not only members of the Church who were overjoyed; outsiders shared their happiness too. Many Protestants and Jews sent letters attesting their great joy at his election.

Only those who saw it know what an enormous amount of work the Holy Father had to deal with at the beginning of his pontificate. It was many days before the receptions and mountains of incoming post slackened off a little. Perhaps it was a good thing that Pius XII was swamped with work during this period since it helped to lift the weight that had burdened his finely strung soul since the day of his election. Since his official duties required him to scan the world's press, he could not close his mind to the fact that the impression his election as Pope had made on the whole world was uncommonly good. The eyes of all were focused in admiration on the man who spoke their language and had traveled their country. During his many years in Germany he had done such untold good that the people felt great admiration and love for him (with the exception, of course, of the man who now was ruling the country and who knew full well that in him he was facing an outright opponent). France was a country he had visited repeatedly. The Hungarians had called him their own since the Eucharistic Congress. The USA was proud of him because he was the first

---

1   The German *"du"* is the familiar form of address in the singular, similar to the French *"tu"*-TRANS.

Pope to have set foot on her soil and traveled the whole country. Spain he knew well and South America was not unfamiliar to him, either. However, above all he had a reputation of being deeply pious and possessing personal authority. "Pastor Angelicus" is what he is called in the Prophecies of Malachy. How well this name fits Pius XII. Years earlier at a Catholic Congress in Germany, a Protestant had said of him: "*Angelus non Nuncios* (He is an angel, not a nuncio)."

Admittedly, the mildness, simplicity and humanity, the self-abnegating quietness and fervor of the Holy Father's asceticism may not have been to everyone's taste and they were perhaps features to be fully appreciated only by those who were permitted always to be around him. Everyone, on the other hand, was forced to acknowledge his extraordinary, truly universal erudition and his intellectual superiority despite all his simplicity, mildness, and kindliness. The higher he rose, the smaller he seemed to become in his own eyes; yet in the eyes of those who had the good fortune to be able to observe him constantly he grew daily. Often the words of Pius XI crossed my mind: ". . . it would be an infinite blessing for Holy Church . . ." And Pius XII always remained true to himself throughout the twenty years of his pontificate. Even now, after being raised to the highest dignity, he did not change anything in his modest, simple lifestyle. However much he disliked all pomp, he nevertheless knew where it was necessary to display genuine splendor when his exalted office and the dignity of his position demanded it.

A few days after his election, the Holy Father gave me a fairly large sum of money. "Put this in the cash safe," he said. "Monsignor Mariani gave it to me, it's intended for the housekeeping." But it was not long before he asked for this or that amount from the sum to help the poor and distressed. Soon there was nothing left of it, and the housekeeping was financed from his private funds as it always had been before.

During Pius XII's almost twenty-year pontificate, it was always the same. All the household expenses and any personal needs—which were, incidentally, very modest—were paid for from his own means.

With Church moneys, the Holy Father was always very economical. They were not his property, he said, he was merely a trustee who would be called to give precise account one day. His attitude regarding gifts was the same, even if they were given expressly for his personal use.

Here is just one incident that I remember particularly well. Soon after the beginning of the war, a Cardinal gave the Holy Father a large sum of money with the express instruction that it was to be used for his own needs and for causes particularly dear to his heart. The Cardinal had even put this in writing and the Holy Father gave me the letter along with the considerable sum of money, instructing me to put them both in the cash safe. Since I also knew the donor, the latter entrusted me with the task of making sure that the money really was used for the Holy Father. Only a few weeks later all that remained in the safe was the Cardinal's letter with the following entries: "For two chapels on the outskirts of Rome: 50 million. For a destroyed school in (name of town): 25 million. For the bombed-out village of X: 40 million . . . " and so it went on. In a few short weeks, everything had been spent that had been expressly intended for the Holy Father personally and donated for him alone.

Similar episodes recurred constantly and the sums of money were never used for anything but to relieve whatever distress was greatest at the time.

Everything else given to the Holy Father—gifts of money or material objects—was immediately passed on to the Secretariat of State.[2]

However careful Pius XII was not to diminish the Church property entrusted to him or to eat into it through unnecessary expenditures, his generosity knew no bounds when there was real distress to be alleviated, and the whole world came to know how magnanimous and charitable the common father of all Christendom was.

The idea of increasing his own property never entered the Holy Father's head; on the contrary, he did not even know what he possessed and it was always possible to ask for what one needed of what he had. Only when it was a matter of a fairly large sum did he ask, "Is there anything left?" Here it was usually a case of requests from priests for their poor parishes addressed to Pius XII via his private storerooms and from bashful people in distress. As long as his private resources had anything left to give, there was no problem about addressing requests to him—"no" was never the answer.

Since the death of his brother, Francesco, the management of his personal fortune lay in the hands of an old and loyal official at the

---

2   Later in the text it becomes apparent that certain gifts went into the private storerooms for distribution to the needy.-TRANS.

Administrazione Beni della Santa Sede. Even after beginning his papacy, Pius XII left the task to him because his nephew, to whom he wanted to entrust it, did not wish to take it on. Commendatore Federici[3] often asked me, "What on earth do you do with the Holy Father's money?" And another time: "You give everything away, so that there won't even be enough left for a coffin." When I told the Holy Father this, he laughed and said, "Tell the Commendatore Federici to look for someone to make me a present of a coffin, then he'll have one less worry!"

After Federici's death, the management was taken over by an official at the Secretariat of State since the Holy Father's nephew Carlo repeated his request not to have to do so. It was only after work had begun on renovating the Holy Father's private apartments that it became clear that there was more to be repaired and seen to than had originally been thought. Since the repairs would take a fairly long time, the Holy Father went to Castel Gandolfo. It was autumn before he could return to Rome and move into his newly decorated papal apartments.

These were simple and unpretentious but nevertheless noble. Pius XII had lacked the time to concern himself with the renovations but put complete trust in those who were to undertake the task. Therefore, he was even happier to find the apartments fitted out completely in accordance with his own taste. He abhorred all luxury and would not tolerate it in either his dress or his surroundings. All he needed was light, air and sun since these seemed conducive to his work. He was delighted that there was plenty of room for his books. He owned a beautiful library and this was his joy. In both his small and large studies, there was room for those books that he needed constantly at hand for his work. The library proper consisted of five large rooms full of exquisite books. The Holy Father knew every book and its rightful place. The priest whose main duty it was to take charge of the library made every effort to arrange everything as clearly as possible since the Holy Father very often went into the library himself to fetch the books he needed for the work he was currently engaged in.

Since the library grew visibly over the course of time, the Holy Father had more metal bookshelves put up across the middle of the rooms so that there would be enough space for his books to be clearly and nicely arranged. Sometimes he was given duplicate copies, which also had their

---

3   *"Commendatore"* is the title given to a commander of an Order.-TRANS.

own place, and if the Holy Father knew of someone who would appreciate them, he would give them away. Since Pius XII spoke all the major languages, he wanted to use original texts only. If he needed to check a quotation and did not possess the book in the original in his library, he would have it fetched from the Library of State or some other library.

Once the Holy Father was given a set of books that were most important for his work, in the original language but in a simple binding. They were immediately placed in the large study. Some time later he received a translation of the same work finely bound in leather. We thought that we ought to place the beautifully bound books in the place of honor and relegate the others to the duplicates, but we were mistaken. "Where have those books gotten to?" he asked.

"Your Holiness, these are the same AND they are more beautifully bound." Pius XI's reply: "Their value does not lie in the binding, and translations are never the same as the original." The books had to be exchanged immediately.

Pius XII treated his books with great care. He was glad that the most beautiful objects in his apartments were the bookcases. He did not bother about anything to be taken to Castel Gandolfo each year except for the books, which he took charge of personally, selecting them and giving instructions as to which were to go with us. Then he would warn us to be careful and to make sure that not a single book was damaged or lost. Every year, transporting all the books required filling a whole truck, since he did not care what was missing at the Castel as long as it was not a book. However tired the Holy Father was on arrival at his summer residence in the evening, he would check that all the books were there and standing in their proper places. It soon became widely known what pleasure the gift of a valuable book gave Pius XII and it "rained" books on all sides, so that the large library was hardly able to hold them all.

Once a group of foreign pilgrims brought with them, alongside all kinds of gifts for the poor, a fairly large number of valuable books. We took these into the anteroom of the library in a hamper. Although Pius XII had not found time to look at the books immediately after the audience, he remembered perfectly well that some had been brought. On returning from his walk, he went straight up to the library to inspect them but was unable to find them. Finally, he discovered them in the anteroom. In the meantime, a telephone call had come from the Secretariat of State. We searched all over the apartments in vain and even checked the audience halls and the library. Nowhere a trace of him. The Holy Father could not have gone out, could he? We were all worried. I was just about to take the elevator into the storerooms when I caught sight of a light in the library anteroom. There, kneeling on the stone floor, was the Holy Father surrounded by the books, which he had already looked through thoroughly and arranged in piles. "Your Holiness, what a fright we've had!"

"Why? You've just come in time. I've finished. Take these books upstairs; the others are for Father to put on the shelves."

When the Secretariat of State rang again shortly afterwards to ask whether we had found the Holy Father, I answered, "Yes, among his books!"

When more and more books kept on coming and we no longer knew where to put them all, I once said, "So, now we'll take them all down into the Cortile di S. Damaso and set fire to them."

"What, Madre, burn the books?" came the horrified reply. "Burn what you like, but don't you dare touch my books!"

It was not only books that had a privileged place in the rooms where he worked; the written documents did too. The cupboards and drawers for them were always kept in meticulous order. During the day the desk, tables and chairs in the study were piled high with letters, papers and other documents, so that there was not a space free. However, when we came to clear up in the mornings, everything was scrupulously tidy. Each item had its own place so that no time was lost in hunting for anything. Lying at the front every morning was the large portfolio containing the papers for the Secretary of State (during the first years of his pontificate) or for a particular section of the Secretariat, depending on whose audience was scheduled to come first. The Holy Father never went to bed without attending to this no matter what the hour. He prepared his audiences with scrupulous care and expected the same of those attending them. "How much time could be saved if people would prepare and consider the subject matter in advance," the Holy Father used to say. He valued not only his own time but also that of others. He could tell immediately whether an official was prepared or not. He knew who simply had the work prepared by the department responsible and then came with it to the audience and who had handled the matter himself and was thus capable of replying to any queries. "How nice it is to work with someone who works himself and how much you get done in an hour if everything has been thought out in advance! On the other hand, what heavy going audiences are when every question is an eye-opener and not a single question is answered!" the Holy Father often said.

Cardinal von Faulhaber once told me after an audience with Pius XI that the Holy Father had said that audiences with his Secretary of State, Cardinal Pacelli, were always a pleasure even when there were difficult problems to solve. The Cardinal was, he said, not only very good and quick at grasping things but also never strayed from the subject or displayed any lack of concentration. Furthermore, he was always meticulously prepared, which made it not only easier but also a genuine pleasure to study and discuss matters with him.

Pius XII wrote all his speeches and addresses himself in his beautiful hand. He always emphasized that he could not memorize them unless he had written them himself. In the first fifteen years of his pontificate, he always spoke without notes no matter what language the speeches were to be delivered in. His prodigious memory allowed him to know his speeches off by heart when it came to making them until he was very advanced in years. Even if they were forty or more pages long, his marvelous memory never failed him. The prerequisite was that he composed and wrote down these speeches personally. With speeches and addresses, this was always the case whereas encyclicals and the preparations for large-scale Church or diplomatic rallies were initially entrusted, with detailed instructions, to the appropriate departments, whose work was subsequently subjected to thorough scrutiny.

Pius XII once said at an audience to a minister from one of the German states who had come with a delegation to Rome, "We have met before."

"Yes," the Minister replied, "many years ago, Your Holiness." Then Pius XII reflected for a moment and said, "It was fifteen years ago, on the twelfth of March in the Munich-Berlin express."

"I was staggered," the Minister said afterwards, "but my amazement was increased when two of my colleagues told me later that Pius XII had named the year, day and place of their meetings with him too."

As Nuncio, he once told of a boy who had been at school with him, who had also possessed a very good memory, but could not stand anyone being better than he was. One day it had happened that this classmate had had to ask the rest of the boys questions on history and had called almost exclusively on Eugenio Pacelli. The teacher, who was listening, had noticed that the questioner was really annoyed that Pacelli answered everything correctly, even when he began to ask things that were not part of the course. Then the teacher himself had begun to put the questions, also on subjects going beyond the curriculum, almost always calling on the pupil who had up to then been the questioner and who now, probably upset at having been seen through, missed a lot of the answers. "But after that I was left in peace," the Nuncio said, "and we became good friends because I told him that it was no credit to anyone personally to have a good memory but a gift of God, which He grants as and where He wants."

Pius XII worked with great precision and would never have used a quotation in a speech without first convincing himself that it was correct. He never considered it a waste of time to check everything thoroughly himself. If he did occasionally ask someone else to do it for him, he always ended up checking again to make sure that there had been no error. "What you don't do properly you regret afterwards," was already his motto as Secretary of State. As Pope, he adhered to it even more avidly and it is understandable that this was not easy for those working with him. Yet Pius XII was exceedingly considerate and whereas he never forgave himself a mistake, he could always show understanding for anyone else who erred. One of his closest collaborators once came out of an audience somewhat downcast. Since he saw that I noticed the fact, he said, "Something very stupid happened to me today and when I admitted it to the Holy Father, he simply laughed and said excusingly, 'Monsignor, when the Germans have committed a blunder, they say they've shot a big buck. It's a pity it isn't a buck, otherwise you could invite the whole Secretariat of State to dinner tomorrow.'"

When the Holy Father was asked to make a speech at a congress or some other event, he would first examine whether it was necessary and beneficial to comply with the request. If it was, he had all the pertinent literature fetched or requested it from other libraries if he did not possess it in his own. Then the material was studied thoroughly and the speech drafted. If the Holy Father knew an authority on the field in question, he was modest enough to consult whoever it was. He was grateful for all suggestions, examined them closely, and made use of them to the extent that he found them appropriate. When the outline of the speech was drafted, the full version was written out—for many years by hand, later on the typewriter, always by him. In the process, a great deal of filing, correction, and improvement was carried out. He then had this version looked through by a scholar he knew in the field in question. If there were no objections or corrections, which was often the case, the Holy Father might ask, "Do you really believe that everything has been thoroughly checked?" This showed the modesty of the Holy Father, who respected and valued the judgment of others. No one had to fear that he would lose Pius XII's esteem on account of a criticism. On the contrary! Even if the criticism turned out to be incorrect, this did not affect the Holy Father's trust in any way. In such cases he would simply say, "Anyone can make a mistake. The main thing is that I can be certain that the whole work has been checked and studied thoroughly." Once an important speech had gone through this process, it was ready to be passed on to the printer. It often happened that a speech, especially a Christmas address or something similar, was already printed before it was delivered. This was necessary so that all the translations could appear at the same time. The proofreading was also undertaken by the Holy Father, who had a sharp eye and seldom overlooked an error. Naturally, it sometimes happened that Pius XII was asked on the spot to say a few words, which meant that he could not prepare anything for the occasion. These short, but sometimes even lengthy speeches had a charm of their own in their simplicity, naturalness and sincerity—not that these qualities were lacking from his prepared speeches! The latter were well thought out and considered, something the spontaneous ones could not be. When Pius came back from an audience at which he had been asked to speak impromptu, he quickly jotted down what he had said so that he would remember it. He intended to have these subsequently noted-down addresses printed one day—if he ever found the time to look them through again carefully—along with a large number of other as yet unprinted speeches that the Secretariat of State was waiting for. In his extreme conscientiousness, he felt unable to hand over anything that had not been checked down to the last detail. Unfortunately, he never did find the time to look all this material through and so these treasures were burned as he had instructed.

Pius XI had often complained to his Secretary of State, "Cardinal, if you knew what an effort all these speeches are for me!" And Pius XII? In the prime of life and healthy as he was during the first years of his pontificate, he had spoiled everyone with addresses in all fields of ecclesiastical and secular scholarship so that in the course of time it became a veritable custom for every congress held in Rome to be treated to hearing his words, seeking his judgment and receiving guidelines from him. The Holy Father did everything, performing almost superhuman feats, to do justice to all.

Who among the millions who listened to him could ever have imagined what it cost him to cope with the vast amount of work that the speeches in particular demanded of him? Only those living close to him were able to see how Pius XII never wasted a minute, never allowed himself a free moment, but lived solely for his duty.

People often asked how it was possible for the Holy Father to be so well versed in every field. The answer was certainly, on the one hand, his supreme intelligence, his quick grasp of things, and his brilliant ability to retain what he had studied. On the other hand, he was filled with an indefatigable eagerness always to be learning new things. There was no field that would not have interested him. Already as Nuncio and Secretary of State he had made use of every moment, but once he was Pope, there was no rest for diversion whatsoever. I remember really well his friendly but firm reply when he was asked to rest a little for once: " There's all eternity for rest; here on earth it is our duty to completely fulfill the tasks entrusted to us by God."

Many years later, I was visited by a bishop who greatly admired Pius XII, to whom he owed his appointment. He asked a lot of questions and wanted to find out more and more about the Holy Father's life. "But now tell me," he said finally, "was there really never an hour in the life of the Nuncio, the Cardinal, and then the Pope without prayer, without business or work, no real relaxation, simply doing nothing with a few friends, perhaps over a glass of wine or something?"

I was forced to reply, "In all those long years, I NEVER knew him to do anything like that."

"But," came the response, "that's not possible. Then he must just have been an exceptional, a perfect person—a saint."

How very fond the Holy Father was of music! Nevertheless he would have regarded it as robbery to listen to a piece of good music on the radio unless it happened to be at mealtimes or during the 15–minute rest that he was ordered by the doctor to take after his walk in the last few years of his life. Everywhere duty came first. The argument that it was also his duty to pay at least a little attention to his health was brushed aside. Even during the quarter of an hour while he was shaving he would listen to "English by Radio" or to a French lesson. The Holy Father needed these languages continually and wanted to keep brushing them up by hearing them frequently. All this conveys an idea of how it was possible for Pius XII to deliver the magnificent speeches and addresses that amazed everyone, even as he was coping with the gigantic task of ruling the universal Church. The wisdom and erudition, the worldwide scope of his knowledge, and the response to thousands of different questions in the twenty volumes of his speeches are gold mines' that will certainly not be exhausted for decades. Pius XII will go down in Church history as a really great figure who sacrificed and consumed himself in the service of God, the Church, and souls.

A noble, pious priest (Father MacCormick), who knew Pius XII very well, said shortly after the Holy Father died, "Everything about him was heroic! No normal person could take the pace he kept up all his life. From my room I used to see the light burning in his window into the early hours. And that for twenty years! When I sometimes had the good fortune to be summoned to him in the evenings, it was always the same picture: the Holy Father at his desk, whether tired or fresh, whether in good or poor health, invariably with the same kind smile. Each time he apologized for disturbing others; he did not realize what a joy it was for me to be called. Today more than ever, now that the Holy Father has gone from us, I cannot help thinking of this heroism." Another saintly priest (Father Capello) said to me, "Give thanks to God that you had the privilege of serving such a great saint for forty years!"

For Pius XII it went without saying to sacrifice his all. "God has given me this office and I must do what is within my powers. A Pope does not have the right to think of himself!" That was his conviction and he lived and acted in accordance with it.

At my first audience with Pope John XXIII he talked a great deal about Pius XII. He praised the simplicity and good taste of the apartments and the typically German furniture, the perfect order in every cupboard and drawer, and in particular the so attractive and appealing chapel. Pope John went around the apartments with me and wanted to know who had given Pius XII the magnificent old paintings and various other objects, questions that were easy for me to answer. Then he was interested in how Pius XII had spent his day. I told him the daily routine and how his predecessor had never wasted a minute. "You don't have to tell me that," Pope John interrupted, "I've seen all the files in the Secretariat of State

containing Pius XII's memoranda, speeches, notes, and letters. It's unbe-
lievable that a human being could be capable of doing all that alongside all
the other work that a Pope has to deal with daily. I can only explain it if
Pius XII worked day and night. I always have this gigantic amount of work
before my eyes. I could never do anything like it. I delivered a speech in
Venice after his death but today I realize that I said far too little. Now I
want to have mosaics and two altars put in the chapel in St. Peter's where
he rests to make it really beautiful." I took the liberty of pointing out that
this was not necessary. "Your Holiness, Pius XII loved simplicity and even
emphasized the fact in his testament. But if Your Holiness wished to promote the cause for his beatification …!" The Pope replied, "That I shall
certainly do, most certainly, but I do not wish to leave the other undone,
either."

Not only books and documents were kept in meticulous order in the
Holy Father's apartments, it was the same with everything else. Adjoining
the small study was his bedroom, in the corner of which stood a large table
where the Holy Father used to lay the speech to be delivered the next day.
All the material relevant to the speech lay there too. When Pius XII
returned to the apartments after making the speech, everything to do with
it was cleared away and the material for the next was laid out. In the study
itself he had his important official documents and reports. Only when all
his official work had been looked through, dealt with, and prepared for the
following morning was it the turn of the speeches.

Pius XII did all his work thoroughly. Nothing was laid aside before it
had been exhaustively examined and checked. In view of the enormous
burden of work he had to deal with this was a way of making sure that
nothing was overlooked. Furthermore, it saved time since he did not have
to return to the document in question.

Unfortunately, the large, spacious bedroom only saw the Holy Father
for a few brief hours. He often said that this would be enough if only he
could really sleep well. However, he suffered very often from insomnia,
perhaps the affliction of all great thinkers. In addition, he had an extremely finely strung soul. Any serious worry—and when is a pope without
one?—any other sorrow, trouble, or a piece of bad news could immediately mean a sleepless night for him. But even after such a night, the next
morning always found him invariably kind, sympathetic, friendly, and
understanding.

Next to the bedroom were the bathroom and dressing-room. A great deal was spoken and written about morning gymnastics. The truth is that the Holy Father never had time for anything like that. His sole "gymnastics" and physical recuperation consisted in the one-hour walk that he took out of sheer necessity. Certainly, there was indeed a small room next to the bathroom containing the aforementioned electric horse, but in all the long years there, this was hardly ever used.

The small room led into a drawing-room with a beautiful painting of Innocent XI, and after the beatification of this great pope, the room was named after him.

Adjoining the drawing room was the dining room. The solid furniture with its skillfully executed German carving was much to the Holy Father's taste. On the sideboard stood the lovely silver soup tureen given to Nuncio Pacelli as a farewell gift when he left Germany by Hindenburg, who was President of the German Reich at the time. The exquisite tableware, the silver, and crystal were all Pius XII's private property. Almost all of it had come to Rome from Germany.

In the dining room, there were three bird cages with the little songsters the Holy Father loved so much. It was in fact Cardinal O'Connell who gave the Secretary of State Pacelli a cage containing two canaries when he was visiting the USA. These two now adorned the dining room. It was not until a greenfinch that had fallen out of the nest entered the house, was reared there, and delighted the Holy Father with its attachment to its new "family" that the little birds became Pius XII's inseparable companions.

Everyone, after all, needs some kind of diversion and relaxation. All of us around Pius XII, knowing that he never permitted himself any distraction, did everything to make the brief breathing space spent with the birds as pleasant as possible. The Holy Father was particularly fond of Gretchen, the beautiful, pure white canary. At first the bird did not thrive very well in her nest, and so we took her into special care. This was no easy matter during the first few days since she had to be fed carefully every two hours. It took some time before the little bird became tame. When the Holy Father came to meals, the little nest with Gretchen in it would be standing beside his plate so that he could give her this feed himself. She stayed there in her nest and cheeped when the Holy Father left. Gradually she made her first attempts at flying and soon came to meet the Holy Father, sat on his hands, head, and shoulders, flew on to his plate, and once—despite all our

HIS HUMBLE SERVANT

precautions—into the hot soup! Fortunately, she was not hurt. What pleasure this little creature gave the Holy Father! She recognized his step perfectly and flew to meet him when he came to breakfast or lunch. She would pull at his hair or even his ear when he was so lost in thought that he did not pay any attention to her. She sat on his hand and sang him a song for all she was worth. If she was thirsty, she would settle on his tumbler or wine glass. She flew on to every dish that was brought in to see if there was anything on it that she liked. When the Holy Father wagged his finger at her, saying, "Gretchen, that's not for you," she would fly off and settle instead on his hand to see if there might be something for her there. After the Holy Father's walk, we sometimes let the birds fly into the study. Usually the Holy Father would be sitting in an armchair by the window busy with the work that was brought regularly from the Secretariat of State after lunch. Gretchen would then fly directly on to the Holy Father's shoulder and from there to the sheet of paper he was holding in his hand, as if she wanted to read it too. Once, a sheet of paper slipped out of the Holy Father's hand and slid across to the door opposite. As quick as lightning Gretchen shot after it and with all the strength she could muster pulled the piece of paper right up to the Pope's feet with her little beak. She would dearly have loved to put the paper on his knees, but that was beyond her strength, so the Holy Father picked up both Gretchen and the sheet of paper. The little bird fluffed herself with joy at the praise she received. There was one thing that Gretchen could not stand and that was for the Holy Father to be busy writing. The little bird would then sit herself down exactly where he wanted to write and peck at his pen, so that he could not write a single word. When the Holy Father opened an envelope, Gretchen at once hopped into it to see what was inside. But the wonderful time in the study did not last long! Soon the Holy Father, with no time to waste, would ring for poor Gretchen to be put back into her cage. At 6:15, the hum of the electric razor was to be heard from the Holy Father's dressing room in the mornings. At the sound of it, Gretchen could not bear to be imprisoned in the cage any longer and was allowed to fly in to the Holy Father even though he was busy listening to a French or English lesson on the radio. There Gretchen would sit on his razor, being rocked to and fro.

In Castel Gandolfo, a greenfinch once flew in at the window and then stayed. It soon became the most affectionate creature imaginable, behaving just as if it had always been with us. It was particularly fond of the Holy

}86{

Father. When he ascended the stairs, the greenfinch did not fly but hopped from step to step with him. It hopped around after him from room to room and one had to be careful not to hurt it. Since it was so tame, we took it with us on to the patio one morning. It stayed with us for a while but then flew up high into the air and was gone. All day we hoped that it would return but on the second evening, we gave up all hope. But then, when the Holy Father came back from his walk the next afternoon and went into his study, where the windows were wide open, what should he see sitting on the arm of the chair at his desk but little Hans—and Hans flew to meet him as if nothing had happened! Affectionate as ever, the little bird remained with us from then on and was a joy to the Holy Father for many a long year.

Nor must we forget our lovely bullfinch. A Protestant couple from Germany who admired Pius XII greatly had heard that he loved birds and brought the bullfinch to Rome and the Vatican personally. At first it sang only for the Holy Father and seemed to know no one but him. Later, however, it would whistle the songs it had learned for us too, even when it was alone in its cage on the patio in the mornings. Down below in the court-yard people stopped to listen and asked who was whistling so beautifully. They could scarcely believe that it was a bird.

Adjoining the study in the papal apartments in the Vatican was the office with the telephones. Next to this lay the kitchen, pantry, and cloak-room. This part of the private apartments could be shut off with a large door and reached via both the staircase and the elevator. Across the corridor, there were two large rooms, in the first of which hung a very beautiful painting portraying the Holy Father as Cardinal. It had been painted by the famous Spanish artist Bacca Flor on the occasion of Cardinal Pacelli's visit to the USA as Secretary of State. The magnificent mahogany furniture there was again solid German workmanship.

The next room contained an oil painting of Pius X. As Pius XII told us, it had been painted during the saint's lifetime and Pius X had said at the time, "That's what I'm really like!"

From here, one entered the large study, which was more like a library with its four large bookcases. Set into the desk was a small silver plaque saying that the contents of this room had been given to Nuncio Pacelli by the German bishops as a farewell gift. Here it was that for many long years Pius XII received the gentlemen from the Secretariat of State in the evenings. The large, beautiful room contained three very old oil paintings by German and

Dutch masters, which were also gifts from dear friends. The floor was decorated with Pius XI's coat of arms, a present from the mosaic factory of St. Peter's. The Holy Father always found this too much for him and wanted to have it removed, but he was unable to find anyone to do him this favor because no one shared his opinion, and so he finally gave up insisting.

A door on the left of the large study led into the antechamber. From there one could get to the Scala Papale and the loggia. It was very rare for visitors to enter the private apartments via the papal staircase, since Pius XII did almost all of his receiving in the official rooms. On the other hand, the gentlemen from the Secretariat of State regularly came to audiences via the loggia.

A further door led from the large study into two spacious rooms full of cupboards. These contained the presents brought to the Holy Father. He would often have had an opportunity to give others pleasure with these but in his conscientiousness he scarcely considered himself to be their owner. Any gift that could be used for poor churches or for the poor in general— and there were a great many such gifts—was immediately put into the private storerooms for distribution. These rooms led into the loggia, part of which was shut off by a glass door. It was here that we always prepared the tree and crib for Christmas.

The beautiful chapel, which invited composure and prayer, was the focal point of the apartments. The furnishings in it had already belonged to the Holy Father as Cardinal. He never allowed anything about it to be changed. Anyone who saw the Holy Father alone there with his God knew whence he drew the strength and courage for his constant, taxing life of sacrifice. Originally the artist had decorated the ceiling of the chapel not only with the coat of arms of Pius XII but also with the Pope's name. This was also too much for the Holy Father. After a few years, he succeeded in getting the golden letters covered up so that they were no longer visible. Only when the chapel has to be renovated will Pius XII's name come to light again. Since the Holy Father loved his chapel dearly, we did everything to decorate it as beautifully as possible. For Holy Mass Pius XII normally used the chalice left to him as a remembrance by Pius XI, in the cover of which was a handwritten card with the words: *"Al mio carissimo Cardinale, con infinita gratitudine. Pius XI"* (To my dearest Cardinal, with infinite gratitude). Like everything else, this most beautiful chalice with a large diamond set in its base remained there.

But of course, the Pontiff very often had to use a chalice that had been sent to him directly or via the Secretariat of State by a priest—usually a newly ordained one—with the request that the Holy Father should use it once for Holy Mass. Such a request was never denied even though the form of the chalice was not always to the Holy Father's taste.

Pius XII preferred to be alone at daily Mass. Only the members of his household were present. "At least for this brief hour leave me alone with my God," he used to say. Thus he could take his time and was not forced, as was otherwise always the case, to take everyone and everything into consideration.

In the early years of his pontificate his relatives were allowed to attend the midnight Masses on Christmas Eve. However, they were soon deprived of this beautiful hour since later the Holy Father celebrated in the Capella Matilda in the presence of the whole diplomatic corps. His relatives saw very little altogether of their eminent brother and uncle. They were already kept very short when he was a Cardinal and they certainly did not see him more often now. I sometimes heard that the newspapers wrote of nepotism, but I can say from my own direct experience that there must seldom have been a pope who took as little care of his relatives as Pius XII did. If we sisters had not prepared some little trifle for them as a Christmas present while we were decorating the tree and the crib, they would certainly have been likely not to have received anything at all. "God has given my family what they need," the Holy Father would say, but all the same, he genuinely shared their pleasure when they expressed their delight at receiving these small tokens. The short time they spent with the Holy Father brought them so much happiness and joy that they longed for Christmas and his name day all year through. We sisters were always impressed by the refinement and modesty of these dear relatives.

The sacristy adjoining the chapel contained exquisite vestments, which had been given to him by dear friends and religious institutions. The Holy Father preferred the light vestments and so the heavy, gold-embroidered ones almost always remained in the cupboard after a single use.

We also took care to provide him with thin, light albs. All objects had to be of good quality and beautiful, serving as they did our greatest treasure on earth when they were used at Holy Mass. Later the Holy Father had a cupboard installed, which was gradually filled with a rich selection of chasubles, albs and altar linen ready to be given away whenever Pius XII was asked for such things in audiences—which was frequently the case—by the bishops of poor dioceses.

The papal apartments were entirely appropriate to their purpose and dignified. How they had been altered to their advantage by the renovations! The windows were now half as high again—they had been restored to their original form—which removed the oppressive atmosphere from the rooms completely. One of these windows, the "vigilant eye of the Father of Christendom" as it was called, became renowned throughout the world. It was lit into the early hours of the morning, bearing witness to the tireless work and worry of the Holy Father consuming himself up there like a candle in the service of God, the Church and souls.

When it was very difficult to get to Rome to begin with after the collapse of Germany and the end of the war, an American officer offered to take Cardinal von Faulhaber with him in his car from Munich to Rome. It was an arduous drive lasting several days. "When we finally arrived in Rome," the Cardinal told me, "it was already late. Nevertheless I wanted to see St. Peter's first and we drove there. The basilica, the Vatican, the enormous colonnades seemed more impressive than ever to me that night. I had never experienced them like that before. Then, as I raised my eyes higher, I saw like a silent, radiant star the lighted window of the Holy Father's study. Oh, that eye of the Father of Christendom watching over the sleeping city, over the whole world, what an impression it made on me! The officer looked up at it too, and asked me who was still up so late there. I told him it was the Holy Father. When I leave Rome again in a few days' time, I shall go to St. Peter's Square again at midnight to experience this again one last time," the Cardinal concluded.

How often the Holy Father blessed the people from this window! Although it was a long way up from St. Peter's Square, the crowds below felt instinctively that Pius XII was among them and blessing them when he spread his arms wide and uttered the words *"Benedictio Dei omnipotentis . . ."* in his clear, euphonious voice. If I happened to be passing, I never missed an opportunity to mingle with the crowds waiting for the blessing. Thus I often witnessed wonderful scenes. Once, just as the window was opening, a woman said to those kneeling around her, "I don't know why you're supposed to kneel here, the Pope is a human being too!" But then the Holy Father appeared and greeted the crowds, raising his arms and waving lovingly to everyone. The woman stared up at the window as if transfixed and gradually sank to her knees. She was still kneeling long after we had all stood up again after the blessing and there were tears streaming down her face. Finally, I went over and asked if anything was wrong with her. "Oh no," she sobbed, "but now I know why people kneel here before the Holy Father—that's our Lord Jesus on the Cross!" When Pius XII gave the blessing, his eyes raised to Heaven, his arms outstretched, he really was like Our Lord on the Cross.

After a canonization or some other great feast day, for example Saints Peter and Paul, when St. Peter's Square was bright with thousands of lights in the evening and the whole city seemed to be gathered there, the Holy Father had no peace behind his lighted window. He was forced to keep opening it to bless and bless! Again and again the window opened and the jubilant crowds called their beloved father. Once we went out on to the square after the evening rosary together in the private chapel to take a look at the spectacle from below. There we bumped into Cardinal von Faulhaber and his companion, who were also in Rome at the time. "We've been here for almost an hour," the Cardinal said. "Can there be anything more beautiful? I intend to stay here as long as the Holy Father keeps blessing."

"It will be midnight, then," we warned him.

"If the Holy Father can bless until midnight, I can hold out that long too," the Cardinal replied, adding rather sadly, "It's likely to be my last visit to Rome, I'm old and ill." But in fact he came several more times.

For Pius XII it was no easy test of his patience to have to keep getting up from his work, opening the window and blessing the crowds. However, if he allowed more than ten minutes to pass, the cars began to hoot so that the noise would have prevented him from continuing to work anyway.

It was often said of the Holy Father that he spoiled people too much, but with his kind, fatherly heart, he could not find it in him to turn a deaf ear. "God will allow blessings to flow from this sacrifice too," he said to those who thought he did too much in this respect.

When the silver trumpets sounded at great Church festivities in St. Peter's and the Holy Father, clad in full papal attire, was carried in on the *sedia gestatoria*, many people probably thought that the Pope's life must be one long, solemn ceremony, far removed from the burdens and travails of everyday life. However, anyone who was permitted to experience the Holy Father's daily routine at close quarters for decades also knows of his quiet, unsuspected heroism.

Let us take a brief look at the Holy Father's day!

At 6:15 a.m. the alarm rings and soon the hum of the electric razor is to be heard from the bathroom. The small radio is also turned on since at this hour there is a fifteen-minute lesson in one of the major languages, which the Holy Father considers it useful to hear repeatedly even though he already speaks them. His favorite little bird does not distract him for it sits on the hand in which he holds his razor. It is allowed to stay with him until he has finished dressing. Then it knows it has to leave and return to its cage. At 7 a.m. the Holy Father goes to the chapel. He kneels down on the large prie-dieu, which makes his tall figure look even slimmer, to prepare for the divine sacrifice. Then he goes to the altar and puts on the sacred vestments. He recites the prescribed prayers so clearly that every syllable is audible, but not loudly or in a disturbing way. Now he begins the prayers at the foot of the altar. Bowing low, he prays the Confiteor slowly, as if laying his soul into every word. Then he spreads his arms wide, raises his eyes and face to the large ivory crucifix and ascends the steps to the altar. I always found the Introit of the Mass of Doctors of the Church so appropriate for Pius XII: "In the midst of the Church the Lord opened His mouth, and He filled him with the spirit of wisdom and understanding; He clothed him with a robe of glory . . ." The Epistle, the Gradual, the Gospel, all the glorious prayers acquired a special solemnity on the lips of the Holy Father. "*Sursum corda*! (Lift up your hearts!)" The Preface follows! Could it ever be prayed more beautifully, more movingly? Then there is silence for a while. The Holy Father remembers all who have asked for and rely on his prayers; he prays for all his children throughout the world. I once asked him why his *Memento* prayers took so very long. His reply: "I am constantly being asked for my prayers. The Divine Sacrifice is the moment when the Eternal Father cannot refuse anything, so I use this time as well as I can."

The Holy Mass approaches its climax. With seraphic fervor in his devotion the Holy Father speaks the words of the Consecration, so quietly yet so clearly, with such strong faith and warm love that all present are drawn under the sacred spell. The Eternal High Priest looks down from the Cross at his vicar and grants him what he implores in fervent prayer. Again a long pause! The dear departed are not forgotten, either. Holy Communion is a most intimate uniting with HIM whom the Holy Father is called to follow and represent on earth.

Then again the arms are outstretched toward our Crucified Lord and the blessing of the Vicar of Christ is given not only for those few present there, but for the entire world. His thanksgiving after Holy Mass is long and ardent. A prelate who once chanced to witness it was so moved that it was a long time before he was able to appear before the Holy Father. He was absolutely set on taking a photograph of the Pope at prayer and returned for that purpose the next day. The picture, which we still possess, has preserved the expression of composed earnestness and unqualified preparedness.

Once the Secretariat of State telephoned after Holy Mass and asked for the Holy Father to call back. Since his thanksgiving took a particularly long time, a second call came. They thought that we had forgotten to pass on the message and so I ventured to go into the chapel and tell the Holy Father. He was kneeling there as always, upright, his eyes raised to the crucifix above the tabernacle. "Holy Father, they are asking . . ."

Slowly his folded hands were lowered, but his gaze remained fixed on the cross and the Holy Father said, "He is nailed fast and cannot free Himself, can only endure and suffer—and He does so without complaint, out of love. The Pope too is nailed to his post and must remain silent." The Holy Father must have been oppressed by some great sorrow but he said nothing more about it. I was deeply moved by this experience. At other times too, when Pius XII suffered injustices, bitter disappointments, hurtful behavior, even calumny from certain sides, indeed even from those around him to whom he was so good, one noticed this only if one happened to be in the chapel at the same time as him, when he thought that he was pouring out his cares to his Lord in the tabernacle alone. It was impossible to forget such incidents, which displayed most clearly his way of thinking.

This calls to mind the kindness with which Pius XII always treated other people when he knew perfectly well that they had done something wrong. One of his nephews had mentioned an obvious lie to him, which the Holy Father could not fail to recognize as such. "Never lie yourself!" he said to his nephew, "What others do is not your responsibility."

When he had finished giving thanks after Mass, at about 8:30, the Holy Father used to have breakfast. His birds kept him company, but they also knew that only fifteen minutes were allowed. Punctually at six minutes to nine, the elevator took Pius XII to the audience rooms on the floor below. Normally it was the Secretary of State or one of the two

Undersecretaries who was received first. This audience usually lasted one to two hours. Then came the "*Udienze di Tabella*," the scheduled audiences. These were primarily with the Cardinal Prefects of the various Congregations, who discussed their problems, presented their work and waited for the Pope's decision. Very few people have any idea of how much work this is. The Holy Father was extremely exact and responsibility weighed heavily on him.

If state visits were expected or other eminent persons to be received, this was entered on the audience list the day before. After these came the private audiences with persons of importance—priests, politicians, ambassadors, creative artists. The length of time taken up by these varied, but then began the semi-private "*baciamano*" audiences. At these, the Holy Father went from one person to another—everyone was allowed to speak to him and received a word, a look, a piece of encouragement that often lasted a whole lifetime. Many people said that they had come to the audience well prepared but then in his presence, held spellbound by the incomparable kindness and understanding benevolence that his eyes radiated, had forgotten everything, fallen to their knees and through their tears had been able to do nothing more than kiss the hand he offered them. All languages were spoken here and in all languages the greeting, the words, and the understanding were returned.

Now it was the turn of the big general audiences. Pius XII gave these too their own special character. The people appeared in the hall in groups, praying and singing. How soon the largest hall became too small! St. Peter's was all that was left and there in the basilica innumerable pilgrims waited for the Holy Father, the focus of their yearning on their visit to Rome. That Pius XII was punctual was long since common knowledge. Naturally, everyone wanted the best places and came early. The great masses of pilgrims really embodied the catholic, all-embracing, universal Church. The silver trumpets announced the approach of the Holy Father. Unbounded jubilation, a storm of enthusiasm broke out. So that everyone would be able to see him, the Holy Father had himself carried in held high on the *sedia gestatoria*. He overlooked no one. He turned to all sides, greeting and waving. Afterwards everyone thought that the Holy Father had looked at him alone, greeted him specially. The *sedia* stopped in front of the throne. Pius XII lightly ascended the steps and, smiling kindly at everyone, waited for the noise of the rejoicing to die down. Now he began to name the groups who had come. They were all to know that the Holy Father was aware that they were there. For each group he had a special word, a special greeting in their mother tongue. All felt they were at home there!

These audiences usually lasted between one and two hours. Very often there were special circumstances leading Pius XII to deliver a fairly long address. When everyone had finally been remembered and everything done, the Holy Father rose and gave the blessing. Thunderous applause broke out. Some shouted for joy, others wept; others still were quiet, asking themselves if the audience really was over. Pius XII descended the steps. Here a lot more people were waiting for him, some with gifts, and others with requests. Those who could not reach the Holy Father's hands tried to touch his cassock or cloak. It would never have ended if the chamberlains on duty had not finally extricated the Holy Father. Back on the *sedia* he was carried slowly toward the exit, where he once again turned to his children and, with arms outstretched and eyes raised heavenwards, blessed them for the last time.

It once happened that as the Holy Father bent right down from the *sedia*, as he so often did, his *zucchetto*—the white skullcap—fell off. Of course, everyone wanted the cap and Pius XII came home without it. From this incident a custom grew up that lasted right up to his final audience: as soon as the Holy Father came into sight on the *sedia*, hands were stretched out to him holding *zucchettos* for him to put on and give back again. At a single audience there were once over a hundred caps to be put on and returned. He complied in order not to spoil the pleasure of possessing a *zucchetto* that he had worn for the people who, as time went on, badgered him more and more.

At such meetings, there were always people who told their common father of their sorrows and suffering in the hope that he would help. Unabashed and in a loud voice they told him what was troubling them. Let one incident serve as an example for many similar ones. Pius XII had just come to lunch after a long audience when Monsignor Montini announced a woman who simply would not be turned away. She said she had to thank the Holy Father. In the general audience she had asked him to help her child, who was seriously ill. The doctor had diagnosed a form of tuberculosis and declared it to be incurable. The disease was already at a very advanced stage. For a month, the child had not been able to either stand or walk. The mother herself was a war widow and had only this one child. At the audience, the Holy Father had consoled the woman, blessed her repeatedly and told her to have great faith and trust in God since for Him everything was possible. "I went home," the woman said, "and on the stairs my daughter already was coming toward me calling out, 'Mama, I'm no longer in pain and I can walk again, I'm well!'"

After these audiences the Holy Father usually came home very late for lunch, which was then simple and short. While he was eating, he listened to the latest news on the radio and his birds kept him company. It was a good thing that Pius XII had a chance to be alone now for he would have been too tired to continue talking. At most, he had to make peace between Hansel and Gretel if they were fighting over a lettuce leaf, or to warn Gretchen not to be constantly after his hair when she wanted to build a nest.

The thirty minutes were soon over. Now and then, someone came from the Secretariat of State or the Antechamber during this time to give him a piece of important news or to ask for a reply.

Now the Holy Father took half an hour's siesta. In the meantime, a bulging portfolio would have arrived from the Secretariat of State with important reports and announcements. Pius XII looked them through and took out what seemed suitable work for his hour's walk. How often the doctor begged him not to work for at least this one hour, to enjoy nature and give his mind a rest. "I can't afford that, otherwise I won't get through my work," was always the reply. Many years earlier, before he became Pope, he asked the doctors whether there was any way of doing without his walk—naturally, in order to save time! None of them knew of one. This was a good thing too, because the walk was absolutely necessary for Pius XII's health—he suffered from gastroptosis (a dropped stomach). This brisk, hour-long walk was certainly one of the reasons why he remained so mobile right into old age that everyone was astonished. At 4 p.m. the Holy Father was back home. After a visit to the chapel he returned to work—and he worked on without respite. All the problems that had been addressed to him at the scheduled audiences, the fat portfolio from the Secretariat of State, the day's post—an immense burden of work—were all waiting to be dealt with. For almost twenty years, the Holy Father bore this burden and coped with this amount of work with perseverance and dedication, never flagging, never tiring. Unless some special exception was called for, no audiences took place in the afternoons, so Pius XII was able to devote these hours to peaceful work. If there was some matter that could not be postponed or dealt with on the secret telephone linking the Holy Father with the Secretariat of State, the official in question would be called to an audience in the Pope's private study.

By this time, it was eight in the evening. Several times a week Pius XII had himself informed about everything to do with the government of the Vatican State since he wished to know all that went on and took an interest in every conceivable field. I often heard it said, "People come to him with the most difficult problems and cannot see a way out. In a few sentences the Holy Father has banished every doubt and found a solution for everything." At 8:30 p.m. the Holy Father would come to dinner. What he ate was so little that we often wondered how anyone could live on it with such a workload, especially since Pius XII neither ate nor drank anything between meals. His little birds were long since asleep and so he just listened to the news on the radio. At this hour there would also have been an opportunity to listen to good music, which Pius XII was so fond of, but it was extremely rare for him to allow himself even a quarter of an hour for this.

Now and then a particularly good film was shown that we wanted the Holy Father to see. If there was no way out, he would come for five or ten minutes but certainly never longer. "You watch it and enjoy it," he would say. "I can't afford to, my work doesn't permit it."

He did not even see the whole of the splendid film entitled "Pastor Angelicus," which was greeted with so much enthusiasm at the time and seen by so many people. A number of gentlemen were allowed to come who he knew would give him an accurate and frank assessment of it—after all, it was about him—but he himself thought that duty called him to his desk.

At about 9 p.m. the Holy Father prayed the rosary with his household in the chapel. Then he continued working until eleven. The hour between eleven and midnight belonged to the Lord in the tabernacle. Then it was back to work until 2 a.m. Now at last the day's work was over for the Pope.

In the window high up in the Vatican Palace the light went out, the Holy Father had gone to bed—after a hard day filled with work. But the new day that would soon begin to dawn was to bring him new labors, and for almost twenty years no other sort of day was ever to greet him.

One episode that belongs here comes to mind. When the Holy Father went to Castel Gandolfo, the doctor wanted to persuade him to stop work at midnight there at least. At last Pius half and half gave in to his insistence. Then, one night, when everyone was fast asleep and no one could check when the Holy Father really did go to bed, there was suddenly a loud, non-stop ringing at ten to two in the morning. We sisters were on our feet immediately. We feared that something had happened since the ringing went on and on. And what did we see? At the top of the stairs—our rooms were on the floor below—stood the Holy Father shaking his head and saying, "I don't know what's the matter, the bell suddenly went off by itself and won't stop ringing!" We saw the cause at once. Lying on Pius XII's desk was a small, round pushbutton bell on which he had laid a heavy book without noticing when he was clearing up so that the bell went off straight away. Now the truth was out: he did not go to bed at midnight! We could not resist teasing him. "Your Holiness, we thought you'd gone to bed long before now!" He understood immediately. Nevertheless, the tell-tale bell had to disappear from his desk.

CHAPTER SIX

THE TIARA AS A CROWN OF THORNS:

THE SECOND WORLD WAR

In the last few months before he died Pius XI had already been extremely worried about the threat to world peace. His successor, burdened with the same worry, saw it as his pre-eminent task to work for peace and the prevention of war. From his very first hour as pope, he dedicated himself totally to the task God had given him. When the outbreak of war destroyed all hope, he did everything that was humanly possible to prevent the war from spreading and to give every conceivable assistance to those affected by it. At the beginning this was far from easy, but love found ways and means enough toward this goal. No stone remained unturned.

Soon after his coronation, Pius XII had addressed an appeal for peace to the world and he spoke on the same subject in St. Peter's at Easter. He let no opportunity pass without appealing for prudence and justice, and he called on the nuncios to do the same. Pius XII, who had lived and worked in Germany for almost thirteen years, knew the German people. Consequently, he shared the nation's suffering sorely when it was subjected to slavery and exploitation and, above all, religious persecution during the Hitler regime.

How happy Pius XII was over the end of the Spanish Civil War, which had brought the country so much suffering and distress. In a fatherly manner, he admonished Spanish Catholics to do their utmost to secure just peacetime policies in their country.

As early as May 1939, the Holy Father called for a crusade of prayer for world peace. His imploring radio address on August 24 is familiar to everyone: "Nothing is lost by peace; everything is lost by war . . ." On August 31, a further appeal followed. Nevertheless, the powerful of the world turned a deaf ear to the voice of reason and saw only their own egoistic aims. These were not empty words that Pius XII addressed to the world. Before he said or wrote anything, his sensitive soul had already tasted everything to the full. Now, in his supreme office and responsible for the good and ill of his children, he suffered doubly and trebly.

How well I remember von Ribbentrop's visit. How incensed we Germans were at this arrogant man! I was consequently delighted to hear a remark made by one of the chamberlains: "He came out of the audience much smaller than he went in!"

Despite all his active charity, the salvation of souls remained Pius XII's main consideration. He let no opportunity pass, whether at receptions, jubilees, canonizations, or beatifications, without calling for a deepening of faith and the interior life. He admonished priests to the fullness of priesthood, religious to a true religious spirit. In this, he saw a possibility of warding off the divine scourge of war. His own life was a living example to the world that bordered on the incredible.

There was no coal for heating and so the Vatican—above all the Holy Father's apartments—was not heated. Many people in the Vatican resented this, but Pius XII believed that he owed himself such hardship as he wished to set a good example. The large rooms were bitterly cold in winter, especially in rainy weather. All the same, the most he allowed himself was a hot-water bottle or an electric cushion for his hands so that he could write. For really cold days we procured an electric radiator, which we switched on in the private apartments in the Holy Father's absence and without his knowledge in order to warm at least his study a little. However, it was completely inadequate in the large rooms, and we also had to make sure not to be caught with the radiator on. The Holy Father suffered badly from the cold and had severe chilblains on his hands. But the soldiers in the field, the people who had been bombed out, the refugees and all the others—did they not have to put up with much worse? And so the Pope did not want to be better off than they were. We in the house moved about as much as possible and worked as hard as we could; the Holy Father, on the other hand, was forced to sit at his desk working and consequently felt the cold much more.

Pius XII took a great personal interest in the Information Office he had set up immediately after the outbreak of war. It was able to help many thousands of families or at least to give them a ray of hope. The Holy Father wished to be kept informed of the work there and was delighted by every piece of good news that could be passed on. How happy he was when a mother wrote that the pontifical information service had finally assured her that her son was alive. At an audience, a man once called out to the Holy Father, "I must tell you something. Holy Father, please read my letter." With these words, he handed Pius XII a letter in which father, mother, brothers and sisters, and grandparents of a soldier who was now a prisoner of war thanked the Pope sincerely that they had received news of him. They also wrote of the soldier's joy at receiving a parcel from the Pontificia Commissione di Assistenza (PCA), the first since he had been taken prisoner. "Holy Father," the happy father wrote at the end of the letter, "my family and I wish that all the happiness and joy that you have brought to our family may return a thousandfold to your own heart." Pius XII immediately had a letter written to the family and another especially good parcel sent to the prisoner. This is just one example among so very many! How much suffering was alleviated, how many tears dried, how many families brought consolation and help!

Unfortunately, it was not possible for the blessings of the information service to benefit everyone. Russia and Germany impeded it wherever they could. Nevertheless, everything possible was done and no sacrifice of time or money was spared. The information service was only a small part of the PCA. One of the Holy Father's great concerns was to help the poor prisoners of war. Every country still rich enough to help was asked for assistance and God alone knows how much the soldiers and prisoners received in the way of warm clothing, food, and medicaments. And it was not only the prisoners who benefited from Pius XII's help; it also went to every country affected by the war. Long cavalcades of PCA trucks were dispatched with donations. The Holy Father sent the gifts of his love to the various regions of Italy, to France, Germany, Austria, Hungary, etc. Whereas to begin with there were only trucks available to distribute the gifts, these were soon joined by railway wagons carrying a steady stream of donations to the suffering and needy in the various countries.

How Pius XII had welcomed it when Monsignor Baldelli had asked for permission to set up the PCA. What a great interest the Holy Father took in it! It was really an ideal for him since its humble beginnings were in accordance with his preference for doing good behind the scenes. Naturally, he soon recognized that in view of the enormous amount of distress it was imperative to expand this relief organization and he supported it in every way, showing his pleasure when it was the first to help whenever new distress appeared. Who today still remembers the glorious adventures of this "Caritas" charity organization from the years around 1944?!

Alongside the large-scale PCA, there were also His Holiness's private storerooms, which from tiny beginnings developed into a gigantic relief organization. Originally intended merely to satisfy the many individual requests received daily, they were gradually enlarged and extended more and more. Our requests to the Holy Father for help were never inopportune, for he always had an open hand. When the large deliveries of gifts then arrived from the USA and other countries, it was in these private storerooms that, with the help of thirty to forty communities of nuns, clothing and linen were washed, cleaned, darned, and ironed to warm the freezing and clothe the naked.

The Holy Father commissioned people to go into the prison camps to bring consolation and help to their wretched inmates. From the storerooms they were given truckloads of medicaments, food, clothing, linen and shoes so that they would not have to turn up empty-handed. Once a high Church dignitary who did a great deal for His Holiness's private stores came and asked us what we needed most urgently. After we had given him an idea of everything, he said, "Rest assured that I'll do what I can. At my audience with him the Holy Father expressed such sincere and heartfelt thanks that I'll gladly go begging for him myself." We often heard similar words from cardinals, bishops, and benefactors from all over the world.

Once a village near Rome had been bombed out and completely destroyed during the night so that immediate help was required. The storerooms were quickly emptied but, even before we could give a thought to what we were going to do the next day if help should be needed, Providence replenished the exhausted stocks again.

Although the Holy Father was overburdened with work, he took the time to come into the storerooms personally and express his gratitude to those who helped so untiringly to enable him to alleviate distress with his gifts. He never missed an opportunity to spur us on to charity or to thank us. He wanted to know exactly where the gifts had come from so that all the donors could be thanked. If he had a chance to do this personally at audiences, the expression of his gratitude was so heartfelt that everyone went away filled with a renewed desire to give generously.[1]

The Holy Father's radio broadcasts to children and adults in the USA are renowned. However, it was not only from the USA that help was received; Spain, Canada, Mexico, South America, and other countries made their contributions as well. All the states capable of sending help vied with one another to enable the great and kind Father of Christendom to distribute aid generously.

At an audience with an American officer the Holy Father had succeeded in being granted permission for the wagons loaded with gifts from the Vatican to be taken to Germany free of charge by military transport trains. What did not remain in West Germany could easily be sent on from there. In this way, a large number of deliveries were also made to the eastern zone, to which it had until then been almost impossible to send gifts even though they were so urgently needed precisely there.

A priest from Thuringia once managed to come to Rome. He told the Holy Father of the inconceivable plight and forlornness of the priests there. We had just prepared a consignment of seventeen goods wagons and now hurriedly packed approximately seventy more parcels, each containing a cassock, linen, shoes, wine and hosts for Holy Mass, and a little food so that these poor priests should receive a Christmas greeting from the Holy Father. We waited in suspense to see if it would be possible to penetrate Soviet-occupied territory and cheer the priests, who had already gone without so much, with these gifts. The resourceful Caritas Director had organized everything excellently and the first letters of thanks arrived over Christmas from those to whom the Holy Father's kind heart had shown such loving care. One day a man handed Pius XII a letter during the general audience. When the letter was opened at home, it read: "Your Holiness, I am one of the priests to whom you sent those wonderful Christmas parcels. We cannot express what we all felt, but be assured that the knowledge of the loving care of a father who is so close to us in our misery gave us all new courage to remain faithful to our calling—even to our deaths."

---

1   The following paragraphs appear to refer to post-war aid, particularly the references to West Germany, the "eastern zone," and Soviet-occupied territory around Thuringia.

"Holy Father," another priest wrote from the Sudetenland, "there are no words to describe what we felt when your fatherly kindness sent us this greeting, which made us forget all the misery in the joyful knowledge that you think of us and are close to us with your prayers, your love, and your understanding! For a long time we had suffered the sorest starvation, not only physically, we were spiritually run down as well. Then came your greeting . . .!"

A priest from France once wrote: "The most beautiful gift we ever received came from you, Holy Father! It was obvious that love had prepared and packed it!"

Every year the Holy Father received a shipment of coffee from Brazil. As a result of an error that was clarified only later, it was once left lying in a storehouse in Naples for a very long time so that a double delivery arrived—right on time to add twenty-five sacks of it to a consignment of gifts that had just been put together. Later a letter came from a camp in France: "Holy Father, can you imagine what your coffee meant for us starving, emaciated prisoners with our heart complaints?"

A letter also came from a military hospital: "Holy Father, if only you could see the faces of the sick here who had not smiled for months and are now radiant with joy over their cup of coffee, all feeling much better. If only you could hear how they bless you and thank and thank you!"

Now Pius XII no longer wanted to drink coffee or see any on his breakfast table (he had hardly ever drunk a cup before and when he had, it was before he had to deliver a long speech) so that we could send more into the field!

These are just a few examples of what was written in love and gratitude. Thousands of letters express similar feelings—and how many more letters may never have reached their destination?

Long after the war was over a priest who had served for a long time as a military chaplain told me in the private storerooms that he had ministered to a dying soldier in his last hour. When he asked the soldier if he had any further wishes, he had told him to reach into his pocket and take out the slip of paper there. It was the card enclosed with every consignment of parcels that went into the field: "From the Holy Father with his apostolic blessing." The priest had put it to the soldier's lips so that he could kiss it once again, for it was with this blessing he had wanted to die.

The spiritual distress of his children oppressed the Holy Father no less than the physical. Innumerable churches and chapels lay in ruins, thousands of Catholics were without all spiritual care. It is all too well known how quickly people become alienated from the Church as soon as they are deprived of a chance to attend Holy Mass and receive religious instruction.

Once again, it was the Holy Father himself who gave what he could and requested money for three hundred emergency churches. The generosity of the American bishops, headed by Cardinal Spellman, made it possible to alleviate the most desperate distress here too. Never shall I forget either the joy with which Pius XII accepted this help and passed it on the very same day, or the sincerity of his gratitude.

The private stores were then able to deliver hundreds of chalices, ciboria, and chasubles as well as altar linen, albs, sick-call sets, and everything necessary to set up an altar, to equip an emergency church. Again and again, when everything had been given away, the empty cupboards in the storerooms were filled up again. We were often astonished that we always had something to give even though the requests we received did not diminish in number. One day a lady came into the private storerooms and gave us a sum of money large enough to pay for a hundred monstrances. She wished merely for her name to be engraved in their bases, which we were more than happy to agree to. Just before she came, we had given away our last monstrance.

With the exception of one full-time employee—who was dedicated to his work with exemplary loyalty and love—all the work in the private storerooms was done by voluntary helpers. Since the goods wagons were transported completely free of charge by the Americans, everything could be passed on in full to benefit the poor. How hard and how gladly everyone worked here! The dear sisters and the one or two men who carried out this great work with me day after day were all very happy to help. They all knew that, next to serving God, they were being allowed to serve the Holy Father, whose love for the poor had created this little kingdom of active charity where so much good could be done. Pius XII knew that he only had to tell us to send this or that here or there. Nothing was ever unavailable in the stores. A great deal of bashful and hidden misery was alleviated here. It was a special joy to the Holy Father when he discovered such suffering and was able to relieve it quietly and unnoticed.

Even though he sometimes complained, "You always have to be looked for in the storerooms," he immediately added, "but it's a good thing that we have them."

No one who turned to the Holy Father with a request was disappointed, but it was his heartfelt need to give abundantly to Rome and above all to the poor parish priests in the suburbs. All these priests soon knew about the private storerooms and turned to them with all their needs. They were regularly able to provide themselves with clothing, shoes, linens, and food for the poor in their parishes. Writing materials, toys, and sweets for the children were not forgotten, either, and everything that the children needed for their First Communion was given them too. The poor priests were also most grateful for the Mass stipends we repeatedly requested for them. The private stores did not possess any money but whenever there was great need anywhere, we knew that a request to the Holy Father would not be in vain since any other expenses that arose were also paid for out of his private funds. What the Holy Father gave to poor priests for an urgently needed chapel, for a clubroom, for the purchase of building land or a sports field ran into millions. Even after the war was over and conditions gradually began to return to normal, the distress was still inconceivably great and it was known and confirmed by experience that turning to the Holy Father was a sure way to obtain help.

The poor suburban priests often complained that they lost almost a whole day if they had to go to the Vicar General's Office or some other office. How pleased they would be with a motorcycle or a small car! However, such a thing was naturally beyond their means. Now and again, the Holy Father was given a motorcycle or bicycle at an audience, but what was that for so many?

The Chairman of the Fiat car works occasionally visited the Holy Father and one day he came down to us in the storerooms. Soon the first car, a "Giardinetta," arrived in the courtyard. One of the suburban priests was allowed to collect his little car that same afternoon. We asked the Holy Father to bless it before going into the garden for his walk. The red light on the elevator announced his punctual arrival. Beside the "Giardinetta" knelt the priest who was to become its proud owner. Pius XII blessed the car, went up to the priest, extended his hand to him, and exchanged a few words with him. The priest could hardly reply for joy and simply gazed up at the Pope, who looked at him so kindly. All the staff were kneeling in front of the storerooms to receive, as always, a blessing and a friendly wave. However, today the Holy Father took no notice of us, did not even look round, and we rose to our feet again without a blessing. The priest, on the other hand, was so overjoyed that he did not even notice our disappointment. He got happily into his car and drove off.

That evening the Holy Father said to me, "How ashamed I felt in front of the priest who got the little car—with my big one standing next to it!"

"Your Holiness," I protested, "the priest would never have wanted that big old car of yours." It had already been in service all through Pius XI's pontificate and must have been twenty years old. "He's a thousand times happier with his little new one."

"Is that true? Oh, if that's the case, then everything is all right," the Holy Father said, visibly relieved. It was clear to see that a load had been taken off him. Now we also knew why he had overlooked us that day in front of the storerooms. That was just like Pius XII! In his humility it preyed on his mind that he, the Pope, had a large car and the suburban priest a small one.

After that Pius XII often blessed new little Fiats before priests received them. Once, when six of them were lined up together in the courtyard, he asked one of the priests who was to become the proud owner of one of them whether he would rather swap it for the papal car. The priest answered quite frankly, "No, no, Your Holiness, that old clunker is no good for anything anymore!" Now at last Pius XII was completely satisfied and took great delight in blessing the more than forty cars given to priests after that. There were also several larger cars sent to poor dioceses since the Fiat Chairman repeatedly displayed his generosity when the Holy Father addressed a request to him.

Mention must also be made in profound gratitude of the very generous silk factory in Como which for many years supplied free of charge silk, linings and braid for thousands of Eucharistic vestments. A large room in the Pope's private apartments was transformed into a tailor's workshop, where we sisters also made a large number of liturgical vestments alongside our duties of taking care of the Holy Father and his household. Several convents also worked continually in order to be able to fulfill the numerous requests for such items. Monstrances, chalices, ciboria, altar crosses, thuribles, candlesticks, and such objects were given to the Holy Father at large audiences. On special occasions, at beatifications, canonizations and the like, people constantly asked what they could give the Holy Father. His answer was always, "Something for my poor churches." When a group of sisters once gave him a magnificently embroidered chasuble as a personal gift, we extolled its beauty in glowing terms. Pius XII looked at it but did not say a word. Then we led him to all the other things, chasubles, albs, altar linen, etc., that the same sisters had given him for poor churches. Now at last Pius XII was happy. After inspecting everything, he returned to the beautiful chasuble, which only acquired any real value for him now that he had seen what an abundance of gifts had also been brought for poor churches. So it was always! The joy of being able to give freely to the needy outweighed all personal pleasure.

As cardinals and bishops from abroad were gradually able to come to Rome and the Vatican again after the war, we in the storerooms also often received a visit. Again and again they all expressed their amazement at how well informed Pius XII was about what their dioceses had sent to the private storerooms and they assured us that they would be happy to continue to help.

None of these magnanimous donors is to be named. Their names are inscribed in the book of Him who can give them divine reward, and the Father of Christendom remembered them daily in deepest gratitude at the altar.

Once at an audience for industrialists a textile manufacturer noticed that the Holy Father's cassock was very shabby and afterwards sent him a length of fine material. "That's much too beautiful," the Holy Father said. "Aren't you always needing material for children making their first Communion?"

"Yes," I replied, "but . . ."

"No 'but'" the Holy Father interrupted. And when, a few weeks later, a group of children came to him wearing their Communion clothes made from this material, he was most satisfied and shared sincerely in their happiness.

When the difficult war and postwar years were at last over, we believed that our work in the private storerooms would end now too. However, Italy's recovery from the aftermath of the war was slow and requests continued to flow in to the Holy Father. Thus the work and the giving went on. Whenever there was a catastrophe caused by floods, fire and the like, cries for help reached Pius XII. We were glad always to be prepared to help and endeavored to replenish the storerooms when everything had been given away. We also soon came to know who to turn to for this.

Exact accounts were kept of the incoming and outgoing goods in the private storerooms. Yet what can figures say? God alone knows how much work, sweat, and toil, how many long nights spent in the stores it cost to prepare everything that for so many years the Holy Father's love distributed to the needy. However, the silent work in the seclusion of the storerooms was amply rewarded by the knowledge that we were being permitted to help the Holy Father in this great work of active charity.

After the sudden death of our beloved Holy Father, we hurriedly compiled a summary inventory of everything contained in Pius XII's private storerooms. The figures showed that there would have been enough to go on distributing gifts for a long time.

Audiences for soldiers! It is impossible to give an impression that in any way does justice to the love and effort Pius XII dedicated to these. How much courage, confidence, and consolation he gave the departing soldiers! No one wanted to go into the field or to any other post without first seeing the Holy Father and receiving his blessing. Every new day saw him among his sons. He shared their sufferings and fears. Often he would return from these audiences unable to touch his meal because he felt so sorry for the soldiers and for their mothers, fathers, wives, and children. He often wept with a soldier who could not believe that he had been ordered to the front. This went on for years. For years, Pius XII held out with his sorely tried sons and allowed himself no rest even when the "*baciamani*" (kissing of his ring) lasted for hours and his entourage could hardly keep on their feet any longer. How on earth did the Holy Father manage it? Even when he returned from such audiences, dripping with perspiration and ready to drop, never a word of complaint passed his lips. The next day new groups of soldiers would be able to come and find in him the same kind, untiring, loving father. It sometimes happened that one or other of the soldiers whispered to him that he wanted to speak to him alone; the Holy Father then took the man aside after the audience and the deep window alcoves in the audience rooms turned into confessionals in which many a soldier unburdened his conscience before going into the field. On other occasions also, when Pius XII returned very late from general or "*baciamano*" audiences and we said in astonishment, "But so late, Holy Father!" he would merely reply, "Now and then one has to be a confessor too."

When the war was in full swing and engendered so much hatred, Pius XII was repeatedly warned not to expose himself to possible danger when walking through the long rows of soldiers. This warning fell on deaf ears. The Holy Father wanted to be close to his sons. He understood what it meant to a soldier to press his hand, kiss his ring, see him at close quarters, and be able to exchange a few words. The fact that he came home with his clothes soiled and even snippets cut off his cassock and cloak did not matter. But the Holy Father also returned with bleeding fingers because in their love they had squeezed his hand so hard that the ring had cut into his flesh.

One Sunday in St. Peter's an American soldier asked us whether there was still a possibility of seeing the Holy Father that morning as he had to leave Rome in the evening. For some reason the large audience for soldiers had been moved forward that Sunday and the American soldier assured us that he had not known about this. He implored us so earnestly that we ventured to telephone the Antechamber, where we were told that he could join a small group. Only after we had given him this news did he tell us that today would be his 112th audience. Seeing our astonishment, he said that he had not let a day pass without attending an audience. He had taken over night duty for comrades so as to be free at the hour of the audience. At his very first audience the Holy Father had addressed him and asked where he came from. Since then he had not had any peace. He had taken instruction to prepare him for conversion (he had been a Protestant) and today he had been granted the joy of receiving his first Holy Communion. Now he wanted to see for the last time the man whom, after God, he had to thank for his happiness. When Pius XII came home to lunch very late and exhausted, we told him of this incident. He simply smiled in happiness and said, "I know, I spoke to the soldier myself. At the large audience this morning, there was also a group of twenty-one who had all found their way back to Holy Church and received their first Communion today. The harvest of souls is worth every sacrifice!"

A dear elderly nun we knew well turned to us to procure a particularly good place for her two nephews at an audience. Since her conversion and entry into a convent, she had heard nothing from her distinguished family as they not only disapproved of her step but also regarded it as a disgrace for the whole family so that they broke off all contact with her. Now came two officers who greeted her as "Aunt" and had but one wish: "We would like to see the Pope!" Did their parents at home know about this? Naturally, they had no idea but it was the dream of every soldier coming to Rome to see the Pope, they said. Since their aunt had been in Rome so long, she must be able to obtain them the privilege of seeing the Pope at close quarters and perhaps being able to speak to him too. The two officers got their "really good place" and Pius XII also spoke to them. Full of suspense, the sister awaited the return of her nephews. When over a week had already passed, she feared that they had perhaps been unable to see the Pope and left again in disappointment. However, ten days later the two of them returned, this time accompanied by a third, a Catholic military chaplain. At their request, he had given them thorough instruction and prepared them for conversion. They had already been to confession and their first Holy Communion was to follow shortly. The sister was absolutely astounded and asked if the family knew about it, to which one of them replied, "I'm of age and my brother soon will be too. We have already written home and told them that our most wonderful experience up to now has been the audience with the Pope and that we go to it as often as we can. After our first Communion we're going to an audience again, along with other comrades who have also converted."

It was at the time when Hitler had forbidden German soldiers to go to papal audiences. This regulation was broken wherever possible but they had to make sure they were not caught; the officers in particular had to be very careful. One morning two officers came up through the Bronze Gate to an audience. A pair of suspicious eyes followed them and, soon afterwards, the guard on duty was asked casually how many exits the Vatican had. "Oh, three or so," replied the guard, who was used to spying going on. Now two spies were posted at the Portone di Bronzo, by Sant' Anna, and at the Arco delle Campane respectively. Meanwhile the two officers were immediately informed and after the audience were let out of the Vatican "by a different route." Late that afternoon one of the spies finally asked the guard when the audience would be over that day. The latter answered roguishly that what he presumably meant was when the next day's began! However, the following day the tricked spies sent a soldier into the audience who had the audacity to ask the Holy Father personally how many exits the Vatican had. Pius XII, who knew about the events of the preceding day, understood immediately and replied with a touch of irony, "As many, my son, as are necessary to put know-alls on the wrong scent!"

There is much more that could be added here. The Holy Father himself told of many an incident. It made him happy to hear again and again, "Now we'll go to the front, to the war, into every danger with courage for we know that your blessing and prayers will accompany us!" The words whispered to him, "I received a parcel from you at the front," or "I heard from my father, my brother through your information service," were for the Holy Father a rich reward for the hours of *baciamano* audiences every day.

Once a soldier held the Holy Father's hand unusually long in his own. Pius XII looked at him kindly and made to withdraw his hand, whereupon the man said quite ingenuously, "I just wanted to see if you really are a human being . . .!"

Another time a soldier said, "Holy Father, I have a wife and children at home. If you pray for me, I'll feel quite safe to go into the field because I know that nothing will happen then."

Or another time: "Holy Father, I'll be back a second time. I'm certain that with your blessing I can be quite calm and reassured." Hundreds of letters and notes pressed into Pius XII's hand express similar feelings and testify to what these audiences gave the soldiers to take with them on their way. They were not ashamed to show their admiration, not embarrassed by the tears that streamed down their cheeks. The trust was boundless that, in their distress, people put in this white-clad figure radiating nobility and dignity and yet also so much human kindness; this figure in which Christ's representative on earth was venerated and loved.

How very moving were the audiences for those blinded and crippled by war! No one who saw these sorry processions crossing St. Peter's Square and entering the Vatican will ever forget the sight. Guided by relatives and nurses, they came to the consoler of the afflicted. For hours on end, the Holy Father walked through the rows, encouraging, helping, blessing them! On countless faces, he conjured up a smile, a look of joy, a ray of sunshine. The world must have seen the thousands of soldiers and suffering who daily climbed the steps of the Vatican, seen the wounded, the blind, the crippled who came to audiences. Nevertheless, the world knew nothing of the sea of pain and bitterness they left behind for the Holy Father, whom God had destined and chosen as their common father and who shared in all their suffering and bore their burdens with them.

Added to the horrors of war were the cruel persecutions. The prisons and concentration camps were filled with the best of the clergy and laity. Every public profession of faith had become impossible and expressing solidarity with those who had been unjustly imprisoned meant sharing the same fate. The worst thing about it was that there was no way of helping these poor people since one heard time and again that the slightest interest taken in them would, if it became known, only worsen their situation. For these unfortunate sufferers too, the Holy Father did a great deal—quietly and secretly, doggedly persevering in small steps. He saved many a life without anyone ever learning of it.

Pius XII left nothing untried to keep Italy out of the war, but everything was in vain; consequently defense preparations were called for. The Holy Father was provided with an air-raid shelter but he himself never entered it. When the sirens sounded at night and an air raid began, the Holy Father always went into the chapel to say Mass. However much it raged and roared around him, the Holy Father remained as calm and composed as if he did not hear anything at all. Filled with reverence, lost in God as if he were not a part of everything that was going on in the world, he offered up the Holy Sacrifice. Once, however, shortly before midnight the noise was terrible. During the whole Mass there was such a crashing and banging that one could have thought it was the end of the world. As the bell was rung for the Consecration, there was a crash that shook and rattled the windows. Someone in the chapel let out an involuntary scream. But even now, nothing disturbed the exalted celebrant. We could not help asking Pius XII afterwards if he had not heard anything at all. He answered calmly, "There has to be a lightning conductor in this great city too."

When the Palazzo del Governatore in the Vatican was bombed one evening, one of the gentlemen from the Secretariat of State was at an audience with the Holy Father. You could tell from the impact that the bombs were falling really close by, but the Holy Father went on working calmly until he was informed of what had happened and what severe damage the bombs had caused.

On another occasion, Monsignor Montini came to Pius XII's private apartments from the Secretariat of State and told me that he had received reliable information that the Vatican was to be bombed during the night. He asked us to tell the Holy Father that he should go into the air-raid shelter immediately the first alarm was given. I reflected on the matter but then thought it wiser to say nothing, but simply to make preparations to be able to go down straight away when the time came. Therefore, as not to arouse any suspicion, I went to bed with the other sisters but then got up again quietly and prepared everything for Holy Mass in the air-raid shelter. The elevator was also ready so that we could leave at once if the sirens were to go off. By about eleven, everything was seen to. As always, the Holy Father was still working in his study. Punctually at eleven o'clock, the door opened and Pius XII crossed the small corridor to go, as was his custom, into the chapel. Since he left the door open behind him, I could see his tall figure kneeling at the big prie-dieu. At the sight of him all fear left me and did not even return when he ceased his prayers and went back to work at midnight. Now I too could go into the chapel without fear of being caught there by the Holy Father. At about 2 a.m. the light went out in the study since it was at last time for the Holy Father to go to bed. Still nothing had happened. I was profoundly happy that I had said nothing, thus sparing everyone a sleepless night. That whole night not a single siren went off. When day began to dawn at about 4:30, I went quietly to bed so that I could get up with the others half an hour later. No one had noticed anything of my night's experiences. Had the information been false or had the Holy Father praying quietly before his Eucharistic Lord once again been able to act as a lightning conductor for the Vatican and the Eternal City?

Then came that terrible day of July 19, 1943, which surely no one will forget who lived through it in Rome. The afternoon sun was shining brightly out of a clear, cloudless sky when suddenly and with incredible speed the humming bombers hurled death and destruction upon Rome and her inhabitants. Everyone was frozen with horror.

The Holy Father was standing at the window and saw the harbingers of death swoop down on his city. He was very pale as he raised his now trembling hand in blessing. From his window, it looked as if it was the district around Santa Maria Maggiore that was burning. He hurried to the telephone but no one knew anything definite. "Have my car sent immediately," Pius XII ordered.

"For God's sake, Holy Father, you can't go out now!"

But he did not listen to any objections. The chauffeur was called. Pius XII took all the money that was in the house and was ready to leave in a flash. He was already in the courtyard before I succeeded with difficulty in reaching Monsignor Montini so that the Holy Father would at least not go out completely alone. The chauffeur, not suspecting where he was to drive to, stood next to the car that normally took Pius XII into the garden and was instructed to drive to the place of death. It was still not clear whether the district that was burning was by Santa Maria Maggiore or by San Lorenzo. In the Vatican, no one had any idea that the Holy Father had gone out. From the window we saw Pius XII's car cross St. Peter's Square. I ran to the telephone to report to the Secretary of State that the Holy Father had left. "*Che cosa?* What? No, no—he can't go out now, under any circumstances!"

"But he left several minutes ago, Your Eminence; he just went off and would not be stopped!"

It soon spread like wildfire through the Vatican and the city: "The Holy Father! The Holy Father!" But he was already among the distraught crowds, the smoking ruins of the collapsed houses, close to the destroyed basilica of San Lorenzo fuori le Mura. The poor people crowded around their pastor and father, who was the first to come to them bringing consolation and help. They hung like bunches of grapes on the running board of his car, climbed on to the hood and roof. At one point, the car came to a standstill and could not be moved from the spot. The Holy Father got out and mingled with his sons and daughters, consoled them and finally knelt down to pray on the smoking heap of rubble that was once the basilica. The people prayed and wept with him. Then Pius XII distributed everything he had taken with him. It was already evening when he returned to the Vatican in a small car because his own had broken down. His clothes were blood-stained and dirty but he was content, despite all the suffering, to have brought a little solace and help to his sorely tried children. To someone who reproached him for having exposed himself to such danger he replied without further ado, "I shall do exactly the same again if—which God forbid—the city is bombed once more."

That evening, when the Holy Father blessed his beloved city from his window as he always did, there were bright tears streaming down his face. It was clear to see that he was experiencing and suffering again all the pain of the afternoon.

From then on, the colonnades of St. Peter's became a refuge day and night for the frightened suburb-dwellers who feared another attack. Every air-raid siren brought a great crowd of people streaming to St. Peter's and the square in front of it. The whole world knows what an enormous effort Pius XII made to prevent a further calamity. Nevertheless, Rome was bombed again and once more the people saw him among them, comforting and consoling them.

What Pius XII did for the persecuted Jews, whose extermination is known to have been Hitler's goal from the start! Accommodation was provided for them in every conceivable way; thousands were helped to escape overseas; the gold was found to set hostages free. Pius XII, who for the sake of the honor and reputation of the Church was forced to do much in public that would otherwise certainly have been done behind the scenes, was always happy when he was able to do good quietly and without making a fuss about it. There would be so much to tell if I did not know that this would be contrary to the great Pope's wishes. It was not without reason that the former Rabbi of Rome, who, inspired by God's grace and the good example of the Christians, converted to Catholicism, wrote: "No hero in history has ever led a more splendid, more combated, and more heroic army than Pius XII did in the name of Christian charity."

One recalls with horror the morning in August 1942 when the newspapers announced in banner headlines the dreadful news that Hitler had reacted to the Dutch bishops' public protest against the inhuman persecution of the Jews by having 40,000 Jews arrested and gassed during the night. Among these was the philosopher and Carmelite nun Edith Stein, whose life Pius XII had followed with great interest. The morning papers were brought into the Holy Father's study as he was about to leave for the audiences. He simply read the headline and turned deathly white. On his return from the audiences—it was already one o'clock and time for lunch—the Holy Father did not go into the dining room at once but first came into the kitchen, the only place with an open fire where things could be burnt. He had two large, closely-written sheets of paper in his hand and said, "I want to burn these papers. They are my protest against the gruesome persecution of the Jews, which was to appear in the *L'Osservatore Romano* this evening. But if the Dutch bishops' letter cost 40,000 lives, my protest would perhaps cost 200,000. I must not and cannot be responsible for that. Hence it is better to remain silent in public and to continue to do everything humanly possible for these poor people quietly."

"Holy Father," I ventured to object, "isn't it a pity to burn what you've already prepared? It might be needed some time."

"I've thought of that too," Pius XII replied, "but if they do come in here, as is constantly being said, and find these papers—and my protest is much sharper than that of the Dutch bishops—what will then become of the Catholics and Jews in German-held territories? No, it's better to destroy them." The Holy Father waited until the two large sheets of paper were completely burned before he left the kitchen.

"He is nailed fast and cannot free Himself, can only endure and suffer. The Pope too is nailed to his post and must remain silent." Who could ever have experienced with more intensity than Pius XII what it means to be the Vicar of Christ?

The world heard Hitler's criminal plan from his own lips when he "prophesied" in his speech to the German Reichstag on January 30, 1939:

> If international Jewish finance should succeed inside and outside Europe in plunging the nations once again into war, then the result will not be the Bolshevization of the world and thus the victory of Jewry, but the destruction of the Jewish race in Europe.

Quite apart from this, his book *Mein Kampf* is crawling with similar hymns of hatred. But among the statesmen in positions of responsibility there was none who put a stop to the fateful developments. Pius XII alone, the ruler without weapons, foresaw the immeasurable horror and set himself against it with all his might; but hatred and national egoism spoke louder than the voice of justice, which had no military forces to back it up. The war was not to be stopped.

A glance at the German newspapers of those years still shows us today that the murder of the Jews—lying though it does on a quite different moral plane—was not to be separated from the other events of the war. For Hitler and his supporters the Jews were *"our misfortune"* and *"world enemy number one,"* as the Nazi publications kept screaming at their readers. The extermination of the Jews was one of Hitler's main war aims and, as his behavior in the Netherlands showed, any protest simply increased the determination and brutal cynicism with which he pursued it. The persecuted repeatedly implored the Holy Father to help them only in secret.

In the above-mentioned speech, Hitler had declared publicly:

> The opinion seems to be held in certain circles abroad that a particularly loud expression of sympathy for elements that have come into conflict with the law in Germany could bring about an alleviation of their situation. Perhaps they hope to be able to exert a terroristic influence on the leadership of the German state through certain journalistic methods. This opinion is based on a capital error. We see foreign support of certain enterprises directed against the State as a final confirmation of their treasonable character! . . . This support thus seems to be intended only for those who mean to destroy the German Reich. For this reason we shall regard every single case merely as an urgent reason to step up our measures.

Are not these statements plain and clear evidence that Pius XII, who in his prudence always considered the precise consequences of his actions, was right to do everything he devised and undertook in order to save the Jews in secret and without causing a stir so as to avoid bringing new misfortunes upon them instead of helping and rescuing them?

September 10, 1943! Who does not recall the day on which the Germans marched into Rome? The fall of Mussolini and the armistice still did not put an end to the horror. For two days the doors of St. Peter's remained closed. The Romans locked up their houses, their shops, everything. Fear and horror lay like lead upon the inhabitants of the whole city. Anyone who was living in Rome at the time knows that people went out of their houses only if it was absolutely necessary and returned home as quickly as possible. But everyone looked toward St. Peter's. How they envied those who were able to live inside the Vatican City. Nevertheless, they knew for certain that their pastor, their father was watching and worrying for the whole city and everyone expected salvation from him alone. The Vatican City now also bordered on Hitler's Germany after the occupation of Rome. The former ally of Italy had become an occupying enemy and the Germans had pitched their tents precisely at the entrance to St. Peter's Square, in sight of the apostolic palace, the home of the Holy Father. Everyone feared for him, of course, but another fear was expressed even more loudly: "Don't go away or we're lost!" If only they had known how little Pius XII entertained the idea of leaving! He worried day and night about his beloved diocese, his Rome, all his children who, in view of the shortage of food, he knew would soon be in the grips of hunger. All conceivable preparations had been made long ago so as not to be caught standing empty-handed if the feared occupation should take place. However, it was clear that these stocks would not last long and that an alternative had to be sought. Food was still to be had outside Rome but the permission of the Germans was required before anyone could leave the city. Pius XII's nephews together with the Superior General of the Salvatorians, Father Pankratius Pfeiffer, and many others helped to bring about the success of this undertaking. In the early morning, every truck that could be found left the Vatican and crossed St. Peter's Square to drive out of the city and bring back bread for the starving population. Since the Allies were closing in on the city more and more, this work of charity was also fraught with great sacrifices and dangers. Many trucks had bombs dropped on them even though they were painted yellow and white and displayed the papal ensign. One driver was killed on this mission of love.

But it was not only hunger that reigned in Rome. The occupying enemy went openly and without any restraint on manhunts. The fear of being arrested and dragged off to some concentration camp or other was so great that it is hard to imagine. People tried to hide in every conceivable way and, again, it was the Holy Father who had every door opened. The Vatican, the many religious houses, the colleges all became places of refuge for hunted and persecuted people. The Holy Father himself helped to provide for those in hiding and make their accommodation tolerable. And everything had to be done in the greatest secrecy for new people kept coming in search of refuge and those who were already in safety must not be endangered. Pius XII wanted to help, to help all who were in need. No differences were made; those who repaid him with ingratitude and even calumny were also taken in. Woe betide anyone found by Pius XII to have hesitated about taking in a person with too bad a reputation. He always wanted to know everything and be informed about what had already been done and what was still left to do, never tiring in his desire to give.

When the distress and misery in the population as a result of the war and the air raids became increasingly worse and the Holy Father saw that the means at his disposal were far from sufficient to help in the way he would have wished and as would have been necessary, he inquired whether there were any valuables that could be sold. He also wanted to have the precious stones removed from the tiaras and miters and replaced with worthless ones. A jeweler was called in to value them but they would have fetched so little that the Holy Father realized that this would be no use. Then he thought of the treasures in the museums and the statues in the galleries. It took all the powers of persuasion of a number of experts to prevent him from handing over these precious objects. In any case, where could a buyer have been found in such times? It would also have been impossible to get them out of the city. And what would malicious tongues have said if these things had been sold? Pius XII countered this last objection with the words, "People will always have something to say and even the best and most well-meant actions can be interpreted wrongly." He did not care about what "people" said; he merely wanted to help his city and everyone everywhere as much as he could. Even the German sentries on guard at the entrance to St. Peter's Square were not excluded from this kindness. When he saw them patroling in the pouring rain, he said with a laugh, "Poor fellows, it's safe for you to go into your shelter, the Pope certainly won't run off."

Pius XII knew full well who it was that they were after most. He was not afraid that the myrmidons might find valuables if they were to get into his private apartments—these existed only in the imagination of journalists. However, the documents had to be taken to a safe place and an excellent hiding place was found for them. The salvage work took days and had to be done without outside help and unnoticed. Everything seemed to be peaceful and orderly. One could have supposed that the Holy Father was not in the least concerned that the voices were becoming louder that wanted him out of Rome and deported to Germany, where everything was said to be prepared for his accommodation. He made it very clear that he would never leave voluntarily, only under duress, even if this were to cost him his life. The Romans knew that they could depend on Pius XII and that it was through him alone that the most terrible fate could be averted.

There was enough terror everywhere in any case. The following are just a few small episodes. One night there was a ring at the door of a convent—the house, which had room for about fifty people, was almost bursting at the seams with "guests." In broken Italian one of the three German soldiers standing at the door said, "We've come to fetch the mattresses from this house."

"We can't help you there," came the trembling reply. "We only have sacks of straw."

"You expect me to believe that?" the soldier retorted.

"Come and see," the sister replied, opening the first door to the former visiting room, which contained about fifteen plank beds with clean sheets and blankets over sacks of straw.

"We don't want that stuff, you can keep it yourselves," shouted one of the soldiers and turned to go, whereupon the sister, in great relief, opened the door kindly for him. However, she went straight to the telephone to inform the other houses in the vicinity in case they also received "visitors."

It did not always turn out so well as this. The soldiers went looking for blankets and sheets somewhere else and the poor "guests" had to get out of their beds to satisfy the Germans' insatiable demands. All the same, they were glad to freeze for a night so long as they were not discovered. Many slept in monks' or nuns' habits or in priests' cassocks so that they would not be recognized if there was a nocturnal raid, as so often happened. Many kept changing hiding places to make sure of escaping any investigations. When it did then happen that someone was found and taken away, it was the Holy Father that this grieved most.

Was it surprising that after the German occupation of Rome and the discovery by the Holy See that Hitler wanted to have Pius XII deported that everyone in the Vatican was aghast when they heard that, at the request of Father Pankratius Pfeiffer, the Holy Father had received, under the seal of utmost secrecy and alone, a high-ranking German officer who had asked for an audience? The revelations made by this officer were, however, of a nature to convince Pius XII that people were right in fearing for his safety. He now heard clearly and unambiguously from the mouth of this officer what was planned against him.

But what store could be set by the assurances of such a man? One thing is certain: Pius XII had asked this officer to spare the lives of two young people who had been condemned to death and were to be shot the next morning. The Holy Father was later informed that both had been set free and could return to their families. It was only many years later that I learned that this high-ranking officer was General Wolff.

Even now that the Holy Father knew exactly what Hitler had planned against him, nothing whatsoever changed in his daily habits. It was repeatedly pointed out to him that he was being watched from the air when he took his walk in the Vatican Gardens and that it was very risky always to go out at the same hour. This was to no avail. "I don't walk for pleasure but simply because I can't work otherwise and I can't choose the time myself, either." Fear for his own person was something quite alien to him. Despite the now confirmed knowledge that Hitler would stop at nothing, Pius XII did not fail to raise his voice ever more imploringly and to make it clear to the warring parties what a terrible crime they would be committing if they destroyed Rome. Alongside this, arduous spade work was carried out via diplomatic channels to fight for the preservation of the Eternal City, but everything seemed to be in vain.

The horrors increased. It was already being said that the Germans had made preparations to blow up all the bridges over the Tiber. If the Allies were to enter Rome, death and destruction threatened the whole city. At this point I feel obliged to state that Pius XII knew absolutely nothing—at the appropriate time—of the taking of hostages or of their cruel murder in the Fosse Ardeatine. If he had known, he would without any doubt whatsoever have taken every humanly possible step to prevent this atrocity.

In this difficult hour, the Holy Father invoked the Blessed Virgin, who is venerated by the Romans as the "Salvation of the people of Rome." He called upon everyone to pray with him. And it was not long before the prayers were answered. What had happened? Only yesterday, German soldiers were strutting proudly and high-handedly all through the city, yet on this Sunday morning, June 4, 1944, it seemed as if the whole burden of the years of war had laid itself on their shoulders. Gasping under this burden, they dragged themselves in large and small cavalcades of vehicles out of the still sleeping city. All preparations for its destruction seemed to have been forgotten. Away! Away! was their battle cry.

The Holy Father, who was about to go into the chapel to offer up the Holy Sacrifice of the Mass, looked out into the street and saw a picture completely transformed since the day before. A "Thanks be to God" coming from the depths of his soul expressed his relief and, on entering the chapel, he joyfully intoned the *Magnificat*. In Sant' Ignazio, at the foot of the *Madonna del Divino Amore*, who had been taken to Sant' Ignazio from her shrine outside Rome, the novena begging for Rome to be saved was to be concluded that day in the presence of the Holy Father. And Pius XII came. His route from the Vatican to Sant' Ignazio led through a turmoil of cars and people such as Rome has seldom seen. In the overcrowded church, the faithful prayed, sang, and gave thanks. The *Salus populi Romani* had repaid her children their trust. After the sermon and the Eucharistic blessing, the Holy Father intoned a grateful *Te Deum*, which re-echoed in the great vaults. The Queen of Heaven had protected the city in which her Son's representative dwelt.

The following day all Rome came to St. Peter's Square to thank the Holy Father, to whom alone it was to be ascribed that Rome was saved. Pius XII was rightly called the *Defensor Civitatis* by the people of Rome. For all time, he will go down in history as the savior of Rome.

However, the war was not yet over; the suffering continued. Only now did it really come to light who had found refuge and shelter in the Vatican and the extraterritorial buildings, in convents, monasteries and institutes, and how generously Pius XII had taken care of them all.

But who today can still imagine the period of terror, fear, permanent uncertainty, the misery and distress of the weeks and months? It all reads so easily today as something to be taken for granted. Only those who lived and suffered through this time know what it means to live under permanent nervous strain; no one knew what the next hour would bring.

When the end of the terrible war finally came, it was possible to see properly what ghastly wounds it had left, what destruction it had caused and what a dreadful calamity it had brought upon the whole world. Now a new and taxing task began for Pius XII, who was the father not only of the victors but also of the vanquished. He had to watch new hatred growing out of the harshness and intransigence of the victors. For this reason, he undertook everything humanly possible, with unflagging patience and total self-sacrifice, in order to achieve acceptable terms of peace and to bring the nations closer to each other.

The Allies had scarcely entered Rome than everyone rushed to St. Peter's. They all wanted to see the Pope, who had done so much for his people. The Holy Father did not spare himself. In spite of his excessively slim figure and delicate constitution, he was extremely robust. He never complained of tiredness. The vast crowds saw him walking very uprightly between their rows, drawing everyone under his spell with his kindness and friendliness.

The immense strain, both spiritual and physical, which was bound to undermine his health, caused his confessor to urge him to take things easier. He was advised not to deliver a speech for every little party of pilgrims; just a few words would be enough. And what did Pius XII say? "No, Father, I don't agree with you there; remember that it's always the Pope who speaks. Every word uttered by the Pope must be worthy of his office!"

Even though Pius XII did not allow himself any recreation, he was sincerely happy to see others relax, enjoy themselves, and take a break. "You can do so, whereas I no longer have the right to since God has entrusted me with this task!" That was his conviction and no one could dissuade him from it.

The world knows in part the notes, letters, speeches, encyclicals and prayers written and published by Pius XII during his pontificate, but there are few who know of the work, worry and effort, of the grief-ridden days and the nights spent watching and working that went into writing them.

Pius XII's achievement during the war and postwar years was enormous. Here he showed himself to the world as a great Pope and one of the greatest benefactors of mankind.

After the war Cardinal von Faulhaber told me about the time he had been received by Hitler in Berchtesgaden. It is well known that Hitler had an elevator installed in the mountain and a house built on the top of it. It was here that he received the Cardinal, who, when he got out of his car, had to allow himself to be blindfolded so that he would not be able to see the entrance to the elevator. The Cardinal told me of the embarrassing and unpleasant conversation with Hitler.

There has been so much talk of the *grande Papa politico*. Pius XII was indeed fascinated by politics as a science—there was no field in which he was not interested—but he was always glad when as a result of a strike no newspapers were delivered for him to have to read. Politics as they presented themselves in everyday reality were diametrically opposed to his upright, sensitive character. Nevertheless, wherever politics encroached on the Church, bishops, priests, Christ's flock, on what man holds most sacred, Pius XII regarded it as his duty to raise his voice and point out with dazzling clarity the legal foundations without which there can be no politics. On the other hand he remained silent, however unjustly he himself was insulted, even defamed and mocked. How he suffered because of the ugly attacks made on him by worthless newspapers! Nevertheless, he regarded it as his duty to read them. How often we tried to clear them out of the way when we heard by chance or when it was pointed out to us that this or that newspaper contained such base attacks, but we were rarely successful.

Who does not remember the 1948 elections? After a lost war, with destruction, poverty, misery and distress everywhere, with passion and hatred dividing the nation, it was easy for the enemies of God and the Church to influence people, to sow discord and strife, to incite even more a nation that was already in revolt. How the Holy Father prayed, sacrificed, and worked, what risks he took, what plans he devised, what preparations he made! Little of this ever became public. Those who had the chance to pray with him in his private chapel and see how this great concern of his was remembered specially at every Holy Mass know what his soul suffered and sacrificed.

In this context, I am reminded of a school essay written by the seventeen year-old Eugenio Pacelli, *"I mei nemici"* (My Enemies). He who, as he wrote here himself, is much more inclined to love than to hate and has consequently not known any serious quarrels, attempts in an essay to imagine his future enemies. The fact that one day he will have enemies is clear to him since some of his ideas, which he is deeply convinced are good, will probably not be liked by everyone. Nevertheless, he intends to proclaim them loudly and clearly:

> However that may be, one thing is certain. I have never attempted and shall never attempt to make everyone my friends through caution carried to the lengths of stupidity, through base flattery and cowardly hypocrisy—in short, by adapting myself completely to the life of conventional deeds, words, and phrases necessary to maintain friendships that do not come from the heart. Not I! Certainly, I shall . . . try for my part to love as many people as I possibly can and to make as few enemies as possible. But I shall never stoop to certain base actions even if this makes me hated by the whole world and persecuted a thousandfold. Anyone who wishes to hate me for this can do so. I shall cheerfully offer up this sacrifice of my heart in order to preserve the nobility of my attitude . . .

I once read in a newspaper that Pius XII wanted to do everything himself and listened to no one, etc. I showed this article to Monsignor Tardini when he came for his audience that evening. He read it and laughed out loud. "You see," he said, "how badly informed people are and how little they know the Holy Father. Yes, he does do a lot himself, but everything is prepared with long, thorough, and total consideration and prayer. He inquires, he asks advice, he analyses the question in every conceivable way, he calls for the opinion of people he is convinced understand the matter and are able to pass judgment on it—not until then does anything new see the light of day. What I always admire most about Pius XII is his prudence. Even with innovations he is introducing and has introduced, nothing sees the light of day before it has run the gamut of pros and contras. I could say a lot more about this, for we who are around him know his method of working."

A well-known priest with whom Pius XII often conferred once said to me after an audience, "Thank God that He has given our Holy Father such a rich measure of prudence, caution, and empathy. In all his decisions one sees that it's really the Holy Spirit who guides him."

I remember very well the Holy Father saying to Monsignor Tardini before taking leave of him after an evening audience, "And now, Monsignor, it will take twenty years of really intensive preparation before it can be begun. And I shall no longer be alive then and perhaps you won't, either." Monsignor laughed heartily and left the Holy Father.

I had heard their parting words because Pius XII had rung for me to show Monsignor Tardini out and I asked in astonishment, "Your Excellency, what needs a whole twenty years of preparation?"

And he replied, "The Holy Father was talking about a future council that he is preparing and he believes that if it is to be done really well, it requires a great deal more intensive work. You know yourself that Pius XII wants everything to be perfect."

If the Holy Father sent for someone and the person in question kept him waiting half an hour or longer, Pius XII was always the same, just taking up his work and smiling. I remember one single occasion when over an hour passed without the person who had been sent for appearing. The Holy Father then rang and said, "Please say that I no longer have any time." However parsimonious Pius XII was with his own time, never wasting a minute, his patience with others knew no bounds.

When one of the gentlemen once left the audience very late and lost in thought, I ventured to say, "Your Excellency, I hope you haven't robbed the Holy Father of his night's sleep with too difficult problems."

"No," he replied, "I don't think so, I'm just amazed at the matter-of-fact way in which the Holy Father knows how to take the blame for something that is obviously not his fault in order to spare whoever really is to blame."

All the same, Pius XII sometimes had to be strict as Pope, where he would gladly have overlooked an error or failure as a private person.

When Rolf Hochhuth staged the sorry distortion of Pius XII after the Pope's death, it was said that Monsignor Hudal had provided him with the material for it. I do not know whether this is true. At the heart of the gossip probably lay the fact that Hudal had never gotten over being advised by the Holy Father to resign his post as principal of the Collegio Teutonico di Santa Maria dell' Anima. Naturally, Pius XII did not do this simply off his own bat, but the continual complaints received from cardinals, bishops and priests, which a thorough investigation had proved to be justified, forced him to do so. That was something Monsignor Hudal was never able to get over.

CHAPTER SEVEN

PREPARING FOR THE 1950 HOLY YEAR

In the first year of his pontificate, Pius XII was forced to move to Castel Gandolfo soon after his election as Pope because the papal apartments in the Vatican had to be thoroughly renovated. As Secretary of State, it would have been impossible for him to remain in his former apartments because the noise caused by the renovations would have disturbed both work and audiences too much. Hence, the best solution was to move to the summer residence. We made every effort to prepare everything well in Castel Gandolfo so that the Holy Father would have all that he needed immediately at hand.

On his arrival at Castel Gandolfo, he was first welcomed by the inhabitants of the little town. Then it was a matter of settling in. Pius XII only knew the residence from audiences with Pius XI. He had never visited either the palace or the gardens, but he soon became very fond of everything although it was some time before he knew his way around completely. Here too he arranged everything so that his work would be sure not to go short.

His sole recuperation in Castel consisted in his having himself driven into the garden if the audiences ended in time. In a shady spot sheltered from the wind a little glass house had been erected with a sunshade over it. A small table with a simple chair in front of it and a rack to lay papers on were all it contained in the way of furniture. Here the Holy Father spent the time remaining before lunch working. In this way he at least got some fresh air. We should dearly have liked to make this spot more attractive and comfortable for him but he did not want us to. "I just need a place to work, not somewhere to make myself comfortable," he said. Even in Castel, Pius XII allowed himself no more than half an hour's siesta. Then he went for his walk. He always took the same path under the magnificent evergreen oaks, which kept off the burning rays of the sun but not the fresh breeze from the sea. In autumn Pius XII used the next section of this avenue, which was bathed in sunshine and pleasant. Even though he did not permit himself to relax completely during this hour either, occasional comments he made displayed his great love of nature and animals. He knew every tree, was pleased that everything was so well tended, and when he once saw two cockerels engaged in bloody combat, he called a man working in the garden to ask him to check that they had not fought to the death. Once he also found a young fox enjoying a good meal of a stolen chicken and reported this to the gardener.

For rainy days, the Holy Father used a covered walk since he never missed going out into the fresh air whatever the weather. On returning home, he would immediately set to work.

Unfortunately, no one ever succeeded in persuading Pius XII to permit himself any real relaxation. Every year at least a fortnight was planned without audiences so that he would be able to rest properly. Every year this came to nothing. Only the *"Tabella"* audiences were canceled for a few days, but all the others continued. He also kept strictly to his work schedule and, as in the Vatican, his day ended at two in the morning.

The first stay in Castel Gandolfo was overshadowed by the terrible events that, despite all Pius XII's warnings and admonitions, were to lead to the most dreadful of all wars. Hence there was a great deal of worry and pain. Nevertheless, the Holy Father's equanimity and tranquility remained unchanged.

At first there were not so many public audiences, since Pius XII was permitting himself more rest in Castel Gandolfo. However, he soon drew more and more people under his spell so that the audiences became more frequent. The daily routine was the same as in the Vatican except that in Castel the Holy Father simplified everything as far as possible. The Master of the Chamber and the chamberlain on duty were present at audiences but once these were over, they left the summer residence and returned to Rome. If there was a special audience requiring the Noble Guard and other staff, these came out to Castel specially. Swiss Guards and gendarmes were present only in such numbers as were required to maintain order.

For himself Pius XII had just one employee, who was Assistant of the Chamber, chauffeur, and valet rolled into one. With what devotion and profound admiration this man in particular was attached to the Holy Father! Nothing was too much for Mario. You could call him at any time of the day or night if necessary; he was always happy to be summoned to the presence of the man whom he saw to be working indefatigably for the wellbeing of all. In the course of his almost twenty-year pontificate, millions of people saw the Holy Father in full papal regalia on the *sedia gestatoria* or mingling unpretentiously and simply with the crowds at some solemn occasion in St. Peter's, in the large square in front of the basilica, or at royal visits or various audiences. Did they have any idea of the modesty and humility of this great Pope, I wonder?

For seven years Pius XII did not even allow himself any longer the slight change of air offered by Castel Gandolfo. "Other people can't afford anything either in these difficult times and I don't want to be better off than they are!" With these words, he brushed aside the advice of the doctor, the entreaties of those around him and many other well-meaning people. During these years the Holy Father stayed in Rome. Not until his weight was down to 58 kg (128 lbs)—although he was 1.82m tall (5'11")—would he accept that things could not continue that way.

The 1950 Holy Year was approaching! How enormously exhausting this was for Pius XII is hardly to be described. He really wanted to refuse to go to Castel Gandolfo that year but finally gave in to the urgent pleas of his doctor and those around him. Nevertheless, he still had to go to Rome for audiences twice a week and to the Vatican three or even four times. It would not have been possible to accommodate the thousands of pilgrims at Castel Gandolfo. However, for the Holy Year pilgrims it was not enough to see their so beloved Holy Father just once and so they came out to Castel every day and "organized" a further audience for themselves. They lined up in front of the palace, began to sing, pray and shout, and were not to be persuaded to leave until the Holy Father was informed. The people were not to know that the Pope's rooms lay on the opposite side of the building so that he could not hear their shouts. Finally there was nothing for it but to tell the Holy Father that there was a large crowd of people waiting to see him. And Pius XII came and blessed them and talked to them. The pilgrims left again overjoyed. What had succeeded yesterday could not fail today, and so people came every day and the famous audiences in the courtyard of the palace had begun: without tickets, without staff, without the Antechamber, without ceremony. How the people loved these audiences! In the courtyard there was no first or last place, they were all the same. Everyone who sang and cheered, gesticulated and waved here would maintain afterwards that the

Holy Father had looked at them in particular, had greeted and blessed them especially. Everyone was convinced that the penetrating eyes of the Pope had been able to read their souls and that with his blessing they could embark confidently on their homeward journey. Soon the courtyard was no longer big enough to hold all the people even when tribunes were put on the roof and the courtyard was filled a second, third and fourth time. The pilgrims were so insatiable that something finally had to be done. The poor tormented Pope would never have been able to get any more work done, since people kept turning up at all hours of the day. If this happened while the private audiences were going on, it was impossible to inform the Holy Father; it then became a matter for the chamberlains on duty and they were harder of hearing! But during the afternoon the "family" had no choice but to keep interrupting the Holy Father. Although it was no small matter for him to have to get up from his pressing work again and again, it was likely that he would have been extremely annoyed if he had heard that we had let people leave without a blessing.

Sometimes it went too far. Once a party of pilgrims who arrived at dusk, kept on singing and shouting and would not be sent away: "We shan't be here tomorrow and we've come a long way" or whatever all the excuses were. However, no one gave in since the Holy Father had already been out five times that afternoon to bless various groups. Meanwhile it was time for Pius XII to go to dinner. He heard the shouting and had the people brought into the courtyard at once. The jubilation of the young people was indescribable. They could not express their thanks enough and the Holy Father took pleasure in the fresh, cheerful young people.

The next morning I had to go into Rome and on the way I met a group of young people walking along praying and singing, their bus driving empty in front of them. Astonished, I asked why they were walking when they had a bus. They said that the evening before Pius XII had recommended prayer and sacrifice so urgently that they wanted to do the journey on foot and pray according to the intentions of the Holy Father. I told the Holy Father this on my return and he was quite speechless with joy.

On another occasion, when a party was told it was too late to ask the Holy Father to come out, they said simply, "Then we'll stay here all night!"

When we realized that they were serious about it, there was nothing for it but to inform Pius XII. He came without delay. As soon as the cheering had died down, he said, "So, you wanted to wait here all night, did you?"

They were all somewhat surprised that the Holy Father knew what they had said, but then an elderly man came forward and replied, "Holy Father, for the chance to see you and receive your blessing it would certainly not be too much to wait here the whole night!"

The audience with forty sailors from Goa in India must also be mentioned. They had gone on land in Naples at about 4 p.m. and had to be back on their ship early the next morning, which meant that they would have to return to Naples in their buses the same evening. It was 8:30 p.m. by the time they arrived at Castel Gandolfo. An English-speaking priest from the observatory brought them in. Without saying a word, they immediately knelt down on the ground and kissed it. They remained on their knees to await the Holy Father, who soon appeared on the balcony. They listened to his words with their heads bowed low to the ground and only raised them again when he had stopped speaking. Although he invited them in English to stand up, they remained kneeling until he withdrew after blessing them, saying a hearty goodbye, and waving. Only when the light went out on the balcony did they rise from the ground. With shining eyes they accepted the medals and rosaries the Holy Father had distributed to them and left the courtyard in profound reverence as silently as they had come. It was so moving that all of us who had witnessed this singular audience had moist eyes.

What things that courtyard has seen and experienced. Formal audiences with the great of the world, with scientists and scholars took place there. Participants at congresses of all kinds gathered in it. The courtyard turned into a throne-room or it was a simple place of encounter between a loving father and his children. It was a rendezvous for all estates and nations. In six or more languages, Pius XII addressed his sons and daughters. Everyone was to hear the language of his own country and feel at home with the common father of all. What delightful dialogues came about now and then! The audiences almost always lasted over an hour and when the blessing had been given, the greeting and waving was never-ending. Once a father lifted his small son up high for the Holy Father to give him a special blessing. The slender hand of the Pastor Angelicus made the sign of the cross as he bent right down. The little boy clapped his hands in delight and the happy father pressed him joyfully to his heart.

A young mother had brought her five children and got hold of a bench by the wall of the house, where she stood her little ones in a row like organ-pipes. They all shouted and waved, and lo! The Holy Father discovered them, blessed them, and waved to them. The happy mother felt her burden lightened, but she had to keep promising her children to come back again the next day. One day when the Holy Father was receiving a prelate, he was informed that it was time for the audience and so he walked with his visitor to the veranda from which he addressed the pilgrims. The prelate, on hearing the singing, said with a laugh, "Listen, Your Holiness, the house is full of glory again." (The German hymn that they were singing begins "A house of glory looks out far over every land . . .")

Pius XII so loved to hear this hymn, glorifying the Church as it does, and said to the prelate, "How happy I always am when the pilgrims sing the Church's praises so enthusiastically! If only they take a great deal of love for our Mother Church home with them, then their pilgrimage will not have been in vain." How magnificently Pius XII's deep love of the Church, the mystical Bride of Christ, manifested itself always and everywhere. No work was too much, no sacrifice too great in order to glorify the Church and just as his testament calls the Church his "loving mother," he for his part was her most faithful and devoted son.

At such times, many people of other faiths who were at the audiences may have gained an idea of what the papacy is. Countless people attended the audiences and went away from them happy and enriched. But who has ever stopped to ponder what it meant for the Holy Father always to be there for everyone, always to display a cheerful, sympathetic, kind smile, constantly to have to spend his strength; what it meant for a man who was over-abundantly burdened with worry and toil for the whole of God's Church? After all, the above merely gives a hint of what went on throughout the year.

The countryside around Castel Gandolfo is also very pleasant. If the sunset happened to be particularly beautiful and impressive, we would perhaps venture to go into the Holy Father's study and ask him to look at the splendid spectacle too. This, however, was a small pleasure and distraction that he seldom permitted himself. Pius XII had always taken a great interest in astronomy. However, I do not believe that in all the years he took the time on more than three or four occasions to climb up to the observatory and admire the starry night sky.

In Castel Gandolfo it soon became known that what the Holy Father liked best was to be able to work in peace without being disturbed. All the staff then took exemplary care to fulfill this wish and in both house and garden everything was so well ordered that—apart from at audience times—nothing disturbed the harmonious atmosphere in any way.

The stay at the summer residence was drawing to a close and Pius XII was preparing to move back to the Vatican. "Holy Father, you haven't allowed yourself a single free moment in all these months whereas the world says that the Pope is returning from his vacation!"

Pius XII was already standing with his hat in his hand at the wide-open window that offered a splendid view of the countryside, which the setting sun seemed to turn to gold, and he said to himself, "How beautiful this patch of earth is!"

"Yes, Holy Father, how beautiful! And all these weeks you've seen nothing of it."

"When would I have had time?" came the almost sad reply. "A Pope has no longer any right to himself." And, as if he had already allowed himself too much distraction, he quickly turned away from the window and walked to the door, where a cheering crowd was waiting to bid him farewell.

And now another little incident, which occurred after Pius XII's first stay at Castel Gandolfo when he moved into the newly decorated papal apartments in the Vatican. As already mentioned, he did not know the apartments in detail in any case and now, after being redecorated, they were more unfamiliar to him than ever. Naturally, he knew all the furniture, carpets and pictures, in fact everything that he had had in his apartments as Secretary of State; for it was his property, but it had all been put into new surroundings and he had to familiarize himself with everything.

He had returned from Castel Gandolfo late in the evening and, as always, his first task was to order his documents and papers. He had not yet been around his apartments and so he did not know that there was a staircase leading from his study down to the library. While looking for a light switch, he fell headlong down the stairs. The member of his household staff who had just come to call him to dinner saw this and was rooted to the ground with consternation. Finally we ran to the staircase. The Holy Father was standing at the bottom looking up at us with a friendly smile. What had happened? He told us that he had noticed immediately that he had stepped in the wrong place but, being unable to catch hold of anything, had simply prayed, *"Madonna mia, salva mi!"* (My Mother, save me!) And then he had found himself at the bottom of the stairs standing on both feet and completely unhurt. On the contrary, the pain that he had felt for over a week in his right leg as a result of a sprain had disappeared. We all went into the chapel to sing a *Magnificat* in gratitude. For almost twenty years, the Holy Father went up and down this staircase to his beloved books without any further misadventure.

When the Holy Year began, Pius XII had already ruled God's Church for over ten years. He was still unbroken, fresh and almost youthful despite his seventy-three years. With his whole heart and with tireless devotion he dedicated himself to all who wanted to take advantage of the graces of the Holy Year, who wished to see him and receive his blessing. And besides this, there were all his other tasks waiting for him. What scenes all the churches and basilicas in Rome, above all St. Peter's, witnessed over this year! As time went on, the audience halls in the Vatican and at Castel Gandolfo became fuller and fuller. The Holy Father did not merely show himself, he also mingled with his flock, allowing himself to be crushed and pushed and jostled just like the pilgrims at such gatherings. If he then came home sweating, tired and with soiled and crumpled clothes, and if anyone ventured to mention this, he would simply say, "I don't want to be better off than all those who have come here." It is impossible to describe all the encounters between the Father of Christendom and his children.

One day the principal of a large boys' college came with about five hundred pupils. It is no small thing to take charge of such a large group of ten- to fifteen-year-old boys. After all, they wanted to see the whole of Rome as well as gain the Jubilee Indulgence. The boys were insatiable! They wanted to enjoy more and more of the splendors of the Eternal City so that the principal and his helpers were so tired in the evening that they could hardly keep on their feet. The next day the papal audience was scheduled. Initially a special audience had been requested and granted but for some reason it turned out no longer to be possible, which was a great disappointment for the boys. At least they were given good places at the general audience in St. Peter's. The Holy Father arrived! There was thunderous clapping and cheering, singing and shouting, a confusion of all kinds of languages and noises so that every trace of disappointment vanished and every eye shone in the direction of the Pope as he was carried in on the *sedia gestatoria*, overlooking no one who waved to him. When he came close to the group of boys, they saw that he knew about them and recognized them. He also understood what they wanted to say to him, for even before he ascended the steps of the throne, he waved to them, greeted them specially, and had cast his spell on them all. When the cheering died down, the Holy Father began to speak—to them first! The boys' eyes grew wider and wider. They simply could not get over it that they, only a small group in the great big Church after all, should receive a speech of their own, meant for them alone, words conceived and formulated especially for them. They almost forgot to thank him when the Holy Father concluded his words to them in order to address all the many others present. Finally everyone had been mentioned, no one forgotten. In the meantime over an hour had passed! After the blessing Pius XII descended the steps of the throne and again went first to the group of boys, greeted the principal, inquired about this and that, mingled with the young people, talked to them and answered when they spoke to him. Only then did he move on to all the other people waiting for him. Back on the *sedia*, he greeted and waved again and again on all sides, and left the church blessing the crowds and surrounded by their jubilation. It was some time before it was possible to leave the overcrowded basilica. As the principal descended the steps of St. Peter's, he kept turning around to make sure that all the boys were there. No one was missing. But what had become of the noisy, chattering crowd of boys? None of them uttered a word. When the principal asked what their further program for the day was, they all said with a single voice, "We haven't got one, Father! We don't want to see anything else; it would spoil the memory of what we just experienced. Let's go home!" The principal saw a lot of moist but happy eyes gazing at him. The next morning he announced that he had a program for them, an excursion to Castel Gandolfo to see the Holy Father again before leaving Rome for home. On hearing this, the youngsters' jubilation was indescribable.

Later one of the boys summed up the experience really well:

> How wonderful it was when, at the end of an audience that we shall never forget as long as we live, the Holy Father descended the steps of the throne and came toward us—no, it was as if he threw himself into the crowd just as we plunge into the sea to swim. He was surrounded by surging waves; he allowed himself to be pushed and shoved, his face radiant! What a father, I couldn't help thinking again and again, a radiant, happy father, and we his sons.

When he had pressed every hand, answered every question, listened to and granted the requests and was finally able to tear himself away from us to go to the thousands of others waiting for him, it was just the same. People tugged at his clothes, pushed and pulled him—and Pius XII seemed to like nothing better than this "bad treatment" for on his radiant face there was simply infinite fatherly kindness. It was here that I realized why the Pope is called "Holy Father"! Pius XII, in any case, has earned this name in the fullest sense of the word!

The climax and crowning glory of the Holy Year was the proclamation of the dogma of the corporal assumption of the Blessed Virgin Mary into Heaven. It was on October 30 when he was returning home from his walk in the Vatican Gardens, Pius XII said, that he chanced to look up from his work and saw a strange spectacle. The sun, which was still quite high in the sky, appeared as a dark, pale yellow ball surrounded by a bright halo. A soft, light-colored cloud floated in front of it. The dark ball moved outwards slightly, either revolving on its own axis or leaving its path to the right and left and returning to it again. Inside the ball, a great deal of uninterrupted movement was to be clearly seen. The whole thing was a wonderful sight. Without being dazzled, the Holy Father had been able to look attentively at the sun.

The following day was a Sunday. Full of expectation we too went into the garden, hoping to see the spectacle as well, but we came home again disappointed. The Holy Father asked at once, "Did you see it? It was just the same today as yesterday!" On the day of the proclamation of the dogma the Holy Father saw it again, and then once more on the octave of the feast. We should dearly have loved to see it too but this was not granted to us. Afterwards Pius XII had inquiries made at the observatory, but there too nothing was known or had been seen. Inquiries made outside at the Holy Father's request were also unsuccessful.

The first day of November 1950—5 a.m.! The eye roved over the whole expanse of St. Peter's Square. It still lay in the half-dark of daybreak, yet it was already beginning to come to life. But what about the sky? Was this a day in May dawning so bright and clear, or was it really the first of November? A quiet rejoicing burst out in the soul: Ave Maria! As the day advanced, the tranquil square turned into an immense ocean into which unbroken rivers of people flooded unceasingly. More and more came, singing and praying, with happy, radiant faces, from every people, race, and nation. They surged and pushed, roaring and murmuring, jubilant and exultant! All the approach roads were already thick with people but the vast square found room for them all; it absorbed all the rivers of people, all of them orderly and peaceful, and it was amazing to see that there was even space to be had for latecomers. The singing and praying of the individual groups, of all the languages and nations were so harmonious as if a single person had been conducting them. And the sky! Clear, radiant, cloudless and brilliant it arched over the colorful picture of indescribable beauty.

The Holy Father's razor was already humming but the shutters were still closed. "Your Holiness, aren't you interested in what the weather's like today?"

"I knew it would be good," came the reply, "I said to Our Lady yesterday, 'Well, now I've done everything for your glorification, you do your share too! Where can I go with all the people I've called together for your glorification from all over the world? There is only St. Peter's Square and that needs sun to be beautiful!'" Then the Holy Father went to the window and his gaze embraced the vast square flooded in morning sunshine. Joyfully he exclaimed, "*Deo gratias*. Our Lady has kept her word!"

How often we had seen Pius XII leaving his apartments on his way to feasts and celebrations, but today was something special. It was in honor of the Queen of Heaven and Earth that he walked through the rooms, arrayed in the most beautiful attire, his head held high, toward the celebration. He loved his Queen and Sovereign and this celebration, probably the most beautiful and splendid that St. Peter's Square has ever seen, was in her honor. What a picture the large, packed square presented from up here! But there was no time to be lost if we wanted to get our places in the loggia. The roaring and surging jubilation had already begun when we arrived there, for now the white procession of bishops in copes and miters set off from the *Portone di Bronzo* followed by the Holy Father on the *sedia gestatoria* and surrounded by thunderous applause and cheering. Then came a further unending procession of cardinals and bishops. What a wonderful picture of Christ's Church on earth! The Father of Christendom amid the faithful from every corner of the globe! Oh, Holy Church, how great and glorious, marvelous and mighty you are! How every heart must leap with joy in the blissful awareness of being allowed to call oneself a child of the

Church, which outlasts empires and kingdoms, standing firm and unshakable in the ebb and flow of temporal tides!

Now the procession had reached the basilica. At the foot of the throne the Holy Father prostrated himself in prayer and the whole of the enormous square, the cardinals, bishops, priests and the vast crowd of people, prayed with him, their sovereign bishop, for the help of the Holy Spirit. They all felt united with the Holy Father as he solemnly proclaimed the dogma of the Assumption of the Blessed Virgin Mary into Heaven in body and soul.

The sea of people in St. Peter's Square was joined in their jubilation by the whole world, to which the radio waves brought the glad tidings. What a unique picture of unity and belonging together! Immersed in all the jubilation, I heard a woman pilgrim next to me say, "I think Our Lady ought to appear on such a wonderful day!"

The day had now fully broken. A deep blue sky arched over the dome of St. Peter's. Beside the sun, the crescent of the moon was to be seen exactly over the cross on the dome! How was that possible? The others saw it too, and were amazed. *"Quae est ista . . . pulchra ut luna, electa ut sol— Who is she . . . fair as the moon, bright as the sun,"* as the office of Prime of the day had said. If the day's warmth and serenity were an exceptional rarity, this crescent moon above Michelangelo's dome during this celebration seemed like a wonderful symbol.

Events proceeded on the large square. After the definition of the dogma, the Holy Father addressed us with words of profound understanding and sympathy, of total community with his children throughout the world. Then he recited the prayer to Our Lady that he had composed himself and which we all now continually pray. After that he went into the basilica followed by a long procession. Those who were forced to stay outside because St. Peter's would not hold this sea of people remained united with him since the loudspeakers carried the words and singing of the sacred sacrifice out on to the great square.

St. Peter's presented a different picture than usual, for it can hardly ever before have accommodated so many bishops within its walls. In intimate communion with the exalted celebrant, we experienced for the first time the Mass for Our Lady according to the new formula for the feast. Enormous exultation both inside and outside the basilica surrounded the Holy Father, who today had set a new and splendid jewel in the crown of the Blessed Virgin. After the end of the Mass, the crowds outside St. Peter's wanted to see their supreme pastor again, and so their untiring father kept going out to bless them and wave to them. The bells, which had rung out for hours that day from every church in the city, were long since silent again by the time the crowds gradually dispersed.

However, it was not quiet for long that day. At three in the afternoon the great square was already bustling again; it seemed as if the people could not tear themselves away from the place where they had witnessed that wonderful, unforgettable event. The interior of St. Peter's sparkled so brilliantly that the people going in and out of the basilica were amazed and overjoyed at all the splendor. An old man holding his wife by the hand so as not to lose her cried out aloud, "Just look, Anna, that's Heaven! Heaven!"

This beautiful day was followed by evening. But now a bustle of activity swept over the city, for everyone wanted to have the most beautiful lights in honor of Our Lady. Rome was transformed into a city of light, glittering and glorious to the joy of all. Now people strolled through the city, gazing at everything in admiration! Everyone wanted to have seen the most beautiful spectacle, St. Peter's Square, which was the center of attraction, in all its wonderful illuminations. Once again everyone gathered in this square and, as in the morning, all languages were to be heard, people of all estates and nations to be seen. No one left the square until a window high up on the right in the apostolic palace opened and—yet again—a white figure appeared and kept spreading his arms in blessing. It was like a vision but nevertheless real. Pius XII continued to bless them until far into the night because the crowds kept calling for him. When the window was closed, one stream of people left the square to make way for the next. They all wanted to be blessed again before the wonderful day ended. Truly, it was a day made by the Lord in honor of His Blessed Mother!

A lot has been written and related about the papal audiences in the Holy Year of 1950. If one recalls the multitudes of pilgrims far exceeding all calculations and expectations, the inconceivable amount of physical and mental exertion demanded of the Supreme Pontiff, then one is surely justified in asking whether any Pope ever gave himself in such measure to the pilgrims, ever spent and sacrificed himself as completely as Pius XII.

First and foremost, there were the enormous, scarcely surpassable mass audiences in St. Peter's. Anyone who experienced all the jubilation and enthusiasm surging around Christ's key-bearer; who saw the thousands weeping; the shining eyes of children; the joy and veneration of young and old; anyone who watched St. Peter's Square turn into a surging sea before an audience and who occasionally mingled with the crowds of pilgrims as they stormed rather than climbed the long flight of steps leading to the basilica so as to make sure of not arriving late—anyone who witnessed all this will certainly agree with the many voices that say that there must seldom have been a Pope who, quite apart from the sacredness and dignity of his office, was so loved and revered for his own sake as Pius XII was.

Next in line came the "courtyard audiences." The strange and unique thing about them is that even today it is not possible to establish with certainty who instituted and planned them. Instead of going through the normal channel of submitting a request to the Master of the Chamber, the pilgrims' instinct told them simply to turn up, to choose a direct appeal to their father's heart and kindness in the conviction that unto them that knock the door shall be opened. And so it really was! Castel Gandolfo spontaneously became the goal of all the pilgrims' yearnings. The masses came, saw, and conquered. They entered the courtyard of the papal villa, sang, shouted, begged, and pleaded until the Holy Father appeared on the balcony and entered into a dialog with his children in a way that was so natural and simple, so unceremonious and open, so enchanting and elevating that it cannot be described in words. One has to have witnessed these dialogs in order to be able to taste and appreciate them in all their compelling charm and heart-warming directness. What has been written about them is but a pale shadow of the sublimity and sweetness of direct experience.

However, there was also another kind of audience about which nothing has been written, a quite special type of audience. In having sprung up without being either planned or anticipated, they resembled the courtyard audiences at the summer residence. But, even more than the latter, they were children of the moment, creations of that clairvoyant improvisation the Romans have in their blood and are past masters in.

"*Udienze di passagio*—audiences of passage"—is what I should like to call them. They came into being as if spontaneously during the summer months of the Holy Year when Pius XII had to make the trip to and from Rome twice or more every week. Since I had to lock up the apartments, I usually rode at the back of the cavalcade and so I was able to witness everything that took place on the drive.

The Romans and the pilgrims, who are watchful observers and quick reckoners, had soon found out when the Holy Father had set off on his way back to Castel Gandolfo after audiences in the basilica or other functions. As if of their own accord, people began to look for ways and means of making "strategic" use of this homeward journey. The crowds of pilgrims streaming out of St. Peter's saw a strong body of soldiers posted at the end of the Via della Sagrestia and behind the colonnades at the Piazza S. Ufficio to keep the exit from the Vatican clear. For them as well as for all the people who had not managed to be admitted to the audience in the basilica this was enough to tell them that they could get what they wanted without a ticket, namely an unscheduled meeting with the Holy Father to receive his blessing.

Willingly and patiently, they wait until the longed-for moment arrives. A car drives out in front of the Pope's car and another follows it. At the head of the little cavalcade rides an escort of eight motorcycles. The car in the middle is brightly lit, showing the white figure inside it leaning to the left and right, blessing, greeting, waving. The car is able to drive only very slowly. It takes sharp eyes, a skilled hand and iron self-discipline on the part of the chauffeur to keep moving at all amid such an enthusiastic crowd without endangering the daredevils storming the car all too recklessly.

Soon the cars have turned into the tunnel leading toward the Tiber. The motorcycle escort speeds up. But here too, consideration has to be paid to those who think that this bottleneck is the very place to achieve their aim, away from the large crowds, of seeing the Pope eye-to-eye and receiving his blessing. They kneel on the cold, damp ground and their signs of the cross and the happy smiles on their faces show that they are highly satisfied with the result of their tunnel tactics.

The exit of the tunnel is always extremely dangerous. The security forces are fewer and weaker so although the men join hands to keep back the jostling crowd, the cordon is broken here and there, allowing several people to creep right up to the Holy Father's car and snatch a glance, a smile, a blessing. And it is not only young people who are reckless. Immediately after the pilgrims' hospice at the Palazzo Salviati the rows thin out slightly, but only for a few brief moments. As soon as the cars enter Trastevere, the relative calm changes to a new storm. When the white figure in the second car becomes visible, the commotion starts. Everyone wants to outdo everyone else in cheering and shouting during the brief span when the papal car passes through his street.

At the same corner I frequently see a venerable old lady leaning on her daughter's arm. Every time, the same blissful smile spreads over her furrowed face when the hand is raised in blessing over her.

A mother kneels with her three children close to the edge of the road. The two girls remain quietly and obediently kneeling beside their mother but the boy is less well behaved. He jumps up, runs to the car, shouts something into it and then stares after it with a radiant smile. As so often, there is an unexpected hold-up so that I hear the mother say in a somewhat stern and reproachful tone, "Because you didn't stay on your knees, you didn't get a blessing!" The boy's reply: *"Nient'affatto! La benedizione ed anche un sorriso!"* (Nothing of the sort! The blessing and a smile too.)

Now we turn off from Trastevere toward the Tiber. On the Ponte Palatine the chauffeur picks up speed. However, at the end of the bridge yet another large crowd is waiting. There is a further hold-up. Leaving Santa Maria in Cosmedin on our left, we pass the Generalate of the Sisters of Charity of St. Joan Antida. Sisters, novices and postulants are standing in front of it with numerous residents of the beautiful Aventine district waiting to greet the Holy Father, whom they have to thank for the statue of their foundress in St. Peter's, and to receive his blessing.

Passing the majestic Palatine, we turn into the Passeggiata Archeologica at the Axum obelisk. Here it becomes a little quieter. However, individuals or groups are still kneeling under the evergreen oaks waiting for the Holy Father to drive past and bless them. At the end of the street, a large group of children is waiting for us with the sisters in charge of them. Their happy rejoicing continues until even the last car following the Holy Father's is out of sight. There are frequently residents standing by the villas that line the streets. An old man with a white cloth in his hand is standing at the entrance to a drive. He waves and waves, his radiant face reflecting the joy with which he says, "He blessed me!"

On the other side of the Porta San Sebastiano a crowd has again gathered. A barely eight-year-old little fellow has clambered up on to a fountain and his *"Viva il Papa!"* is to be heard over the shouts of the rest of the people. When the papal car has passed, he shouts triumphantly into the crowd, "He saw me and blessed me best!"

At the crossroads by San Sebastiano, a truly biblical picture presents itself: mothers with little children on their arms, overjoyed to have the representative of the Divine Lover of Children among them here outside the boundaries of Rome and to receive his blessing for themselves and what they love most on earth.

We enter the quiet Via Appia Pignatelli. The motorcycles prepare to put on speed but someone who is stronger than they are forces them to brake. Once again the shouting begins, the cloths are waved. We are amazed where all the people come from to collect the toll of his love and his blessing from their common father. A young father lifts up his smallest child to the Pope: *"Padre santo, benedici tutti, tutti—tutta la mia casa!"* (Holy Father, bless all, all—all my house.)

Near the end of the Via Appia Pignatelli a small estate had sprung up the year before. Its modest houses are set back somewhat from the road. At the junction with the Via Appia Nuova, the residents of the estate have gathered so as not to miss seeing the Father of Christendom drive past. Once again the papal car stops, once again his blessing descends like an evening prayer on the heads of young and old bowed before him in sincere reverence.

On the broad Appia Nuova, we meet long rows of cars driving toward Rome. The occupants of packed coaches—pilgrims and other visitors to Rome—wave and shout and are delighted at the unexpected blessing. Most of those who notice in time stop, get out of their vehicles and kneel down beside them to receive the blessing. Others wave and shout a greeting from their cars to the passing Pope. Everyone receives what he wants since the white figure in the middle car has finally given up switching off the light and responds to every shout. (Admittedly, I afterwards heard something resembling mild regret on the part of the Holy Father that the rosary he always prayed on the homeward journey had been interrupted so often by these "audiences of passage.")

Just beyond the Frattochie, the cars turn into the impressive hilly road leading to Castel Gandolfo. Here at last the driver of the papal car can give free rein to his engine. In the few minutes in which we gaze up enchanted at the star-spangled sky arching over the Alban Hills, we have reached the village road. To the right and left of the entrance to the papal villa crowds of villagers have gathered, the young ones above all not wanting to miss the moment of the Holy Father's return. The southern sounds and passionate enthusiasm of the crowd show how happy and proud they are to have their "fellow citizen number one" back among them.

Pius XII's car disappears behind the large iron gate and the clatter of the motorcycles returning to their quarters is drowned in the joyful cheering of the crowd, which takes a long time to die down. Behind us lies a simple, yet in its uniqueness delightful Holy Year experience. Out of the public eye, away from the grandiose central functions running through this Anno Santo like a string of pearls, it allows us a glimpse of one of its quiet sides. The love of the Father in Christ appointed by God has once again celebrated a meeting with the sons and daughters united with him in faith and loyalty, one of those meetings that are not of this world and whose grace-abounding fruits will certainly live on in many souls—long after the bells of St. Peter's have sounded the end of the *Anno Santo* 1950.

There came the closing of the Holy Door and with it the end of the Holy Year. After his farewell audience following the proclamation of the dogma, Cardinal von Faulhaber told me that he had asked Pius XII how he had managed to keep up the pace throughout the year. The reply was: "If I was able to contribute in any way to restoring Christ to pride of place in men's lives, then certainly no sacrifice was too much!"

CHAPTER EIGHT

A FEAST AS A SYMBOL:

SAINT JOSEPH THE WORKER

Even now, the Holy Father continued to work with total dedication and unwavering love. His ever-watchful eye always discovered opportunities to reject errors, to give advice, to comfort the dejected and persecuted and, through audiences, encyclicals, letters, messages and radio broadcasts, to strengthen faith or kindle it anew.

Pius XII welcomed it particularly when workers requested audiences. The liberation of the working class from inhuman working and living conditions and the establishment of a social order in keeping with the norms of the Gospel had already been a burning concern of his great predecessors. Nevertheless, the calm voice of reason and justice as a rule takes much longer to be heard than the hate-filled propaganda of false prophets. Pius XII took up the concern of his predecessors and developed it, in accordance with the needs of the time, into a comprehensive Christian social doctrine. In the chaos of the war and postwar years it was perhaps more necessary than ever to protect working people against the enslavement of false doctrines and misguided political and economic systems and to make them aware of the great dignity that is their right especially in the light of the Gospel. Hence, the Holy Father took every opportunity that offered itself to stand up for genuine social justice. Best known are perhaps his radio broadcasts on social questions. However, personal encounters with various occupational groups also repeatedly offered him a welcome opportunity to point out workers' worth, their rights, and their duties within the great family of mankind. He found a special word for every group and was able to enter into every situation. Factory workers, farmers, butchers, bakers, tram-drivers, various groups of craftsmen and laborers all came to him and the Holy Father never tired of informing himself about the interests of workers in humble occupations. People were often amazed at how the Holy Father could put himself in their positions, understand their particular worries and difficulties, and how familiar he was with their sphere of work, which they expected to be quite alien to him. But he was the father of all and wanted to be close to everyone. Consequently, he informed himself thoroughly in advance about what might interest each group and what they might be happy to hear from his lips. Nothing was too much for him in this respect, and in spite of all the other demands made on him he did not rest until he was able to relate to each field of work.

After one of these audiences—it was the butchers to whom he had spoken that day—Pius XII came to lunch very late and laughing. He told us how all the men had wanted to kiss his ring after his speech and say something to him. One of them had said ingenuously, "Holy Father, if I didn't know that your job is being Pope, I'd really believe you'd once been a butcher since you know absolutely everything about it!"

Pius XII did much more for the material well-being of the workers than is generally realized today. Numerous audiences given to leading figures in politics and business dealt specifically with this urgent concern. Thus when after his death there was so much talk about new pay increases in the Vatican, we were greatly surprised that no mention was made of the fact that the plans for them had been drafted by Pius XII and were simply waiting to be put into effect, nor mention that there had already been various wage and salary increases while he was alive.

An unforgettable experience was the large audience with Catholic Action members in St. Peter's Square on September 7, 1947. The weather had been bad for days with rain showers and unusually low temperatures for that time of the year. Several newspapers were already scoffing: "Men, equip yourselves with raincoats, galoshes and winter woolies!" The Holy Father was worried that his guests might get wet and catch cold. However, as usual when he held an open-air audience, it was a beautiful sunny day and the thousands of men, from the Minister of State to the simple laborer, enjoyed the bright sunshine. Pius XII was happiest of all and spoke warmly to his dear guests, who cheered tirelessly.

One Easter it was quite stormy and Pius XII looked out worriedly from his study onto the large square, which was already beginning to fill with people. "And what if it rains?" he asked. A prelate standing near him said with a laugh, "But, Your Holiness, what does a little bit of wet matter? The people aren't made of sugar, after all."

Nevertheless, Pius XII was not satisfied, "No, no, I don't want it to rain; they might catch cold and perhaps they're wearing their new Easter clothes too." It did not rain and only after that danger was banished was the radiant joy of Easter visible upon the Holy Father's face.

On May 1, 1955, the world was surprised with a new feast in the Church's calendar. May Day, the festival of labor, was to be dedicated to the Lord's foster-father, who worked hard throughout his life to earn the daily bread for himself and his family. The hallowing of this day surely reflects again Pius XII's great concern to defend the dignity of working people in the light of the Christian Gospel against tendencies that amount to making the worker the slave of production or society and that alienate work from its original meaning. *"Unless the Lord build the house, they labor in vain that build it,"* says the Introit of the feast.

The evening before the feast Monsignor Tardini said to me after his audience, "I have given the Holy Father to understand that tomorrow it is, above all, the prime laborer who ought to take a day off. I believe that few people—perhaps none of those who will be celebrating tomorrow—work more than the eighteen hours he does. Hence he ought to set a good example. The Holy Father was not at a loss for an answer and said with a laugh, 'I'll see if I can manage to stop work five minutes earlier tomorrow.'"

I recently read in a newspaper that the Holy Father did everything hastily and hurriedly in order to save time. It is true, of course, that Pius XII never wasted a moment. However, he did everything calmly, with consideration and attentiveness. He was never hasty, no matter how pressing anything was. Only a few months before his death I heard him say, "I've always tried to follow the advice given to me by my confessor when I was still a young priest and celebrate Mass in half an hour, but I've never succeeded!" Everything about him was poised, spiritualized calm. He emanated holy peace even when he was extremely busy. His calmness gave the impression that he had nothing at all to do. Again and again it was said that if someone had the good fortune to talk to him, it seemed as if the Holy Father was there for him alone, had only him to listen to. One lost all sense of time with him. He did everything fully whether it was something important or something insignificant. Everyone who was allowed to be near him felt this. It probably also explains the far-reaching good influence he exerted on everyone. Let us just recall the soldiers' audiences! A high-ranking officer—not an Italian—said to the Holy Father, "Your Holiness, if it became known how many conversions there have been among our soldiers since they've been coming to audiences, I don't know whether we'd be allowed to continue coming to them!"

This single-minded, conscientious work demanded full physical strength but also outstanding knowledge. Pius XII, who was very well versed in every field, saw that all circles turned to him to hear a word from his lips. Priests, religious, doctors, scholars, politicians, technicians, artists, workers, sportsmen, persons of all denominations, estates and nations received from him what they desired. One could only stand amazed before such knowledge but also before such fatherly kindness and pastoral love as were manifested in the twenty years of his pontificate.

On the fortieth anniversary of his ordination the Holy Father consecrated the high altar of the new church of Sant' Eugenio given to him as a present by his diocese. He praised the architecture of this house of God but he was less pleased with some of the modern altars and he said so without reserve. Pius XII wanted beautiful churches and altars inviting devotion, attractive statues and paintings that elevated the heart and spirit. He had a most refined taste and a well-developed appreciation of art. However, he resolutely rejected modern aberrations. Today Rome, his city, now possessed one more house of God and, what is more, in a district where it was urgently needed. This filled his high-priestly soul with joy.

CHAPTER NINE

CREATION OF CARDINALS

AND FIRST ILLNESS

When the Holy Father created twenty-four new cardinals in January 1953, his main concern was to make the Sacred College of Cardinals reflect even more the worldwide, living Church and to incorporate into it as far as possible representatives of the various nations and continents. At his first creation of cardinals in 1946, there had already been criticism that so many non-Italians had been admitted to the College. Pius XII knew full well that the large number chosen from all over the world would not meet with everyone's approval this time either. Nevertheless, he did what his conscience considered just and right. There were to be cardinals all over the world to display clearly the universality of the Holy Church. The fact that among the new cardinals there were two whose appointment delighted right-thinking people throughout the world showed particularly well the far-sightedness and goodness of the Holy Father.

One of these two cardinals was Archbishop Stepinac of Zagreb. How Pius XII suffered that he was unable to do more for this Archbishop! He often talked about it, seeking ways and means of helping him, and was so happy to be able to show his fatherly love and great esteem by raising him to the purple. He sincerely admired this confessor bishop, who stayed with his flock although he knew for certain that nothing could be done for his health, which had been wrecked by long imprisonment, unless he would leave Yugoslavia for good medical treatment.

The other one, the "Lion of Münster" as Bishop von Galen was called, had given the Church and his fatherland a wonderful example of loyalty and steadfastness in spite of all the abuse, calumny and injuries he had to suffer. For his diocese and the whole of Germany, he had been a paragon of the true spirit of sacrifice and of genuine charity.

At this point, I recall vividly another martyr among the first cardinals created by Pius XII. When I asked the Holy Father in amazement on the occasion of this bishop's being made a cardinal (February 21, 1946), "But how could Your Holiness know what you were saying to the Cardinal? Isn't it terrible for him to hear such a prognosis from the Holy Father?" Pius XII replied that he had been startled himself when he heard himself say, "Among these thirty-two you will be the first to suffer the martyrdom symbolized by this red color." When pictures later appeared in the newspapers of the terrible show trial dragging the tortured Cardinal and Archbishop of Esztergom before the eyes of the world, Pius XII said with tears in his eyes, "My words have come true and all I can do is pray; I cannot help him in any other way."

However, the Holy Father did not remain silent! The stirring questions he addressed to the enormous crowd gathered in St. Peter's Square on February 20, 1949, in protest against this inhumanity remain unforgettable to me, and certainly to thousands of others who heard them as well:

> Do you want a Church that remains silent where she should speak; that diminishes the law of God where she is called to proclaim it loudly, wanting to accommodate it to the will of man? Do you want a Church that departs from the unshakable foundations upon which Christ founded her, taking the easy way of adapting herself to the instability of the opinion of the day; a Church that is a prey to current trends; a Church that does not condemn the suppression of conscience and does not stand up for the just liberty of the people; a Church that locks herself up within the four walls of her temple in unseemly sycophancy, forgetting the divine mission received from Christ: *Go out to the crossroads and teach the people*? Beloved sons and daughters! Spiritual heirs of numberless confessors and martyrs! Is this the Church that you venerate and love? Would you recognize in such a Church the features of your Mother? Would you be able to imagine a successor of St. Peter submitting to such demands?

In reply to the Holy Father came a single cry like thunder still ringing in our ears: "No!"

And once again this is just one example. Cardinal Frings told me on his first visit to Rome after the war how terribly the Holy Father had suffered because he was constantly forced to remain silent as prudence demanded, so as not to bring even greater harm to Hitler's victims. The Cardinal added that the Pope's letters to him had expressed themselves extremely clearly on this point, which history would one day prove a hundredfold.

One day, when the newly created cardinals were still in Rome, I met Cardinal von Galen quite by chance. "Come along with me," he said in his affable way, "there's something nice I want to tell you." When we were sitting together, he recounted how Pius XII had recited from memory various passages from sermons given by the Cardinal during the Hitler regime as if he had learned them by heart; how he had kept thanking him for everything he had done, suffered and gone through; how he had shared his experiences and feelings! He had reminded the Cardinal of things that he himself had long since forgotten. "Yes, Holy Father," he had said to him, "but think of the number of priests I sent to concentration camps, even to their deaths because they circulated my sermons!" Pius XII had replied that precisely the awful certainty that thousands would suffer reprisals had forced him to remain silent. After the Holy Father had then inquired about the state of Cardinal von Galen's diocese, he had started to talk about their days in Berlin and the Cardinal had been obliged to confess that when the Nuncio left the city, he had no more shared his fears about the future course of National Socialism than many others had. But how right Pius XII had been! Then he had recalled so many consultations, so much collaboration at the Berlin nunciature or at various events—things the Cardinal had forgotten long ago. It had been such a cordial and friendly meeting that the Cardinal had not noticed that over two hours had passed. With moist eyes, the Cardinal concluded his account of the audience, "I wouldn't have missed those two hours for anything in the world—not even for the purple!"

For the Holy Father the creation of cardinals was the fruit of long, intensive prayer, a great deal of mature consideration, long examination and reflection, thorough and detailed inquiries. Only when the pros and contras had been carefully weighed up, did he proceed to execute his plans. Those chosen had to be, as far as the Holy Father could ascertain and judge, in every way excellent and a credit to God and the Church. This again displayed in what high esteem he held the papacy and how intent he was on making sure that only men who would contribute to its honor and glory should be admitted to the Senate of the Church. It was clear to see what a matter of great concern it was to the Holy Father to choose only the very best. Such an appointment was never influenced by personal interest or liking. A well-known religious whom Pius XII often called for consultations even said to me on such an occasion, "Anyone who wants to get on in the world must make sure not to be a friend of the Holy Father's."

The people who had hurried to Rome from all over the world to thank the Holy Father and pay their respects to those who had been raised to the purple were naturally waiting eagerly for an audience. One of the new cardinals who was at this audience with members of his diocese (Cardinal Wendel) said to me afterwards, "How on earth does the Holy Father stand it? I was right at the back of the hall and could not help thinking all the time, 'For Heaven's sake, don't kill him!' The poor Holy Father! It really is a considerable physical exertion too, to stand up to such an onslaught. Is it always like that?"

Pius XII then came home dripping with perspiration, but he hardly had time to change as there were a lot more audiences awaiting him. When he returned from his walk in the afternoon, he said that he had a pain between his shoulder blades. The next morning he already had a severe headache. This was an alarming sign since the Holy Father only had such symptoms when he had a temperature. He still did not want to succumb since he had a long list of audiences waiting. However, by evening he was forced to give in as the thermometer rose to 40°C (104°F). A severe attack of pneumonia in both lungs was on its way. His temperature rose even higher and he began to cough up a great deal of blood. Everything possible was done but the illness had struck an already very weak body. The penicillin and other medicaments succeeded in averting serious danger but they were also considerably debilitating. The Holy Father had no choice but to allow himself to be nursed since he was so very tired that it was simply impossible to stay up long. From his sickbed—with a temperature of 40°C—the gentlemen from the Secretariat of State were received and all-important work attended to. In sickness as in health, he did not spare himself. In everything concerning him personally, his demands were simple and frugal; as far as possible, he continued to work in bed and later in a chair. Nothing that required attention was left undone. Until mid-March, it was not possible to hold audiences but the work of governing the Church was not affected in any way. We hoped that the Holy Father would now decide to slow down his work pace, but we were mistaken. "How could I?" he asked, "the work is there and I have to do it!"

When the well-known physician Dr. Paul Nathans came to Castel Gandolfo with his wife for an audience, he said afterwards that the Holy Father had not seemed well at all, in far worse health than when he had seen him a year before. Pius XII told a prelate he knew well who had recommended this doctor to him that he would be glad to be examined by him; however, the pressure of work never allowed this actually to be carried out.

On the Gianicolo, the construction of the new North American College was nearing completion. In October, the first three hundred or so students from all the North American dioceses were to move in. The building in the Via dell' Umiltà had long since become too small and so the North American bishops were obliged to have a new one built. The training of good clergy had always been a matter dear to Pius XII's heart and he shunned no sacrifice to this end. He always pressed for clerics from all over the world to be trained in Rome—in a spirit of deep religiosity and familiarity with customs at the central seat of Christianity. It was consequently not surprising that the Holy Father was happy to comply with the rector's request for him to dedicate the new building. Even though he did not stay longer than was necessary, he took note of everything right down to the last detail. He was full of praise for the modern church, which inspired devotion, for the light and airy studies and recreation rooms. Everything seemed to him to be practical and appropriate to receive the throng of young people who, after several years of thorough training, would return home as true and complete priests to show what Rome had taught them for their work in their homeland.

Along with other guests and a large group of students, cardinals, bishops and a great number of priests who had come over from America—most of them ex-students of the college in the Via dell' Umiltà—expressed their gratitude to the Holy Father for the honor and joy of having him in their midst.

CHAPTER TEN

THE MARIAN YEAR

AND A FURTHER ILLNESS

On December 8, 1953, the Holy Father opened the Marian Year in the basilica of Santa Maria Maggiore. For him, the great venerator of Our Lady, this was a particular pleasure. The route to this greatest Marian shrine in Rome and the world led through the Piazza di Spagna, where the car stopped and Pius XII recited aloud the prayer he had written for the Marian Year while the crowd of many thousands stood in reverent silence. From her tall column the Immaculate Virgin looked down upon her so loyally devoted son, who did everything he could to honor and glorify her. Then the drive continued to the basilica, which was bright with a thousand lights. Here the Holy Father repeated his prayer and after giving the solemn Eucharistic Blessing went to the picture of the *Salus Populi Romani*, where he had once offered up his first Holy Mass at the altar of the Queen of Heaven with joyful, youthful ardor. After giving the blessing *Urbi et orbi* from the loggia of the basilica he set out on his return journey amid the ringing cheers of the population of Rome and all the pilgrims; the whole city seemed to have been transformed into a sea of light in praise of the Queen of Heaven and Earth. Undismayed by the criticism of an unbelieving world, Pius XII had opened this jubilee year in order to bring people closer to Christ through Mary.

It was nearing the end of 1953 when the Holy Father once said on returning from an audience, "People find that I look well whereas I really haven't felt well at all recently." Since we were not accustomed to Pius XII talking about himself, let alone complaining, this comment disturbed us all the more. Only a few weeks later, he started to hiccup badly and asked for Dr. Niehans to be called. I shall never forget the expression on the doctor's face as he entered the room and looked at Pius XII, who had just returned from the audiences with a severe attack of hiccups. He asked the Holy Father to lie down at once in his clothes and held him in a certain position for a while. The hiccupping subsided and Pius XII fell asleep for a few moments. The doctor, holding the Pope's hand tightly in his own and never taking his eyes off him, grew more and more serious and pale as sleep brought back a little color to the cheeks of his exalted patient. After about ten minutes the Holy Father awoke, delighted that his hiccuping had stopped. "Now, Your Holiness, you must go and rest at once, it's high time," said Dr. Niehans.

"I can't do that, Doctor," Pius XII replied, "there are people waiting for audiences downstairs, I've lost too much time already."

The doctor, who was there for the first time, did not dare to contradict him and looked to me for help. I then asked the Holy Father if he would allow us to telephone the Antechamber and cancel the audiences, but Pius XII said that he could not do that and in any case he felt better again now. And so he went. The doctor, however, said to me, "I hope I haven't come too late."

When the Holy Father returned from the audiences, he was once again hiccupping badly. Now he himself felt that something would have to be done! The following morning there was to be a large audience that could not be canceled, but after that, there was no alternative but for the Holy Father to go to bed. That evening Dr. Niehans personally gave him the injections he considered necessary and said at once that everything depended on how the five weeks were bridged that would be needed for the injections to take effect.

Now the race with death was really on. The Holy Father was exhausted from overwork, which meant that the serious illness encountered an organism lacking all strength to combat it. Soon his stomach rejected all food. Constant vomiting and nausea alternated with the continual, cruelly debilitating hiccupping. The only periods of respite were the brief half hours of sleep. He had to be artificially fed to take all the strain off his stomach and so at least the constant vomiting stopped. Long, harrowing weeks passed before the gastritis finally subsided and the Holy Father was gradually able to take food again. Slowly the hiccupping also decreased a little; it did not disappear completely until the end of the five weeks that Dr. Niehans had forecast for the injections to work and there were gradually a few hours of truly refreshing sleep again. Dr. Niehans and the papal physician were constantly in the vicinity of their exalted patient. In the course of time the nights became calmer and the days less wracking.

How many prayers and sacrifices were offered up for the Holy Father during these weeks! All day long and very often at night too, one group would follow another down below in St. Peter's Square, kneeling on the ground, their eyes raised to the window behind which they knew the Holy Father to be suffering. Here they prayed, imploring Heaven for his recovery. Anyone who thinks the Holy Father allowed himself genuine rest during this period of most severe illness is mistaken. Summoning up his last strength, he received one of the Undersecretaries of State every morning and for an hour or more discussed with him all the new work that had arrived and any other problems that cropped up. He looked through the correspondence personally even when he was hardly able to hold the sheets of paper in his hand. Once the doctor wanted Pius XII not to work and told the gentleman who was due for an audience this. "I'll see to that," said Monsignor Tardini, taking the papers out of the portfolio and leaving them in the antechamber; but when he came out of the sickroom, he admitted, "Hmm . . . he didn't exactly believe me when I said that nothing had arrived today."

The doctor always allowed the Holy Father to get up briefly in the afternoons and walk up and down the corridor a few times. Before he went back to bed, he looked through the documents sent by the Secretariat of State and signed the letters after he had read and checked them carefully. Dr. Niehans was always amazed that the Holy Father managed to do this in spite of the wretched state of his health. "Only heroic self-discipline and a sense of duty for which no name can be found are capable of that," he would always say. Very slowly there was an improvement, much too slowly for the man who always said that a Pope neither could nor should allow himself any rest. Ever more frequently, we heard him say, "Dear God, I am ready! Fetch me home!" More and more often, he instructed me to do this or that and set things in order. However gladly I carried out every instruction of his, I was simply incapable of "clearing up" as if the Holy Father would no longer be able to do this himself, and I was quite unable to accept the idea that Pius XII might not recover from this illness. The little book of St. Ignatius's spiritual exercises, which the Holy Father loved dearly, lay within reach beside him and he would often read out a passage from it to us. His constant prayer day and night was the *Anima Christi*.

"Tell me the truth, do you seriously believe that I shall recover completely and be able to fulfill my duties fully?" the Holy Father asked Dr. Niehans, "If not, I shall not hesitate to resign. I have just brought the Sacred College up to full strength so the cardinals will not have any difficulty in electing a Pope; in times like these only someone who is completely fit can be Pope." The question was answered in the positive and God be praised, the Holy Father was soon feeling better again and soon he no longer spared himself again, either.

It was not until July 31, 1954, when the worst heat was almost over, that we succeeded in persuading Pius XII to go to Castel Gandolfo. But his stay there was fuller than ever with work, audiences, and addresses, and for him there was nothing but generous willingness to carry it all out. This time the doctor and everyone around the Holy Father had counted on his permitting himself a little relaxation after the months of serious illness but all he saw was work, forgetting himself completely.

Pius XII had opened the Marian Year with great ceremony and now he looked forward to being able to conclude it after his return from Castel Gandolfo with beauty, solemnity, and dignity. But hardly had he returned to Rome than his old complaint flared up again, this time even more severely. Dr. Niehans came and did all he could. Once again, the Holy Father's stomach refused all food and his hiccupping did not allow him a moment's peace. The injections, we knew, would take five weeks to have any effect. The whole Church feared, trembled and prayed anew for the beloved life. The Holy Father suffered unspeakably day and night. There seemed to be an improvement but then a symptom suddenly appeared that gave rise to grave concern. Dr. Niehans asked the Holy Father to allow him to consult several colleagues. Pius XII replied quite unambiguously, "Bear in mind. Doctor, that this will bring us complications, but do so if you feel you must. However, remember later what I've said!"

Only an hour later four famous physicians appeared. In the meantime, however, the Holy Father's condition had improved. Consequently, the four of them found nothing alarming, merely an extremely weak patient. This was not in the least surprising. The terrible hiccups, which none of the four doctors could explain, made it almost impossible to take any kind of nourishment. The doctors then sat down together to compose a communiqué for the press while Dr. Niehans remained hour after hour at the bedside of his seriously ill patient with the sister on duty, trying to do everything that would bring him some sort of relief.

The following day the patient was thoroughly X-rayed, which was a terrible torture for him. Fortunately, the operation that one of the doctors considered necessary was not carried out since the Holy Father would certainly not have been up to it in his weak condition. However, the blood transfusions he was given strengthened him considerably and the stomach irrigation gradually made it possible for him to take light nourishment again. The case of hiccups, on the other hand, was not cured; it recurred from time to time with alarming violence. It was only after the requisite number of weeks necessary for Dr. Niehans' injections to work had passed that this complaint ceased.

CHAPTER ELEVEN

ANIMA CHRISTI . . . AND TESTAMENT

One evening—it was December 1, 1954—when we were kneeling around the Holy Father's bed after saying the rosary and receiving his blessing, Pius XII said, "Now I've heard a voice again; there'll be a vision!" We did not understand what the Holy Father meant. Once everything was prepared for the night, we left the sickroom.

The sister on night duty was in the adjoining room and always left the door a little ajar so as to be prepared for all eventualities. Hardly was everything quiet when she heard the exalted patient again praying, "*Anima Christi, sanctifica me . . . O bone Jesu exaudi me . . . In hora mortis meae, voca me . . . et jube me venire ad Te . . .!*" Over and over again he prayed it. Suddenly everything went quiet . . . The Holy Father had fallen asleep and spent an extremely good night. The next morning his face shone with happiness as he was prepared for Holy Mass. The altar had been set up between his study and his bedroom so that he could follow the sacred liturgy. (Pius XII felt it would be unseemly for the Holy Sacrifice to be celebrated in his bedroom and so we always placed the altar directly in front of the wide open door dividing the study and bedroom.) The celebrating priest always gave him Holy Communion. About half an hour later, we would bring in the Holy Father's breakfast. So it was that day too. When no answer came to my knock, I simply entered. My greeting received no reply either, but I saw that the Holy Father was lying in bed, his eyes wide open and glowing. I set the tray down on the table, went to the foot of the bed, and asked in astonishment, "Your Holiness, what's the matter?"

"*Dove sta Lei adesso, é stato il Nostro Signore!*" (Where you are standing Our Lord stood) was the reply.

"*Che Signore, Padre Santo?*" (Which Lord, Holy Father?) I inquired, "Our Savior, Jesus Christ?"

I looked and looked at the transfigured face of the Holy Father and waited for something more to be said, but nothing came. Then I knelt down where, as Pius XII had just said, Our Savior had stood, and kissed the floor, hoping that I would hear some more after all. However, all remained silent so I left the room quietly and went to the chapel.

After about a quarter of an hour, the Holy Father rang and asked for his breakfast. Now I said nothing further and did not dare to ask any questions either. But the blissful expression remained on his face and after breakfast he suddenly said, "Now I want to get up!" I looked at him questioningly but he merely nodded kindly. Dr. Niehans had just arrived and I told him of this. The doctor was quite satisfied and said, "If the Holy Father wants to of his own accord, then gladly." The Holy Father never said a further word about this vision to me nor has anyone heard anything about it from me.

It is a fact that from now on there was an enormous improvement in Pius XII's condition. He no longer spoke of dying, "going home," or of being prepared either. No, he again took an interest in everything. Meanwhile the Church prayed incessantly to God to be allowed to keep her pastor.

When the end of the Marian Year was marked by a thanksgiving service in Santa Maria Maggiore on December 8, 1954, which concluded with a *Te Deum* sung by the many thousands present, the voice of the Holy Father was heard through the radio quivering with profound emotion:

> In the presence of the whole of the Catholic world, which lies today like a single family at the feet of the Immaculate Virgin, We express Our gratitude to God that it has pleased Him to accept suffering and sacrifice from Us as a service of love to set a seal on so many prayers and good works that have ascended to Him in this year of grace. Afflicted with illness and with a spirit of sacrifice in Our heart, We are happy to conclude this Marian Year and We repeat with all Our children throughout the world *Ave Maria, gratia plena . . .*

When the Holy Father prayed the *Ave Maria* thus, in a voice that clearly betrayed the suffering he had gone through, everyone was deeply moved. We who were near to him and able to observe him could assess what it cost him not to be present in person at Santa Maria Maggiore to bring to a close the splendid triumph of his Sovereign and Queen.

It was about nine in the evening and we were kneeling at the Holy Father's bedside just having finished our rosary when we heard him say as if to himself, "She does just the same as her Divine Son; everything one devises and does to honor her she repays with sickness, suffering, sacrifice, disappointment, renunciation . . .!"

As soon as the Holy Father was stronger again, he could hardly wait for the moment when the doctors would leave. Nevertheless, he asked them whether he could become fully fit for work again and they answered him positively. If they had not done so, no power on earth would have prevented him from taking the appropriate step; everyone around him was fully aware of this.

Once again, the miracle had happened! (The many people who spent all those days and often also nights kneeling on the bare ground in St. Peter's Square to beg for his recovery certainly played their part in this.) Pius XII had been preserved for the Church and the whole world and was to continue to be a great blessing for both. He had already resumed his duties in full. Addresses and speeches alternated with hard work at his desk for the government of the universal Church. It almost seemed as if he had not merely recovered from his illness but that it had given him new strength. Despite all this intensive outward activity, the Holy Father was a most retiring person. He used every minute left to him, working without respite in silence and solitude—like a monk. But even in this retirement, he remained the same person as the Pope on the *sedia gestatoria* or at other great occasions. That was the great thing about Pius XII. Always and everywhere, in everything he said and did he was aware of his supreme task and acted in accordance with his total conviction of the exalted nature and divine institution of the papacy.

Now we had seen what the Holy Father was like during really serious illness. Here too, he remained the same: undemanding, self-forgetful, humble, high-minded and refined. Mustering his last reserves of strength, he continued to work even in the hours of his greatest suffering, constantly sacrificing himself. Dr. Niehans, who had stood by the Holy Father day and night during these harrowing weeks, said to me later, "I've been called to very many of the great of the world, I've traveled almost the whole globe and come into contact with a great number of people but before I came to Pius XII, I didn't know that such a wonderful person could exist anywhere on earth. The months in which I was allowed to be with him and help him were the most beautiful in my long years as a doctor and I thank God for this wonderful period of my life! It was a special grace for me."

The pontificate of Pius XII was interspersed with beatifications and canonizations. For the Holy Father these also meant more work. Not only must he thoroughly study the preparations and proceedings themselves, he also had to produce lengthy speeches to be held at the audiences following the celebrations. He was sometimes asked about details of the life of the saint in question and so he wished to be well informed. Nothing was unimportant for him.

However, it was also extraordinary how the otherwise so kind, forbearing and understanding Holy Father could utter an inexorable "no" where something was concerned that ran contrary to his distinctly fine sensibility.

One example was the beatification process of a very well known founder of a religious order. The proceedings were concluded and waiting for the Pope's decision. On looking through the documents Pius XII now found some most distasteful words often used by the servant of God, which, however, were in general use in the region where they had been uttered and not regarded as objectionable, as he was assured from various quarters. Pius XII remained deaf to every request and representation. "I cannot," he said simply. Although all the preparations had already been made, the beatification did not receive the "*Placet Eugenio.*"

Nor was this an isolated case! I remember well once entering the study because the Holy Father had rung for me to come and receive instructions and seeing the Holy Father close the book he had been reading, pick up the telephone and say, "Monsignor, it's useless your presenting the cause of . . . to me. He will not be beatified as long as I am Pope." Seeing my look of amazement, he said simply, "I've just read that . . . was a heavy smoker, I can't beatify him." In this case too, the preparatory work had been completed and it was no easy thing for those interested in the beatification to hear such a verdict. What is more, the man in question was a member of an order that Pius XII was extremely fond of. Once the Holy Father had examined and studied a matter and was convinced in his conscience that his decision was correct, he would not allow himself to be swayed to change it no matter how many requests were addressed to him or how much it grieved him personally.

The two saints to whose canonization Pius XII attached special importance were the little heroine of virginity, Maria Goretti, and above all Pope

Pius X, of whom he cherished such dear memories and whose shining example was constantly before his eyes. The Holy Father had often talked to us about Pius X and it was he who pressed for the work on his canonization proceedings to be concluded, despite all the obstacles to be overcome.

The beatification of Innocent XI was also his work. How happy he was that this great Pope could at last receive the public veneration denied him for centuries. The Holy Father spared no sacrifice until every obstacle had been removed. It was extremely gratifying for him to see this Pope, who had suffered so much during his lifetime and been subjected to such persecution, now find his final resting place, clad in Pius XII's robes, opposite Pius X in St. Peter's. Pius XII also had proceedings opened for the beatification of Pius IX. When the body of Pius IX, which has remained completely incorrupt, was exhumed and reburied, it was again Pius XII's linen and clothes that were chosen to cover his venerable body.

Pius XII's first canonizations were those of the great religious foundress Maria Euphrasia Pelletier and the simple girl Gemma Galgani. He was clearly gratified to be able to permit the public veneration of Maria Euphrasia, a so gifted and yet so simple woman who did not allow herself to be deterred by any obstacle and who opened up quite new ways of practicing charity. He had made a thorough study of the life of this woman, who showered her love and mercy precisely on those whom society branded as fallen or guilt-ridden, so as to help them regain their honor and respect. Now he was able to place her at the side of the great holy men and show the world by canonizing her that when a woman does not obstruct God's grace and love, she is capable of achieving a great deal for both Church and society. Pius XII himself specified where the statue of St. Maria Euphrasia was to be erected in St. Peter's.

In contrast to this energetic woman stood Gemma Galgani, an inconspicuous and almost unknown girl whose life of suffering, sacrifice and penance Pius XII knew probably to count for no less in the eyes of God than the tireless activity of Mother Maria Euphrasia.

What a gift Pius XII gave to the world and mankind in his glorious Holy Week Liturgy! How gratified he was to hear of the warm interest with which the faithful attended it! An extremely Eucharistic soul had once asked him to permit Holy Communion on Good Friday. At the time, he gave no answer since the matter was not ripe for one. But when the decree on it appeared, he said to me since I knew about this request, "Write to her at once. Just think how joyfully the news will be received!"

Although permission to celebrate Mass in the afternoon was perhaps initially intended only for the difficult war years, it was presumably retained because its great usefulness was recognized, and the Holy Father was profoundly happy to hear repeatedly how full the churches were at evening Masses.

The considerable relaxation of the Eucharistic fast certainly cost Pius XII a great deal. When someone once confided in him that he considered that the new regulations almost went too far, not retaining enough reverence for the infinite holiness of Christ in the Blessed Sacrament, I heard the Holy Father say, "Even though permission has been given for a fast of a mere three hours before Holy Communion, you and I—and I hope very many others with us—should keep to the practice as it has always been." When the Holy Father later heard from an overseas bishop with a large industrial diocese that hundreds of workers went to Holy Communion on weekdays, too now, because they had to fast for no more than three hours, it was not merely a consolation but also a source of profound joy to him.

It was in the night of May 14/15, 1956. At 1:30, the bell rang. What had happened? The Holy Father never called during the night. We quickly dressed and hurried to the study. The Holy Father was sitting there at his desk and said, "I shall die quite suddenly one day—and I haven't made a testament."

"Oh, Your Holiness, if it's only that, there's time enough tomorrow! It's quite all right for you to go to bed. We'll remind you first thing tomorrow morning."

"No," Pius XII replied very calmly and seriously, "it must be done now." It was soon written and the Holy Father asked me if I wanted to read it.

"No, Your Holiness," I said, "there'll still be time for that in ten years." He then put the piece of paper he had written it on in his desk, dismissed us, and said that he was going to go to bed now too.

The following morning he returned to the matter, saying, "I slept well for those four hours because I'd done what I was supposed to do. I shall die quite suddenly one day and I'm glad I've written my testament. All I need to do now is to copy it out again. I've asked God for a day . . ." I could not manage a reply as I was close to tears.

Had Pius XII received some kind of instruction so that he could say with such certainty, "I shall die quite suddenly one day . . . I've asked God for a day"?

The Holy Father never mentioned the subject again and I did not think of it any more.

His testament! How simple and unpretentious—just as Pius XII was himself! Nothing artificial or contrived, just crystal clear! And what humility!

> *"Miserere mei, Deus, secundum magnam misericordiam tuam."*
> (Have mercy upon me, O God, according to thy loving kindness.)
> These words, which I spoke in full awareness of my unworthiness and inadequacy when with trembling I accepted my election as Pope, I repeat with greater justification, now that the realization of my shortcomings and mistakes during such a long pontificate and in such difficult times has displayed my unworthiness more clearly to me. I humbly beg forgiveness of those whom I may have injured, harmed or offended by my words and deeds.
>
> I request those responsible not to take pains to erect any kind of monument to my memory. It is enough for my miserable mortal frame simply to be buried in consecrated soil, which I shall like all the better the more obscure it is.
>
> Nor do I need to leave behind a "spiritual testament," as so many assiduous prelates are in the laudable habit of doing, since the many statements and speeches I have made in fulfillment of the duties of my office suffice to communicate my thoughts on various religious and moral questions to all who may wish to become acquainted with them.
>
> And now I name as my sole heir the Holy Apostolic See, from which I have received so much as from a loving mother.

May 15, 1956 Pius XII

Everyone who knew Pius XII also knew that he loved his family. Nevertheless, in the same way as he had said when he was alive, "God has given my family what they need so I don't have to worry about this," likewise in death, he bequeathed everything he possessed to the Holy Church, his "loving mother." What dispossession, what freedom from everything a human heart can cling to is required to perform such an act!

Recently I read that Pius XII had himself specified where he wished to be buried. That is absolutely incorrect. I remember perfectly his adamant reply to a question on this point in the presence of several persons: "When I'm dead my miserable remains can be put wherever anyone likes, it's of no interest to me. All that is necessary is to save the soul and that is no easy matter." Count Galeazzi, who had also heard Pius XII say this, told me that after the Holy Father's death he had made every effort to have as simple and humble a sarcophagus made as possible to hold his mortal remains so as to comply with Pius XII's wishes.

Since it was on Pius XII's instructions that the excavations were carried out in the grottos under St. Peter's and thus due to him that the niche opposite the grave of St. Peter was discovered, it was here that he was laid for his final resting place.

CHAPTER TWELVE

EIGHTIETH BIRTHDAY

AND FORTIETH EPISCOPAL JUBILEE

Does time pass more quickly when every minute is used to the full? Our Holy Father was approaching his eightieth birthday. His brilliant mind, his firmness of character, his permanent presence for everyone and for all suffering, his almost miraculous gift of speaking all the major languages, and his excellent memory had all remained true to him undiminished. The tall, slim figure in the white cassock and the pale face with its finely chiseled features perhaps gave more than ever an impression of someone spiritualized in the extreme, to the limit of his physical powers. Yet even now this delicate frame emanated a strength formed of strong will and kindness, and despite his outward appearance of fragility, Pius XII continued to be completely equal to the tasks and crushing responsibility of his office.

On one of the last days before March 2, 1956, Monsignor Tardini left the audience very late. Simply for the sake of saying something I remarked, "It's gone on late today." Laying his portfolio down again, Monsignor Tardini replied, "I've seen the Holy Father really laugh from the heart again. There's something wonderful about the Holy Father's smile! His whole face is transfigured and his soulful eyes radiate his saintly nature. People keep telling me repeatedly that they carry the Pope's smile with them and never forget it again. Likewise, the way he smiles is the way he prays. No matter how many cares and troubles have been laid on him, when he gets up and, raising his arms and face toward Heaven, speaks the blessing, it's as if one saw the heavens open above this blessing man, who seems for a few moments no longer to be here on earth."

Now came Pius XII's eightieth birthday. He had in all seriousness hoped that the world would overlook it. It sounds incredible but it is true. The gentlemen in the Secretariat of State could tell many a tale about this!

Nevertheless, in spite of his forbidding it some preparations had to be made. One could not stand there empty-handed. Pius XII had such an abhorrence of everything that concerned and honored him alone that, sensitive and refined though he was, he could utter an unbending "no" if a request was addressed to him regarding anything of the kind. For everything that was undertaken, a different name had to be found. And yet the world—and not only the Catholic world—celebrated the eightieth birthday of Pius XII. Thousands of telegrams and radio messages as well as even more letters brought congratulations from every continent. A wealth of love and admiration unfolded, so great and wide, so deep and beautiful, that in the end the Holy Father too could not help being happy to see such sincere affection and profound admiration.

Early in the morning, wonderful music was already to be heard! At first it was impossible to tell whether it came from St. Peter's Square or from the garden. The Holy Father cannot have failed to hear it too, but he said nothing. In spite of everything, the private chapel was resplendent in its festive finery. Magnificent white lilies adorned the altar and the statue of Our Lady. On entering it, Pius XII shook his head a little but said nothing, probably so as not to spoil our joy. We had not dared to congratulate him before, as we knew that he would not wish us to. Holy Mass was elevating as always. However, today we felt that the sacrificing priest had more to say, special thanks to offer for it took longer than usual. His thanksgiving afterwards also seemed to be never-ending. When it was finally over, we all told the Holy Father together that we had prayed specially for him and would continue to do so as well as we could. Not a word of congratulation—but he understood what we meant. When he entered the dining room, his little birds sang for joy—a birthday concert he could not refuse.

The music outside the house had meanwhile become louder. Yet Pius XII still did not know what a morning greeting was to await him later. But he ought not to have liked children so much if he was not going to allow himself to be delighted by the parade of the tiniest tots from all over Rome: children from all social backgrounds, little boys and girls from all over, with beautiful flowers in their hands. Playing happily, dancing and singing, they gathered around the Holy Father's chair. One of them said to him confidentially, "Mama and Papa would have liked to come too, but they weren't allowed to."

A little boy said, "If only you had a birthday more often!"

"What are you going to do with all the flowers?" another child asked.

"When you see God, please ask Him to make Mama well," one little one said. And so it went on. When the Holy Father finally stood up and gave the blessing, one of them looked up at him sadly and asked, "Why can't we stay with you? Please call us again very soon!"

All the wonderful pictures we retain in our memories really show us Pius XII as the image of the Divine Lover of Children!

But not only the little ones wanted to congratulate him, the grown-ups followed, absolutely everyone who could came and the audience halls were not empty the whole morning. People wanted to see him, thank him, assure him of their prayers and above all express their hope that he would remain for many years to come a father, leader, lofty example and kind helper to them. When Pius XII came to lunch, very late and exhausted, it was clear to see that all the sincerity and affection throughout the morning had after all filled him with joy.

We were looking forward to the afternoon, when a celebration in honor of the Holy Father was scheduled in the Palazzo Pio XII. The splendid music added to the festive atmosphere in the packed hall. When Cardinal Siri then mounted the rostrum and with warm words painted a picture of the life of the Holy Father, displaying not only his beautiful use of language but, above all, his deep affection and genuine admiration for the object of his praise, the applause in the large hall was overwhelming.

When we returned home from the uplifting celebration, we found Pius XII sitting as always at his desk over his work, toiling for those who were celebrating in his honor. The attitude of his closest collaborators toward Pius XII is displayed in one simple incident. As already mentioned, the Holy Father often called one of the two Undersecretaries of State to him in the evenings. The servant was usually off duty at this hour and so the gentlemen were received by one of the sisters. As soon as it became chilly, Monsignor Tardini was always wrapped up very warmly and I once asked, laughing, "But, Your Excellency, how many coats and woolen scarves do you put on?"

"Madre," he replied in his usual way spiced with humor, "I'm a chilly soul and catch cold easily. But if I have a bad cold, I can't come to the audience—and the audience is my life. A day without an audience lacks all sunshine!" Monsignor Tardini spent almost thirty years as a close collaborator—first with the Secretary of State Cardinal Pacelli and then with the Holy Father.

Pius XII took very little trouble about himself and consequently scarcely knew what belonged to him. A minimum was enough for him as long as it did not prevent him from working and fulfilling his duty. A dentist who once had to be sent for during a particularly hot spell expressed his surprise that everywhere else in the Vatican there was air-conditioning to maintain a tolerable temperature whereas the Holy Father, who lived so high up and was most exposed to the sun and heat, had no such installation. This seemed to offer us a welcome opportunity to mention this to the Holy Father along with the doctor's opinion that one worked more easily and productively when not tormented by the heat. And the reply? "I don't work less because of it and work accompanied by sacrifice is more valuable. Moreover, I'm doing the same as the poor, who certainly can't afford such a privilege."

What an effort it was to persuade the Holy Father to try on a new cassock. The old one would do for a long time yet. "Your Holiness, you've promised Monsignor Tardini a cassock, so you need to have another."

"Yes, in God's name! But give him the new one and leave me my old one!"

"That's no good, Holy Father; Monsignor Tardini wants a cassock that's been worn." So the new cassock was worn a few times and then given away, while Pius XII kept the old one and continued to wear it. And his shoes! If a pair was needed for giving away, the Holy Father put them on a few times and then they could be given away. His own shoes, the old ones, were worn for years until they were really no longer "papal." "But, Your Holiness, a poor man wouldn't wear shoes like that anymore, only a tramp," I once said. And on coming home from the audience—I had cleared the old shoes away—the Holy Father asked, "Please, where are my tramp's shoes?"

Despite all his simplicity and modesty in his clothing and everything else, Pius XII was cleanliness and exactitude personified. He was refined and dignified, and even in his simple house cassock he never let himself go. No matter how hot it was, he never permitted himself to take off any of his clothing. He never complained of the heat or cold although he must have felt both twice as much in view of his delicate constitution. We always admired Pius XII for managing to go for his walks precisely between three and four in the afternoon even in the hottest weather for, as already mentioned, he was not fully fit for work until he had taken this exercise in the fresh air. The fact that it was an inconvenience to have to go out in such heat was simply not taken into account.

Today I believe it was a pity that Pius XII could so seldom be persuaded to sit for artists, whether painters or sculptors. It was time wasted, he would say, and his work was much more important and necessary. However, a famous sculptor, Professor Vigni from Florence, once succeeded in being granted a sitting. He said that he would only need half an hour and that the Holy Father could carry on working at his desk, he would not disturb him. And so the Professor came, set everything up in the deepest window alcove and when Pius XII came, he worked away quietly modeling a chalk bust he had brought with him. After half an hour, I went as arranged to open the door cautiously but since I saw the Holy Father working and the sculptor in the alcove, I went away again. After a further thirty minutes, I repeated the exercise but again saw the same picture. After about two hours, the Holy Father finally rang. Engrossed in his work, he had completely forgotten the sculptor. The Professor was very happy to have had so much time to make his model and thanked the Holy Father warmly. Thus it was that the very beautiful bust was created that adorned Pius XII's study. Various copies would be made of it.

A few years later the Holy Father came home from a large audience in St. Peter's and said, "Several times already an artist has been working on a portrait of me during the audience and I believe that he's really caught me as I am." This was a revelation for us since Pius XII's usual reaction to paintings or busts of himself was, "They ought to write under it who it is; otherwise I certainly shan't be recognized." So I dropped everything and rushed to St. Peter's so as perhaps to be able to see the portrait. But when I was halfway there, a gendarme came up to me and said, "Madre, this gentleman wishes to speak to you." It was Professor Boden, the artist, and he was also carrying his portrait with him. He asked if it would not be possible to be allowed at least ten minutes for a sitting with the Holy Father so as to be able to complete the painting. I asked for the portrait and his telephone number, telling him that I would do my best. I first asked Monsignor Tardini and Monsignor Dell' Acqua to look at the painting and both found it excellent. Together we now asked Pius XII to grant the short sitting, which was at once scheduled for the following morning since we feared that the Holy Father might withdraw his consent. The artist came very early and prepared everything. The sitting took place before the Holy Father left his private apartments for the audiences. After ten minutes the painter said to the Holy Father in English, "There are ten minutes, Holy Father," but a friendly gesture of the hand indicated to him that he could go on working. Two minutes before nine o'clock the Holy Father got up since it was time for the audiences to begin. The artist was overjoyed—especially because he had been allowed more time—and it turned out to be a splendid portrait that everyone likes. The life-size painting had been commissioned for England. The small one, a half-length portrait, was given to me as a present by Professor Leonard Boden.

Pius XII possessed a large number of beautiful and valuable pectoral crosses, chains, and rings but he always wore only the simplest and most modest. One of the most valuable pectoral crosses was probably the one given to him by his brother when he was consecrated bishop, which he still continued to near as Nuncio and Secretary of State together with a ring set with a large, very lovely amethyst which had once been an ear-pendant belonging to his late mother. Both of these he later gave away. The many other objects constantly given to him by dear friends and admirers lay untouched in cupboards and his testament says to whom they were bequeathed. In every picture and photograph, Pius XII is to be seen wearing a cross, a chain, and a ring that could not have been simpler or less valuable.

For a particularly festive occasion in St. Peter's we once laid out a beautiful ring set with a precious emerald for the Holy Father to near. Since there was no other ring there, he had to put it on. However, he was very resourceful: he turned the stone inwards so that at the blessing only the gold ring was visible on his finger. We saw quite clearly how the Holy Father carefully bent his finger to conceal the magnificent stone. However, the episode had a sequel. The following day an ambassador and his wife came to an audience with their children and the little boy, who was about eight years old, held the Holy Father's hand for a long time in his own. The child looked closely at the ring and then said, "Holy Father, you weren't wearing this ring yesterday but '*la fede*' (the wedding ring)!" Pius XII understood immediately what the child meant, remembering that he had turned the stone inwards so that only the simple gold band was to be seen that the boy called "*la fede*."

From that time on, he never again turned a stone inwards. I remember clearly how an archbishop once came into the storerooms after an audience with Pius XII wearing what must certainly have been an extremely valuable pectoral cross and ring for he was all a-glitter. I must have gazed a little too long at this sparkling splendor before kneeling to kiss his ring for His Excellency asked, "Do you like the cross and ring?"

"Ye-es," I replied.

He must have read my thoughts for he went on, "You're thinking of the Holy Father's modesty; I won't come like this to him again." In fact, he never came again at all since he was soon afterwards imprisoned by the Bolsheviks.

How often bishops told us after an audience how impressed they were by Pius XII's simplicity. Many bishops visited us in the private storerooms, coming either from war-ravaged countries to which the Holy Father's charity gave bountiful assistance or from countries that helped him to do good.

The terrible suffering that 1956 brought upon Hungary struck hard at the heart of the Father of Christendom. Here too, he did what he could and the awareness of how restricted his ability to help was caused him great pain. It is common knowledge that Pius XII alone stood by the Hungarians in their uprising against Communist rule. His 1956 Christmas message bears eloquent testimony to this.

The famous Jesuit Father Lombardi displayed great initiative in founding the Centro Internazionale Pio XII per un Mondo Migliore (Pius XII International Center for a Better World). The Holy Father took a warm interest in the Father's work and supported it. In a very beautiful location high above Lake Alban and Castel Gandolfo the new buildings for the central offices of the movement were nearing completion. Pius XII honored the center with a personal visit. He looked around the beautiful church, the house and the facilities belonging to it, blessed them all, and expressed his hope that a great deal of good would continue to flow from the center in every direction. On January 21, 1957, the Holy Father visited the Collegio Capranica, where he had studied as a young man. He often told us that in his day the college had been simple, modest, almost unsightly. Today he now saw it renovated and modernized, equipped with a new chapel and all kinds of new installations. He was happy about this but said that in spite of its simplicity the young people of his day had certainly not been less content. He engaged in lively conversation with the students and enjoined them to prepare for their lofty calling through avid study, prayer, and meditation, and to emulate all the exemplary priests who had been trained at the college. The elevator (which had not been there before either) was all ready so that the Holy Father would not have to walk down the stairs when his eye lit upon the large crucifix, which in his day every student had kissed reverently on entering and leaving. He immediately went over to the staircase, descended the steps and kissed "his" crucifix as he had once done as a young man. An alert photographer took a picture of this. The beautiful photograph will forever preach to the students and to us with what devotion and love one of the greatest sons of the house venerated the Crucified Lord whose representative on earth he now was. As the fortieth anniversary of his episcopal consecration approached in May of that year, the Holy Father hoped that the day would be passed over in silence. But apart from countless congratulations from all over the world, the President of Catholic Action, Professor Gedda, had carried out an ingenious idea. Throughout the night, the Cortile San Damaso was a hive of industry and by the morning, the courtyard had been transformed into a flower garden of exquisite beauty. Enormous carpets of flowers depicted in wonderful floral pictures all the events in Pius XII's pontificate. It was so enchantingly beautiful that even the Holy Father, whom we had asked to look at the glorious display from above first, cried out in amazement, "How on earth is that possible!" Then he went around the whole courtyard accompanied by a number of people close to him, looked at and admired everything and expressed his gratitude as only he knew how to all who had contrived this excellent plan and carried it out to such perfection.

When a dear acquaintance congratulated the Holy Father at home later, he said almost sadly, "People do not think enough about the enormous responsibility that forty years as a bishop—the fullness of the priesthood—place on one's shoulders. Pray for me, I tremble before being called to account."

"Your Holiness," came the reply, "if you talk like that, then who can stand the test?"

"Believe me," Pius XII answered, "the responsibility of a Pope is gigantic!"

CHAPTER THIRTEEN

SERVIENDO CONSUMOR

In 1957 too, it was the end of July before the Holy Father found time to move to Castel Gandolfo. If only he had ever really relaxed there! But unfortunately, the same rhythm of work and audiences was maintained. As the years went on, Pius XII did find working without interruption more difficult, even though he would never admit it. Whereas his excellent memory remained unchanged in its freshness, it seemed as if his exactitude increased, inasmuch as this was possible. Now there were occasions when he would return to a piece of work that had already been dealt with—something that had not happened in the past.

Pius XII loved young people! He never missed an opportunity to be good to them, to encourage them, to make them happy and fill them with enthusiasm for everything noble and beautiful, to speak to them.

The Young Christian Workers (international abbreviation JOC, from the French "Jeunesse ouvrière chrétienne") had made a pilgrimage to Rome for a joint gathering. Young people from eighty-seven nations had collected in St. Peter's Square and for over an hour had already been delighting the eyes and hearts of the thousands who had come to watch this enormous group playing and singing. What they presented was the most beautiful entertainment imaginable. The Holy Father had driven in specially from Castel Gandolfo to greet the young people and speak to them. Before he went on to the square, he took a look at the scene from above, from his apartments. For a while, he watched the merry gathering attentively, but then the happy expression on his face grew serious and sad. "Yes, that's youth!" he said. "Now I'll go and speak to them, and what has been put together and worked out in hours and days of arduous work will soon be forgotten . . ." The Holy Father had a splendid speech prepared for the young people, thought out as usual with the utmost care and love after he had informed himself thoroughly about everything that was of interest to them. As on so many other occasions, Pius XII asked himself whether the toil and effort, the many nights spent working would bear the fruit they ought to. If some things did perhaps go unheeded, it is certain that this unique, almost miraculous ministry of Pius XII's will still bear fruit for many generations to come. The Holy Father went down to St. Peter's Square and addressed them. The enormous jubilation of the young people and the great attentiveness with which they listened to his speech, which was repeatedly interrupted by storms of applause, must certainly have banished the sadness that had weighed on the Holy Father before.

On October 27, the Holy Father went from Castel Gandolfo to Santa Maria di Galeria to solemnly dedicate the new Vatican radio station. He went there via "La Storta" especially to please Cardinal Tisserant, the Dean of the College of Cardinals, by paying a visit to his new cathedral.

Before Pius XII left Castel Gandolfo that year, he blessed the new telescope at the "Specula," the Vatican observatory. He inquired about everything in detail and surprised the astronomer with questions that only a specialist in the subject could ask. He was also extremely interested in the valuable archeological findings made during the digging for the installation of this telescope. Then the Holy Father put the poor brother in a predicament by asking him jokingly if he had not prepared some "refreshment" for him after such a long conversation!

On November 16, the Holy Father returned to Rome. On the seventeenth, he already addressed an audience representing the abattoirs of Rome; on the twenty-second, he delivered a speech to the participants at the pasta producers' convention; and on the twenty-fourth, gave a very important speech to anesthetists. This is just an example of how the Holy Father never missed an opportunity to fulfill the duties of his office in every way.

He always prepared his annual Christmas addresses most conscientiously and down to the last detail; no effort was spared. However, these addresses made the whole world, not just Catholics, sit up and take notice.

It will forever remain one of the most beautiful expressions of praise for Pius XII to say that he always put the general interests of the Church before any personal interest. Anyone who investigates his pontificate using original sources will come to the verdict that this Pope was one of those great spirits to whom their own person is nothing, the cause they serve everything. Everything else receded into the background before the office he held.

Again and again, he emphasized that he felt responsible before God for every soul. Amid shattering external storms, he was indefatigable in caring for the eternal salvation of every hard-pressed Christian. His pastoral love embraced the whole world.

No less than any other year, 1958 was marked by and filled with work and worry but every morning still began with the sacred sacrifice at the altar, which unfailingly gave the exalted celebrant new strength and energy. For March 2, the birthday and anniversary of the election of Pius XII, we had decorated the chapel particularly festively. Today's Holy Mass, which was always uplifting because the sacrificing priest simply inspired devotion, was an especially moving experience for us. When it was over, the Holy Father showed us a letter from a boy, which read, "My heartfelt congratulations on your birthday, Holy Father. I have the same one as you but I am only eight years old. Now I imagine that you as the Vicar of Christ can certainly speak personally to God on your birthday. Then tell Him that I am going to be allowed to make my first Holy Communion this year and that later I want to become a priest. God is certain to hear your prayers. Please do not reply to me, however, since Papa says it is very stupid to become a priest, but dear Mama is on my side." The Holy Father had had the letter with him during Mass, so as to be sure not to forget the child's request.

The celebrations for the anniversary of his coronation on March 12 had been canceled by Pius XII that year. However sad the reason for doing so was for him—the trial of the Bishop of Prato scandalized everyone who knew about it—Pius XII was nevertheless happy to have grounds for dropping the celebrations.

That year the Holy Father took a lot of persuading to go to Castel Gandolfo. Was it merely the many speeches and addresses, the innumerable requests for audiences that oppressed him or did he suspect what was awaiting him? Later we often asked ourselves whether we did right in pressing him so urgently to leave Rome. And yet even here God certainly had His plans, for even in death He wanted to prepare for His humble representative a triumph such as no mortal had perhaps ever seen.

I recall this last "move" to Castel Gandolfo particularly well. The Holy Father entered his study just as I was storing away in a packing case the boxes containing his unprinted speeches and addresses, which were taken with us to Castel every year. "Your Holiness," I said with a laugh, "couldn't these stay here? With everything you have to do during your 'vacations' there certainly won't be time to look them through."

"You're right," he replied, "I'll scarcely get around to it." And I was just about to unpack all the boxes again when he said, "All the same, it's better for them to be in Castel."

Toward evening, when Pius XII was ready to leave the apartments and drive to Castel, he went around all the rooms and made sure that everything was in order. I was always the last to leave so that I could lock everything up and, most surprised that the Holy Father should take the time to do this, I went back to him and said in astonishment, "Your Holiness, I come back here almost every day so if anything has been forgotten, I can fetch it."

But he merely smiled kindly and continued his round. Finally he went back into the chapel, from which the Blessed Sacrament had already been removed, knelt for a while at his prie-dieu, went to the Stations of the Cross, stood still briefly in front of the beautiful statue of Our Lady, turned once again to the magnificent ivory crucifix over the altar, and left the chapel to go to the elevator and get into the car. This made such an impression on me because the Holy Father had never done so before, and hardly knew several of the rooms because he never had to pass through them before. When I arrived at Castel Gandolfo about two hours later, Pius XII was already seated at his desk. He said kindly, "Everything's in perfect order at home, now it doesn't matter what happens."

"But what should happen?" I asked in astonishment.

The Holy Father, however, made no reply.

Nothing gave cause for concern during the first weeks in Castel and if only the Holy Father had permitted himself even a little rest, perhaps—who knows?

There were up to three fairly long speeches to be prepared and delivered each week. Only those in his immediate proximity could tell what an effort these and all his other work cost the Holy Father. It soon became clear that this workload was simply too much now. If only he had let someone help him! But everything had to be formulated, checked, revised, and corrected by him personally.

Although the Holy Father admitted himself at the end of September that he no longer felt well, he continued to work. What we all feared happened: the hiccupping returned, a sign of complete overwork and exhaustion. No doctor could explain this phenomenon and no one could prescribe anything for it, but I am convinced that Dr. Niehans was correct in saying that the cause of the complaint lay in the brain (in the hypothalamus) and that total overwork triggered it off. Cardinal Spellman had also made inquiries to the best doctors in New York and they came to the same conclusion as Dr. Niehans: the seat of the complaint was in the brain, in the hypothalamus. The New York doctors said that no cure was possible. Dr. Niehans, on the other hand, maintained that the illness could be cured with live hypothalamus cells. After all, the result of this cellular therapy four years before Pius XII's recovery proved him right. (It must be added that Dr. Niehans wanted to repeat the therapy after a year, to which the Holy Father consented, but that it was never possible to do so.)

Now Dr. Niehans was not there; perhaps it would in any case have been too late and the Holy Father showed no consideration for himself. The audiences and speeches continued. Cardinal Spellman, who had come with a group of pilgrims, said after the audience that he had wanted to leave again with his party immediately after the address but that the Holy Father had kept him and, despite the hiccups, had talked to him as if nothing was wrong. The following day there was another big audience at which Pius XII was to deliver a very important speech. On Sunday morning, the notaries from all over Italy were due. The Holy Father had already been planning and preparing the address for them for a long time.

CHAPTER FOURTEEN

CONSUMMATUM EST

The night from Saturday to Sunday, October 5, was not good at all and we were all extremely worried that Pius XII would not be able to deliver his speech. At Mass, it was clear to see that he was having great difficulty remaining upright. Nevertheless, at nine o'clock he appeared on the balcony—the audience had to take place in the courtyard because the large hall was simply not big enough for all the people—very pale but with his usual kindly smile. Although constantly interrupted by hiccupping, he delivered the lengthy address. We knew how wretched he felt and so we sisters remained close by, worried all the time that he would not be able to finish the speech. Summoning up his last strength of will, he concluded it and then sank into the chair standing behind him. But even now he carried on waving and greeting for a long time and before leaving the balcony he called loudly—something he had never done before—*"ADDIO! ADDIO!"* It was dedication to the extreme, to the very end!

Later the then-Archbishop of Milan, His Excellency Montini, was to allude to this *"ADDIO"* in his farewell words to the deceased Pontiff when he wrote:

> *"ADDIO"* . . . *Ci ha lasciato, il Padre, il Maestro, il Pastore, il Difensore, il Capo. La penombra del Venerdi Santo sembrò distendersi sulla terra e nei cuori dei Fedeli, sia pure nell'attesa sicura di una vicina rissurezione . . . Se nessuno, infine, scorderà quanto nella sua voce abbia risuonato in ore tremende e fatidiche il grido della coscienza umano—questo non lo scorderà soppratutto la Storia—tutti ricorderanno quel che più appartiene agli affeti nostri: il vibrare nella sua voce, sempre, il palpito di una carità pia e dolce come Quel supremo "ADDIO"!*

("ADDIO" . . . We have been left by the Father, the Master, the Pastor, the Defender, the Head. The shadow of Good Friday seems to spread out over the earth and in the hearts of the faithful, even though in the certain expectation of an imminent resurrection ... If in the end no one forgets how much the cry of the human con-science sounded in his voice in those terrible and fateful hours—history above all will not forget this—all will remember what most moved us: the trembling in his voice, always, the throb of sweet Christian love like that final, supreme *"ADDIO."*)

"But now, Your Holiness, lie down, lie down," we begged him when the speech was over.

"No, I can't, Monsignor Dell' Acqua has an audience." This lasted until 11:55. When the door at last opened and the Holy Father was about to enter, there was another knock. "Your Holiness, the Supplication," said the Master of the Chamber—it was the Sunday when the Feast of Our Lady of the Holy Rosary was being celebrated. And Pius XII went out, deathly pale but upright, as once our Lord and Savior must have gone to Golgotha—to the Cross! That last picture taken at the Supplication shows in all clarity Pius XII's *"Consummatum est."*

At last the door opened again and, when it was closed behind him, the Holy Father said, *"Adesso non posso più!"* (Now I cannot go on). With his last reserves of strength, the Holy Father went to his room and sank on to a couch. If it had not been for the tormenting hiccups one could have thought he was no longer alive. The previous evening, the doctor had given him an injection that was supposed to stop the hiccupping but, as usual, it had not helped. After a while, we took the Holy Father a little light refresh-ment. He probably accepted it simply in order not to disappoint us. A little later, he tried to go into the study but was unable to do so. He then dragged himself into the chapel and from there back to his bedroom. There he had his work brought to him in his easy chair. He began to look through it but it kept slipping out of his hands. All his efforts to master his exhaustion were to no avail. Finally, he laid the work aside. "I can't go on," I heard him say softly. I pulled the little table with the work on it aside and the Holy Father tried to rest. He actually managed to sleep a little since the hiccup-ping was less severe. After an hour, he even asked to take some fresh air. He did go out but with great difficulty, having to keep sitting down and resting. Despite his wretched condition, he forced himself to stay outside for his usual hour. On returning home, he paid a visit to the chapel and then went to work as every other day.

We could watch him from the anteroom through the wide-open door. He read and wrote, stood up now and again to fetch a book or document. Occasionally he rested briefly, but he went on working until a book fell out of his hand. I hurried in to pick it up and was greeted with a look of astonishment. "Your Holiness, don't you want to take a short break?"

"No," he replied, "I'm not getting on very well anyway." He continued working until dinner.

"Holy Father, we'll bring everything into the room next door so that you don't have to go downstairs."

"No, I'll come down," was the reply. Pius XII sat down at the table and ate a little, but it was very obvious that he had to force himself to do so. For him eating was also a duty, so as to keep up his strength in order to serve God, the Church, and souls.

For almost forty-one years, I was able to observe how little it took to satisfy the Holy Father, how undemanding he was, especially at the table, and I often wondered whether there could be anyone at all who was more moderate and frugal regarding food and drink than Pius XII.

That evening as usual we joined the Holy Father in the chapel for the daily rosary. Above the tabernacle hung a beautiful painting of the Black Madonna of Czestochowa, whom the Holy Father venerated deeply. Years before, he had told us sisters the exact story of the miraculous Madonna and also had explained the two splendid murals executed by a great Polish artist. All the furnishings of the chapel were a gift of the Polish people to Pius XI, who for several years had been Nuncio to Poland.

The tall, slim figure at the prie-dieu before the tabernacle slowly slumped a little and then the Holy Father sat down—something he never otherwise did. But he held out to the end, knelt down again and then after a while got up to bless us all as he did every day. We followed the Holy Father out of the chapel, hoping that today at least he would go to his bedroom. But, although dragging himself tiredly, he set off for his study. Our request for him to go and lie down received the answer that the work for the next day's audience was not yet dealt with. One sister remained on night duty and stayed near him, but it was midnight before the Holy Father, after his devotions in the chapel, at last made his way to his bedroom.

The night was restless but not particularly bad. The constant hiccupping did not allow much sleep but it was less tormenting than the night before. The doctor was due early in the morning, as he wanted to pump out the Holy Father's stomach, which had to be empty for this. (He hoped this would stop the hiccups.) The Holy Father would not be able to celebrate Mass until afterwards. Everything was ready and the doctor commenced his work. Pius XII was as cheerful and kind as always. I was struck by his unusual pallor, but soon the doctor had finished. The Holy Father was at rest in his high-backed armchair when his eyes suddenly closed, his head fell forward, and he slumped down unconscious. He had just thanked the doctor warmly, and this kind expression remained on the deathly-pale face as he was laid on the bed next to the chair. The doctors immediately did all that is to be done in such cases while we suffered and wrestled in passionate prayer for his precious life.

A priest who was close to the Holy Father was called at once to administer extreme unction against all eventualities. It was impossible to tell whether the Holy Father was conscious of receiving the sacrament or not since he did not show any reaction. No one can conceive of the suffering during these hours and none of us wanted to leave his bedside for even a minute in the certain hope that the firmly closed eyes would open again.

Hour after hour passed. The doctors came and went but the agonizing uncertainty remained. At 4:30 p.m. the Holy Father at last stirred a little. He opened his eyes and looked around him in wonder. Then he ran his hand over his eyes, opened them wide and asked in surprise, "What's the matter? My spectacles, please." He must not have been able to see clearly yet. Once again, he looked around in astonishment and asked, "What's the matter, then? It must be morning, time for Mass." When we broke it gently to the Holy Father what had happened, he calmed down and allowed the doctors to do what was necessary. Gradually his movements became natural again, his voice once again clear. On the doctor's instructions, we brought the Holy Father some refreshment. After that, he wanted to get up and to bless all the people who came regularly every evening. When he was told that this was not possible today, he submitted but wanted to know exactly whether the people had been properly informed in the appropriate languages.

Poor Holy Father! Little did he know that from the time the news of his serious illness broke thousands had been rushing to Castel Gandolfo all day long in order to find out how he was. How happy they all were when it was now possible to announce better news. All the same, it was not quiet around the Castel until late at night. Everyone was weighed down with worry about the beloved Father of Christendom.

We did not leave his side for a minute. God be praised, the hope that the Holy Father might once again recover grew with every hour. As he was beginning to regain consciousness, Pius XII had not recognized people. Cardinal Tisserant had rushed quickly to his bedside but afterwards the Holy Father could not remember anything about it. Later, however, he recognized everyone again and spoke quite naturally and easily to them. He would have liked to look through the work that arrived every day but the doctor did not allow it; it cost the Holy Father a great deal to obey him in this. We brought what the doctor had instructed in the way of an evening meal and then prepared the bedroom for the night. Since we thought that we ought to let the Holy Father rest, we went quietly into the chapel for the rosary. However, he wished to pray it together with us all as usual and so we opened the door of the chapel, knelt around his bed and said the rosary with him—for the next to the last time. It was good that we did not know this! Certainly no one would have been able to pray aloud! As it was, however, our *Ave Maria* sounded confident that our dear Lady, whom the Holy Father venerated so deeply, would once again work a miracle. Repeatedly we kept looking at the pale face on the white pillows radiating so much devotion and reverence, and at the beautifully folded hands passing the beads of the rosary through their fingers. For many years, we had been in the habit of giving the Holy Father a new rosary every evening so as to be able to satisfy the many people who asked for one that he had used himself. Pius XII, who always carried a rosary on him, often returned from an audience without it because some visitor had asked him for it. So it was that today too, he first blessed the rosary before he gave the sign to begin.

We thought that today we ought to omit the litany and the other prayers but the closed eyelids opened and the Holy Father said, "Pray to the end!" Then he raised his almost transparent hand in blessing. With a heartfelt, "Goodnight, Holy Father," we left the room.

The sister on night duty heard the Holy Father go on praying for a long time before a light slumber brought him a little rest. Again and again, the hiccupping woke him but toward morning, he fell asleep properly. When he awoke after seven o'clock, he thought he was strong enough to celebrate

Holy Mass. "It's the Feast of Our Lady of the Holy Rosary," he said with a friendly smile. However, the doctors would not allow him to get up so we prepared everything for him to receive Holy Communion, which he did with a devoutness that edified all present. The doctor had prescribed a cup of beef tea. After a while, I brought this in, but a quarter of an hour later I had to fetch another, as the Holy Father was still praying and meanwhile the first had gotten cold. The second cup fared no better. On bringing the third, I ventured to say, "Your Holiness, the doctor wants you to take some sustenance." He obediently sat up a little, still absorbed in God, and drank what was placed in front of him. I inquired how he felt. The kind and friendly answer was, "Well." He remained silent for a while and then said all of a sudden, "*Questa e la mia giornata.*" The Holy Father never spoke Italian with us sisters and so I tried to fathom out what he had meant. It was some time before it struck me. I rushed out of the room so as not to burst into loud tears. As I came out of the door, I bumped into one of the doctors, who said, "Oh, you can set your mind at ease. The Holy Father is really very well today, much better than yesterday led us to expect." But this could not reassure me. I went into the chapel, poured out my troubles and cried my heart out; then, a little calmer now, I kept telling myself that I could have misunderstood him. It had struck me like a flash of lightning what the Holy Father had said on that memorable night of May 15, 1956: "One day I shall die quite suddenly . . . I've asked God for a day." Was today that day? Again and again it rang in my ears: "*Questa e la mia giornata*" (This is my day)!

The doctors were now in the bedroom and the Holy Father was talking to them. He wanted to receive one of the gentlemen from the Secretariat of State, which, however, the doctors forbade. Scarcely had everyone left the room than the Holy Father began to pray again. I did not dare to disturb him however much I should have liked to start a conversation in order to rid myself of my terrible fear. The doctors were full of confidence and everyone in the house was happy and full of hope. Thus I did not dare to confide in anyone, so as not to mar their joy. But I could not banish my anxiety. On the contrary! I kept feeling drawn back to the bed on which the Holy Father lay with a peaceful, almost cheerful expression on his fine, pale face, his eyes lowered and his hands folded in prayer.

What would the next hours bring? There were so many people waiting for information and his dear relatives in particular expected that I would be the one to announce the good news of an improvement and encourage them. I did so too, but this did not diminish my own great anxiety. Whenever it was possible, I took refuge in a corner of the sickroom so as not to have to talk to anyone.

Twice before the Holy Father had been very seriously ill. Although very many people feared for his life, at that time I was confident, indeed certain that he would recover, which surprised many. This was said to me quite openly and one high-ranking prelate wanted to know where I got this confidence from. I told him that I did not know myself but that I was quite certain about it. Today the opposite was the case. Everyone around me, including the doctors, was full of cheerful hope, which I alone could not share. Only someone who has had a similar experience can imagine the torture these hours held.

It was time for the Holy Father to take some nourishment. I was glad that he had to interrupt his prayers, hoping that a brief conversation might ensue. A lot of people entered the room again and the Holy Father spoke to them in a kind and friendly, almost cheerful manner. However, what I longed for did not take place. Now he wanted to rest a little. We kept watch with the Lord in the tabernacle—the chapel adjoined the bedroom—and through the open door it was possible to see every movement and hear almost every breath. For a while, a few words of prayer were audible, words from the *Anima Christi,* but then all fell quiet and the regular breathing revealed that the Holy Father was sleeping a little. After an hour, he wished for light to be let into the room again and the doctors returned as well. When they had left, he asked if the transcript of his important Pope Benedict XIV speech was ready. When I said that it was, he would have liked to look through it, but the doctors would not allow this. Although reluctantly, he submitted. In order to provide him with a little diversion, we asked to be permitted to play a recording, since we knew how much he loved good music. He kindly agreed but, so it seemed, only in order to satisfy us. Anyone who was able to observe with what interest, what understanding and attentiveness he listened to good music can judge what a sacrifice it was for him constantly to have to forego this pleasure because everywhere duty came first. Today he did listen but it seemed to us that he was not always enjoying the music. His thoughts must have been elsewhere. My anxiety increased from minute to minute.

Later he wanted to look at a document and gave his instructions with characteristic matter-of-factness and precision—proof that he knew exactly what he was doing. But then he lowered his eyes again and folded his hands. What might he have been saying to his Lord and God that day? Suddenly he picked up the clock. "It's time to give the people the blessing," he said, "Would you go and look in the courtyard?"

"Your Holiness, we'll ask the doctor first."

"Yes, do that, but say that I can easily get up."

Naturally, the question to the doctor was answered in the negative and so the Holy Father gave precise instructions as to what was to be said to the waiting crowd and how sincerely he blessed them all. If only he had suspected how expectantly the thousands of people had been waiting all day long for news and how they were filled with joyful hope, since things seemed to be going so well.

After a while, the Holy Father asked in astonishment, "How is it that you're here so much today? You still have to copy . . . and the . . . has still to be dealt with." He forgot or overlooked nothing. Accordingly, I withdrew from his sight but however hard I tried to force myself, I could not manage to do any real work and so I returned to the chapel, never in my life having prayed more fervently than during these hours.

At about noon Dr. Nichans had arrived by plane from Paris. He had heard the news of Pius XII's illness there and telephoned us immediately before leaving for Rome on the first flight he could get. Pius XII welcomed him most warmly and displayed great happiness that he had come.

That day too, as evening fell we prepared the very light meal that the doctor had prescribed. The Holy Father ate it obediently and without any fuss, entertaining us in his friendly manner as he did so. He also inquired about his favorite little bird, which had refused to eat since the Holy Father no longer came to meals.

Since no one was capable of proper work that day, we all went to his bedroom a little earlier for the rosary. Pius XII said immediately, "It's earlier today!"—once again proof that he was in full command of all his faculties. Then he crossed himself, with the same generous, beautiful movement as always, and we prayed the rosary with him—the last here on earth!

For twenty years, we had always been allowed to pray the rosary with the Holy Father at this hour. Just as he did everything to perfection and always edified everyone by what he did, this was the case in particular when he prayed. He articulated every word clearly, was never either too fast or too slow but borne by a fervor that showed how deeply he was convinced of and imbued with what he was doing.

The rosary was finished and we prayed a further three *Ave Marias*, adding "Thou health of the sick, pray for him!" Then the Holy Father looked at each of us in turn, with what seemed to me an infinitely wistful eye. Then he raised his hand to bless us. It was his last "goodnight blessing" on this earth! One after the other we approached the Holy Father's bed and kissed the almost transparent white hand—for the last time.

The sister on duty opened the window to air the room for the night. The Holy Father looked at the star-studded sky and said, "Look, how beautiful—how great God is!"

Today the sister did not leave the sickroom. The doctor also stayed next door so that he could be on the spot at once. As always, Pius XII prayed until he fell asleep, which was relatively soon. But his sleep was very restless and did not last long. He could be heard whispering again and again, even though the exact words of his prayers were not audible. However, as morning approached, he fell asleep quietly. When he awoke, he almost had a little color in his cheeks. He returned the morning greeting heartily and happily. He asked immediately if he could celebrate Mass or at least receive Holy Communion but the doctors thought it necessary to apply their treatment first. The Holy Father submitted but I noticed that he began to look worse and worse from one minute to the next.

When the doctors had left the room, I set about preparing everything for Holy Communion. But then the Holy Father said to me, "*Mi sento tanto, tanto male . . .*" (I feel very, very ill). Never shall I forget that look, that last look before the Holy Father closed his eyes forever and his head fell slowly forward.

What the doctors whom I called did after that I do not know. For a time I was incapable of speaking, thinking or doing anything. When the doctors had left again, I returned to the bed and asked, "Holy Father, can you hear me?" I took the white hands lying on the covers and I believed that the Holy Father gently returned the pressure. Oxygen was brought and for hours we held the tube to his slightly open mouth. Sometimes his breathing came sporadically and with a rattle. We prayed unceasingly out loud to the Holy Father, hoping that he might understand us. We moistened his burning lips, mopped his brow, but no sign came that he understood us. Yet hope lived on in us! Perhaps . . . perhaps later . . . as it had happened two days before.

His dear relatives came, as well as cardinals, bishops, prelates, dear friends, we did not know who else. At midday, it grew quiet in the sickroom, a relief for us all.

"Come and eat something," I was told, but who could eat on such a day? When I was alone again in the sickroom for a time, I once more took the white hands in mine and asked, "Holy Father, can you hear me?" and this time too, I thought that I felt a slight pressure in reply. Go and rest a little, I was told, it is sure to be another long, hard night. Rest? Now?

At last I went down to the cloister on the floor below. Hardly had I entered my room than there were three firm knocks one after the other. What could it be? There was surely no one there. When I opened the door, there was indeed no one to be seen. What was it then? All at once, something struck me that I had remembered earlier that morning. The Holy Father had given strict orders, "If one day I should not have time, then burn this . . ." Since there had been so many people in the anterooms all morning, it had not been possible to get into the Holy Father's study. Now everyone had gone to lunch. We quickly took three hampers to put the carefully and neatly stacked papers in and take them away. The only order the Holy Father had given was carried out. Should he, as we all ardently hoped, regain consciousness as he had two days before, it would be easy to put everything back again. These were all the drafts for speeches and addresses that Pius XII had delivered during the twenty years of his pontificate without ever having them printed. This had not been done simply because he had not found the time to look them through again and, if necessary, put the finishing touches to them. As already mentioned, he always took these papers with him to Castel Gandolfo in the hope of finding time to do this work. But every year they were taken back again untouched. How often the Secretariat of State had asked about these in order to be able to complete their collection of his speeches and addresses. However, Pius XII had always consoled them with the words, "When I find the time." What it cost us to burn all this—most of it handwritten, the rest typed by the Holy Father personally—cannot be told. But it was on Pius XII's orders. When I was later asked about these papers, I said without reserve, "The Holy Father ordered everything to be burned and it has been."

"Do you realize," I was asked, "that you have burned a great treasure?"

"We know that better than anyone, but it was an order of the Holy Father's, who was sacrosanct to us throughout his life and is no less so after his death!"

Hardly had we rescued the three hampers than the Antechamber and the other anterooms filled with people again. Sister Ewaldis, Sister Maria Conrada, and I returned with a certain feeling of relief to the sickbed now that we had carried out Pius XII's order. We asked Dr. Niehans if there was any sign of improvement and received "no" as an answer. "But," he said, "no deterioration either." Soon, however, the Holy Father began to sweat profusely and his temperature rose. We mopped the perspiration from his face, neck, and hands. Those standing and kneeling around the bedside kept requesting the cloths used for this. We prayed and suffered and hoped—against all hope—along with the many others with us there. Did the Holy Father hear us praying? We prayed softly, but from time to time more loudly, trusting that something would perhaps after all penetrate the deep coma, which—according to the doctor—held him prisoner. His breathing became more and more difficult and painful, and we were forced to watch His Holiness suffer without being able to relieve the suffering or do anything else for him. Our helplessness in the face of such suffering was so bitter that only the thought, "Lord, Thy will be done" made it tolerable. Hour after hour passed. When we could no longer bear to watch without being able to help, we took refuge in the chapel again, offering the Lord in the tabernacle a thousand times over our own lives if only He would let a miracle happen. The hour approached at which the Holy Father's condition had improved two days before. Dear God, let him open his eyes again, once again! But this hour also passed. Perhaps it will take a little longer today but then come after all; that was our hope. But the contrary was the case. His temperature went on rising, the rattle in his breathing increased. And still we prayed and hoped. All we saw now was the dear face marked with suffering, the lips parched with fever, the image of Him who—after surrendering everything for man's salvation—sacrificed Himself to His Father on the Cross.

It was whispered to me that the Dean of the College of Cardinals had already sealed His Holiness's study. So they had abandoned hope! In us it lived on, the hope of a miracle! How glad we now were that we had fulfilled our Holy Father's last instructions and removed the papers. Now it would no longer have been possible.

People came and went; one had to attend to this or that visitor, however difficult it was. They had to be consoled, but who could do so in these so difficult and dark hours with a heart overflowing with suffering? How good it was that the chapel was next door with the Lord in the tabernacle, the only support in these hours of inexpressible pain. This day filled with suffering was also followed by evening, by night. For hours already dear relatives and faithful friends had been kneeling with us around our Holy Father's bed of pain. We prayed silently and then out loud together with the prelates and priests all his favorite prayers, especially his *Anima Christi*.

As midnight approached, Monsignor Tardini, who had also already been at the bedside for hours, said that he was now going to say Holy Mass and implore God, if it be His most holy will, to preserve the Holy Father for the world or to take him to Him, whichever was decreed by His divine wisdom. We were all to unite with him in this intention. This Holy Mass was to be broadcast on the radio so that all the thousands and thousands foregoing sleep and repose with aching and sympathetic hearts throughout the world should be able to join in our prayers. Everyone all over the world who participated spiritually in this Mass and listened to the voice of the celebrant, often choked with tears, knows of the nobility and pain of this hour. We had opened the double doors to the chapel wide and could thus assist at the sacred sacrifice without letting the exalted sufferer out of sight. All of us received Holy Communion for the Holy Father, who lay there on the white pillows and—although without being aware of it—offered himself up with HIM whom he had represented for almost twenty years here on earth. Like his divine example, he had offered up everything, given himself, right to the final sacrifice.

This comes out in what one of the doctors (Professor Gasbarini) said to me that day. "The Holy Father is not dying of any real disease, he's simply worn out. He has worked himself to the limit of what a human being can give. He has a perfectly healthy heart and likewise healthy lungs. If only he had taken things a little easier, he could have lived another twenty years." But in contrast to this was Pius XII's maxim and conviction: "A Pope no longer has a right to himself. He belongs to God, the Church and souls. Here on earth there is no rest for him."

The Holy Mass was over. We resumed our places around the sickbed. Monsignor Tardini and the other priests also joined us again. With passionate prayers, we sought to hold back the fleeing life, to move the Lord over life and death to allow the world to keep the Holy Father. But his breathing was no more than a rattle even though his whole body glowed with fever. Over two more hours passed but no one grew weary of praying.

It seemed as if the expression on the deathly pale face was becoming increasingly pained, although Dr. Niehans, who never left the bedside, thought that the coma was so deep that the Holy Father could not feel anything. In hours of such inexpressible suffering, one sees quite clearly that all that is left to man is hope and trust in the Eternal Love that surpasses all human impotence and gives us the strength to bear even the heaviest burden. The Holy Father's death rattle was interspersed with our prayers, which, right to the end, were not without hope of a miracle.

Now the rattle ceased for a time, but it began again—there was a slight opening of the firmly closed eyes—a gentle closing of the mouth into a wonderful smile that transfigured the waxen-pale face—a bowing of the noble head—a last breath.

Now he is seeing God!—it escaped my lips. Then Monsignor Tardini began in a loud, almost joyful voice, "*Magnificat anima mea Dominum . . .*" and we joined in and prayed with him. And now, "*Salve Regina . . .*" and "*Sub Tuum praesidium . . .*" Then we all approached the bedside and kissed the still feverish hands of the exalted deceased for the very last time.

No one was weeping. Not until the *De profundis* was intoned did an aching sobbing go through the room. Then the doors were opened and we were forced to watch streams of people pour in.

Soon Cardinal Tisserant arrived. After praying for a while beside the deceased, he wished to say Holy Mass. Numerous Masses followed all morning. The Dean of the College of Cardinals had given us permission to wash and clothe the exalted deceased and we were infinitely grateful for this favor. The doors were closed again and we sisters, together with a male nurse, were allowed to render this last service of love to the man whom we had been permitted to serve for almost the span of a human life and whose lofty example had spurred us on to every virtue.

Since the whole body was still very warm from the fever, which had risen to the extreme, it remained light and supple for a long time so that we had absolutely no difficulty in handling it. Soon everything was done. We knelt down silently for a while in ineffable pain—but already there was a knock and we had to open the doors again to allow all the people to enter.

It was good that no time was left for reflection. Cardinal Tisserant had finished celebrating Mass and after he had prayed before the tabernacle for a time, he asked if I knew anything of a testament. I recalled very well that night when Pius XII had written his testament and said, "One day I shall die quite suddenly . . ." He had also showed me where he had put the document. After I had found the key to the Holy Father's desk in the pocket of his white cassock, I was later able to show His Eminence where I suspected that he would find what he was looking for.

That day I drove back along the route I had traveled hundreds of times, this time in inexpressible pain. It was as if the world had assumed a different face, and I was surprised that time had not stood still in view of the event of the past night. Was it all perhaps just a terrible dream, or was it true? Was it reality? On arriving at St. Peter's Square, I heard the great bells tolling, and every stroke hurt beyond words. But I also saw crowds of people with genuine, profound mourning over the beloved and revered deceased written on their faces.

How glad I was, no longer to be able to hear the tolling of the mourning bells once I was in the elevator up to the private apartments. I opened the door to the so familiar rooms, which our Holy Father had filled with life for almost twenty years. These so familiar and well-loved rooms seemed cold and dead to me and I was glad when Cardinal Tisserant arrived with Carlo Pacelli. With trembling hands, I opened the drawer of the desk and His Eminence took out the document he sought. He read it and then took charge of it. He walked all through the apartments and said that he would return a little later to seal everything. He gave us sisters permission, once we had seen to everything in Castel Gandolfo, to return to the private apartments to order our own belongings and to stay there until we had taken care of everything. If we should encounter any difficulty, we only needed to go to him and refer to what he had said. We shall always remember this great kindness and friendliness with gratitude.

When everything was sealed and locked up and His Eminence had left the private apartments, I returned to Castel Gandolfo. The death room was full of people. No matter how much we should have liked to stay quietly in a corner near the Holy Father and pray, this was impossible on account of all the people. To talk to them was even more impossible. So we began to clear up a little; since Sunday no one had been capable of working properly. But everything was a reminder of the Holy Father, who lay still and lifeless nearby and would soon be gone from us forever. Nevertheless, the thought that the Holy Father was still in the house was consoling. We longed for midday, when the stream of people would slacken off somewhat and we should be able to see the dear, still face again for a short time and pray near it. Since the chapel was always full of praying people, it was not even possible to take refuge there.

The great figures of the Church and the world came to see Pius XII for the last time, whom they revered as the Vicar of Christ and head of the Church, but also as a very great and noble person, as a saintly priest, an excellent scholar, a kind and loving father. It did one good to the bottom of one's heart to see so much genuine and profound grief. It was very painful to know that thousands were having to stand outside waiting for hours because it was simply impossible for such vast crowds to get into the death room. It was already late when the radio announced that the doors would have to be closed. The poor people who slowly withdrew weeping were consoled with the promise that they could come back the next day.

In the meantime, Pius XII was taken into the largest room in the building and laid out there in state. Now that only the Noble Guard and the Privy Chamberlains along with students from the various national colleges were standing around the bier, we were also able to kneel down and pray again.

Back in the cloister, we discovered that from the window of one of the rooms we could look directly into the Swiss Room and see the Holy Father lying in state there. With burning eyes that had not seen sleep for nights we looked into the brightly lit room where the Holy Father lay amid candles and flowers, mourned by the whole world but certainly greeted joyfully in Heaven. Hour after hour passed in this solitary wake.

At daybreak, we returned to the Swiss Room and knelt at the bier of the Holy Father until the room filled with people again.

In front of the residence there were thousands upon thousands waiting to be let in. How good it did us in these hours of deepest suffering to see the sympathy of all these people who spared no effort and sacrifice and waited hour after hour just to be able to see once more the revered and beloved face and to thank him who had given them so much when he was alive.

And again it was a feast of Our Lady—the Motherhood of the Blessed Virgin Mary! She, who knew that it was not God's will for Pius XII to be preserved for the world, wanted one of her feasts for the triumphal journey of her loyal son into the Eternal City. Everything inside and outside the house was astir. All the preparations were made for the Holy Father to be taken to Rome. For him who always chose only the simplest for himself, who never liked any fuss as far as his own person was concerned, for him who wanted to be so modest and go unnoticed a triumphal procession was now prepared such as very few mortals may ever have been given. It must certainly have lain in the plans of Divine Providence that the Holy Father was not to die in Rome but in Castel Gandolfo so that this unique spectacle of his last journey to the Eternal City could take place.

In the courtyard of Castel Gandolfo, where thousands had awaited Pius XII daily for audiences, a beautifully decorated hearse stood ready. Up in the Swiss Room the candles were just being extinguished, a sign that the coffin had already been closed. And already the men were descending the steps with their precious burden to lay it on the hearse. It was simply impossible to grasp that what was taking place here in the courtyard was real. For years, we had been present at the farewell from Castel Gandolfo. We had seen joyful, happy people cheering their beloved father, overjoyed to receive a last blessing and already looking forward to the next year.

And today! Since early that morning, the square in front of the Castel had been black with crowds waiting not for the kind, loving, blessing father but for the coffin adorned with the tiara that was just being driven out of the gates. A loud sobbing went through the crowd and then everything started moving, following the hearse as it slowly drove off. Everyone who could manage it at all wanted to be there. It could be read in their faces that these last respects were not only being paid to the Supreme Pontiff. All these thousands of people loved this rare person who, the more God elevated him, bent down closer to suffering humanity and sought to become everything to each and every one. The genuine and deep mourning was not only for the great Pope, the great Roman, who despite his exalted position and refinement truly belonged to them; it was also for the noble man, whose spiritualized figure had almost nothing earthly about it any longer and who nevertheless drew everyone to him with a look or a gesture because they felt that he lived completely for them and the salvation of their souls.

Slowly the hearse bearing the exalted body rolled through the Roman Campagna in the direction of his city, his home. And Rome was waiting for him; Rome greeted her rescuer and liberator and the man who, not heeding the danger to his own life, had been the first to hurry to San Lorenzo during the heavy air raid to comfort the hard-pressed and homeless and who, on returning home, had immediately let the world know that regardless of the danger to himself he would do the same again if there was another air raid. And the world knew that Pius XII would keep his word. It was thanks to him alone, as the Romans knew full well, that their city was saved.

A Good Friday atmosphere lay over the otherwise so bustling and noisy city. Everything seemed to be focused on the deceased father who was now silently entering San Giovanni, the Lateran Basilica and the main and mother church of the world. Here the prayers of absolution and the funeral orations were said for the first time: "Enter not into judgment with Thy servant. Lord . . . Absolve, O Lord, the soul of Thy servant from every bond of sin that, restored to life in the glory of the resurrection, it may live in the midst of Thy glory . . ." The warm, sincere sympathy of everyone was so moving that it also cast its spell on those who were perhaps taking part more out of curiosity.

The sea of people outside the basilica now formed into an immense procession through Rome. The Holy Father had drawn millions to him when he was alive, blessed and greeted millions—perhaps more than anyone else in the history of the world. He now passed once more through the city that he had loved, for which he had suffered and sacrificed so much, and it seemed that the whole city was following him.

The procession arrived at Santa Maria Maggiore. Who could fail to remember the wonderful opening of the *ANNO MARIANO*! Here at the altar of the "*Salus Populi Romani*" the young priest Eugenio Pacelli had celebrated his first Holy Mass.

The route led past the Coliseum, then the church of Il Gesù, where Eugenio Pacelli had sat for hours at the feet of the Madonna della Strada as a boy, confiding everything in her and discussing everything with her, as his own mother once acknowledged.

It was already growing dark when St. Peter's came in sight. For the last time Pius XII was escorted past the obelisk. How often he had been carried past it on the *sedia gestatoria* to large rallies, mass audiences of workers, young people, pilgrims from all over the world! How often he had blessed the jubilant crowds here! And today! The mourning bells tolled dully over the wide square, accompanied by the sobbing of the vast crowd. Those who witnessed this unique spectacle know how great and majestic it was.

In his modesty Pius XII would never have imagined that his last journey into his city would become a great event such as even Rome, rich as she is in extraordinary and unique occasions, can scarcely ever have seen.

Now the Holy Father was received by St. Peter's. How dear this holy place was to his heart and what he had done for the basilica! Now he was entering it for the last time, surrounded not by the customary jubilation but by sobbing and sorrow. The coffin bearing the precious burden was set down in front of the Cathedra Petri.

St. Peter's has seen countless people within its walls, especially during the twenty years of Pius XII's pontificate, but the crowds pouring in and out now must have outstripped all that had gone before. The stream of people went on for days without diminishing. On the contrary! Gradually people arrived from all over the world wanting to see the Holy Father again or at least pay their last respects to him. They did not want to leave this privilege to the Romans alone before the quiet, simple tomb directly below the dome of St. Peter's received the Holy Father, who had meant so much to them during his lifetime.

The mourning bells tolled out over the city, which seemed to take days to awaken from the stunned state that had taken hold of it. The stream of people did not lessen until the doors of St. Peter's were closed at noon on October 13, although thousands of weeping mourners were still waiting to go in. Then followed the funeral of the Pope, which, according to the Church's age-old ceremonial, takes place only in the presence of cardinals, bishops, and priests.

When the doors of St. Peter's opened again, only the catafalque was to be seen, crowned with the tiara. But even now, a dense, continuous stream of pilgrims filed past in somber silence. Right to the last, their love wanted to prove its affection and gratitude. And even here Our Lady accompanied her faithful son—that memorable October 13 was Fatima Day. The "*Novendiali*," the nine days, followed, ending with the burial in the quiet, plain tomb.

Pius XII's simple place of rest, so much in keeping with his testament, has in the meantime become a center of attraction for many people. Those who kneel there in silent prayer know how much love is brought to the great Pope, whose whole life was consumed in the service of God, the Church and souls.

ABOUT THE AUTHOR

Sister M. Pascalina (Josefine) Lehnert (1894–1983) was born in Ebersberg, Germany, which is not far from Munich. She was the seventh of twelve children. At the age of 19, she entered the Franciscan teaching order, Sisters of the Holy Cross (Menzingen) in Altötting. After the Order's customary period of novitiate formation, she worked briefly as a teacher.

In March 1918, her Provincial unexpectedly sent Sister Pascalina with two other young sisters to provide housekeeping services for the new Papal Nuncio, Eugenio Pacelli. Beginning in Munich—then in 1925 in Berlin, and after 1929 in Rome—Sister Pascalina faithfully served for forty years as housekeeper and assistant to Pope Pius XII, until his death in 1958. As superior to the sisters serving with her, by the time she and the sisters moved to Rome, everyone called her "Madre" ("Mother") Pascalina, including the Pope.

A few months after the death of Pope Pius XII, at the request of her superior, Madre Pascalina wrote down her memories of her years in the Pope's service. Finally published in German in 1982, her book about those years offers a uniquely personal portrait of Pius XII.

After the Holy Father's death, Madre Pascalina stayed in Rome and was, from 1959 to 1969, Mother Superior of the Holy Cross sisters working at Pontifical North American College. Beginning in 1969, her superiors assigned her to build a residence for single women called the "Casa Pastor Angelicus," where she lived and worked for the rest of her life. Although she provided little information about her own accomplishments, in 1958 Pope John XXIII recognized her great service to the Pope and to the Church with the papal honor *Pro Ecclesia et Pontifice*. She also received state honors from West Germany, Austria, and the state of Bavaria.

In 1983, she traveled from Rome to Vienna to attend a memorial celebration of the 25th anniversary of the death of Pius XII, and appeared to be in excellent health. As she prepared to fly home, however, she suffered a brain hemorrhage, collapsed, and was rushed to a hospital in Vienna, where she died on November 13, 1989. The obituary published by her motherhouse praised Madre Pascalina's life as one of "prayer and indefatigable commitment to others. She helped wherever she could, above all also in the war and post-war years by dispatching a great quantity of relief supplies on behalf of the Vatican all over the world."

SELECT TABLE OF EVENTS

In the Life of Pius XII

2 March 1876
Born in Rome as the second of four children of the Consistorial Advocate
Filippo Pacelli and his wife Virginia Graziosi.

2 April 1899
After studies at the Collegio Capranica, the Seminary of S. Apollinare and
the Gregorian University, ordination to the priesthood.

1902
Doctor utriusque juris (Doctor of Canon and Civil Law).

1 October 1903
Secretary in the Secretariat of State.

1909–1914
Professor of Ecclesiastical Diplomacy at the Pontificia Accademia dei
Nobili Ecclesiastici.

7 March 1911
Undersecretary of the Congregation for Extraordinary Ecclesiastical
Affairs (1 February 1914 its Secretary).

3 April 1917
Appointment as Apostolic Nuncio to Bavaria.

13 May 1917
Consecrated titular Archbishop of Sardes by Benedict XV in the Sistine
Chapel.

1 May 1920
Appointment as (the first ever) Nuncio to the German Reich.

29 March 1924
Signing of the Concordat with Bavaria.

14 July 1925
Departure from Munich and move to Berlin (in addition, Nuncio to Prussia).

9 July 1929
Acceptance of the Concordat with Prussia by the Prussian Diet.

16 December 1929
Appointed Cardinal-Priest of Santi Giovanni e Paolo, and on 7 February 1930 Cardinal Secretary of State.

20 July 1933
Concordat with the German Reich—the "attempt to save for a most uncertain future the concordats with the states Bavaria, Prussia and extend their scope both geographically and in content" (Pius XII, 19 July 1947).

5 November 1936
Franklin Delano Roosevelt, since 3 November President of the USA, receives the Cardinal Secretary of State during his visit to the USA, beginning a lifelong correspondence with Pacelli.

14 March 1937
The encyclical *Ardenti cura* ("Mit brennender Sorge"), in the writing of which the Cardinal Secretary of State played a significant part, condemns the violations of the Concordat, the un-Christian teachings and practices of National Socialism.

2 March/12 March 1939
Election and coronation as Pope.

18 February 1946
Creation of thirty-two cardinals from all over the world.

1 November 1950
Apostolic constitution *Munificentissimus Deus* defining the dogma of the Assumption of the Blessed Virgin Mary into Heaven.

12 January 1953
Creation of twenty-four cardinals (among them Angelo Roncalli).

8 September 1953
With the encyclical *Fulgens corona gloriae*, the following year—the centenary of the proclamation of the dogma of the Immaculate Conception—is declared a Marian Year.

9 October 1958
Death of Pius XII.

In the Church and the World

7 February/20 February 1878
Death of Pius IX, succeeded by Leo XIII.

20 July/4 August 1903
Death of Leo XIII, succeeded by Pius X.

28 June/28 July 1914
Assassination of the Austrian heir-apparent, Archduke Franz Ferdinand, and his wife at Sarajevo; Austria-Hungary declares war on Serbia, from which the First World War develops.

20 August/3 September 1914
Death of Pius X, succeeded by Benedict XV.

23 May 1915/28 August 1916
Italy declares war on Austria-Hungary and Germany.

21 November 1916
The Austrian Emperor Franz Joseph dies, and is succeeded by Charles I.

6 April/7 December 1917
The USA declares war on Germany and Austria-Hungary.

13 May 1917
First appearance of Our Lady at Fatima.

7 November 1917
Outbreak of the Bolshevik Revolution in Russia.

10/11 November 1918
Kaiser Wilhelm II goes into exile in Holland; Emperor Charles I of Austria renounces any share in the government of Germany-Austria.

11 February 1919
Friedrich Ebert is elected President of the German Reich.

22 January/6 February 1922
Death of Benedict XV, succeeded by Pius XI.

28 February/26 April 1925
Death of the German President Friedrich Ebert, succeeded by Field Marshal von Hindenburg.

10 April 1932
Hindenburg is elected President of the German Reich.

30 January 1933
Hindenburg appoints Adolf Hitler German Chancellor.

24 March 1933
The Reichstag passes the Enabling Act giving the German government power for four years to issue decrees without approval of Parliament (even ones not in accordance with the constitution).

10 February 1939
Death of Pius XI.

1 September 1939
Beginning of the campaign against Poland, from which the Second World War developed.

8 December 1941
The USA enters the war.

25 July/10 September 1943
Mussolini is overthrown; German troops occupy Rome.

4 June 1944
Allied occupation of Rome.

7 May/9 May 1945
Unconditional surrender of the German armed forces.

23 May 1949
Establishment of the Federal Republic of Germany.

25 March 1957
The treaties for the establishment of the European Atomic Energy Community and the European Economic Community are signed in Rome.

BIOGRAPHICAL AND HISTORICAL

BACKGROUND NOTES

Benedict XIV
Prospero Lorenzo Lambertini, 1675–1758
1727 Bishop of Ancona; 1726 Cardinal *in pectore* (published 1728); 1731
Archbishop of Bologna; from 17 August 1740 Pope.

Benedict XV
Giacomo Paolo Giovanni Battista della Chiesa, 1854–1922
1907 Archbishop of Bologna; 1914 Cardinal; from 3 September 1914 Pope.

Bertram, Adolf Johannes
1858–1945
1906 Bishop of Hildesheim; 1914 Prince Bishop of Breslau (Wroclaw);
1916 Cardinal *in pectore* (published 1919); 1930 Prince Bishop and
Metropolitan of the Province of Breslau; from 1919 Chairman of the
German Bishops' Conference in Fulda, and consequently in an exposed
position during the Church's struggle against the Nazis.

Boden, Leonard
1911–1999
Renowned British portrait painter, who in 1957 painted the only portrait
for which Pope Pius XII granted sittings. Other subjects included Queen
Elizabeth and Margaret Thatcher.

Dutch Bishops' Protest
Aspects of Sister Pascalina's account on p. 116 have been disputed. She was
correct about the retaliation and the international news reports
regarding it. On 31 July 1942, calling this action a countermeasure

("*Gegenmaßnahme*") to the Dutch Bishops' pastoral letter, Reich Commissioner for the Netherlands Arthur Seyss-Inquart reported to his superiors the arrest of "around 4,000 [not 40,000] Christian Jews and their transport to a camp [Westerbork] in Holland, where they are being held for the time being." The Dutch bishops' protest was known and reported internationally, for example in the *New York Times*, 23 September 1942, page 10.

Epple, Sister Friedberta
1890–1957
Began working as one of the housekeepers at the nunciature in Berlin in 1927.

Faulhaber, Michael von
1869–1952
1910 Bishop of Speyer; 1917 Archbishop of Munich and Freising; 1921 Cardinal; defender of the Church against the Nazis. Collaborated with Cardinal Pacelli in drafting the 1937 papal encyclical for Pope Pius XI, *Mit brennender Sorge*.

Fiordelli, Pietro
1916–2004
1954–1991 Bishop of Prato; lawsuit brought against him for his 1958 public denunciation of a couple who had a civil marriage, which he termed "a state of concubinage." The court awarded the couple damages but an appeals court later overturned the verdict.

Frings, Josef
1887–1978
1942–1969 Archbishop of Cologne; 1946 Cardinal; 1945–1965 Chairman of the German Bishops' Conference in Fulda.

Galen, Count Clemens August von
1878–1946
1933 Bishop of Münster; 1946 Cardinal; a courageous opponent of the religious persecution and anti-Semitism of the Nazis. Beatified 9 October 2005.
Gasparri, Pietro
1852–1934
1877–1879 Professor of Ecclesiastical History and Theology, Pontifical

Roman Seminary; Professor of Canon Law, Pontifical Urbaniana Athenaeum de Propaganda Fide and Pontifical Roman Athenaeum S. Apollinare; 1870–1898 Professor of Canon Law at the Institut Catholique in Paris; 1907 Cardinal; 1914–1930 Cardinal Secretary of State. Major achievements: the Codex Juris Canonici and the Lateran Treaty.

Grabmaier, Sister Maria Konrada
1914–1995
Served as a housekeeper with Sister Pascalina at the Vatican from 1938 until 1958.

Guarducci, Margherita
1902–1999
Archaeologist, researched and published on epigraphy of St. Peter's tomb. Specialist in Classical and Christian History, professor at the University of Rome; a member of various learned academies (Accademia Nazionale dei Lincei, Papal Roman Academy for Archaeology, British Academy in London, Mainzer Akademie der Wissenschaften); a full member of the German Archaeological Institute in Berlin; President of the Commission for Italian Inscriptions of the National Academic Union (Unione Accademia Nazionale) of Italy.

Hettich, Sister Edgar
1896–1955
Replaced Sister Theodosia Weber as cook for the Berlin nunciature in 1927, and moved with Sister Pascalina to the Vatican, where she worked until 1929.

Innocent XI (Bl.)
Benedetto Odescalchi, 1611–1689
1645 Cardinal; 1646–1650 Legate in Ferrara; 1650–1654 Bishop of Novara; from 21 September 1676 Pope. Beatified 7 October 1956.

John XXIII (St.)
Angelo Giuseppe Roncalli, 1881–1963
1925 titular Archbishop of Areopolis and Vicar Apostolic in Bulgaria; 1944 Nuncio in Paris; 1953 Cardinal and Patriarch of Venice; from 28 October 1958 Pope.
Beatified 3 September 2000; Canonized 27 April 2014.

Kaas, Ludwig
1881–1952
1918 Professor of Canon Law at the diocesan seminary in Trier; 1928–1933 Chairman of the Center Party; from 1934 Secretary of the College of Cardinals; 1936 Administrator of St. Peter's Basilica, Rome (in this capacity responsible for the archaeological excavations under St. Peter's).

Kolb, Sister Johanna
1894–1985
Assigned in 1917 to the nunciature as cook, but stayed only briefly before leaving for a mission assignment in Africa, where she served for the rest of her life. Sister Antonia Reichenberger replaced her in Munich.

Leiber, Robert, S.J.
1887–1967
From 1924 a collaborator of Eugenio Pacelli in Munich, Berlin and Rome; 1930 Professor of Church History at Pontifical Gregorian University, Rome.

Mindszenty, József
1892–1975
1944 Bishop of Veszprém; 1945 Archbishop of Esztergom and Primate of Hungary; 1946 Cardinal; 1948 sentenced to life imprisonment as an anti-Communist, freed in the 1956 uprising; asylum in the American Embassy until 1971, when he moved to Vienna.

Mit brennender Sorge
"With burning concern"—1937 encyclical of Pius XI, written in German rather than the usual Latin. Most available English translations do not adequately convey the powerful message of the original German, nor the impact the document had at the time. The final text was smuggled into Germany and quietly printed at locations across the country. It was secretly distributed to all the Catholic churches in Germany and read from the pulpits on Palm Sunday, 21 March 1937. Retaliation was swift: printing companies were raided and forced to close if evidence was found that they had printed copies of the encyclical. *Time* magazine reported the encyclical on 29 March 1937, and mentioned the Nazis' angry response in a footnote on 5 April 1937, Vol. 29 Issue 14, pp. 51–52: "Angered by the Pope's charges that his concordat with the Reich had been violated, Nazis

last week threatened to void or revise it. In Rome German diplomats boycotted Vatican Holy Week services."

Niehans, Paul
1882–1971
Swiss doctor who worked for the International Red Cross during World War II; developed "cell therapy."

Pacelli, Prince Carlo
1903–1970
Doctor utriusque juris, Consistorial Advocate; worked on the Lateran Treaty with his father Francesco Pacelli; from 2 April 1938 "Councillor General of the Vatican City."

Paul VI
Giovanni Battista Montini, 1897–1978
1922–1954 in the Papal Secretariat of State, one of the closest collaborators of Pius XII; 1952 Pro-Secretary of State; 1954 Archbishop of Milan; 1958 Cardinal; from 21 June 1963 Pope.

Pfanner, Sister Ewaldis
1898–1991
Served in Berlin and Rome from 1927 until the death of Pope Pius XII.

Pius IX (Bl.)
Count Giovanni Maria Mastai-Ferretti, 1792–1878
1827 Archbishop of Spoleto; 1832 Bishop of Imola; 1840 Cardinal; from 16 June 1846 Pope.
Beatified 3 September 2000.
Pius X (St.)
Giuseppe Sarto, 1835–1914
1884 Bishop of Mantua; 1893 Cardinal and Patriarch of Venice; from 4 August 1903 Pope.
Canonized 29 May 1954.

Pius XI
Achille Ambrogio Damiano Ratti, 1857–1939
1888 elected to the College of Doctors at the Ambrosian Library, 1914

Prefect of the Vatican Library; 1918 Apostolic Visitor to Poland; 1919 Nuncio to Poland and titular Archbishop of Lepanto; 1921 Cardinal and Archbishop of Milan; from 6 February 1922 Pope.

Preysing, Count Konrad von
1880–1950
1932 Bishop of Eichstätt; 1935 Bishop of Berlin; 1946 Cardinal; defender of the Church against attacks by the Nazis and Communists.

Reichenberger, Sister Antonia
1893–1981
Served as cook in the Munich nunciature from 1917–1920. When she was sent to Africa in 1920, Sister Theodosia Weber came to replace her.

Schoch, Sister Maria Berchmans
1903–1994
Began working at the Munich nunciature in 1924 and then served with Sister Pascalina in Berlin.

Sonnenschein, Carl
1876–1929
1900 ordained priest; from 1918 in Berlin, where he organized pastoral work among academics and city-dwellers.

Spartacists
Communist revolutionaries of the Spartacus League, founded during World War I by Karl Liebknecht, Rosa Luxembourg, and others.

Spellman, Francis Joseph
1889–1967
1932 Auxiliary Bishop of Boston; 1939 Archbishop of New York; 1946 Cardinal.

Stepinac, Alojzije (Bl.)
1898–1960
1937 Archbishop of Zagreb; 1953 Cardinal; 1946 sentenced to 16 years' forced labor, from 1951 on interned in Krašiæ.
Beatified 3 October 1998.

Tardini, Domenico
1888–1961
One of the closest collaborators of Pius XII in the Secretariat of State; from 1952 Pro-Secretary of State; 1958 Archbishop of Laodicea di Siria, in the same year Cardinal and Secretary of State.

Tisserant, Eugene
1884–1972
1908–1936 at the Vatican Library; 1936 Cardinal and Secretary of the Congregation for the Oriental Churches; from 1951 Dean of the College of Cardinals.

Wagner, Sister Hilaria
1901–1985
Began working in the Munich nunciature in 1924 and continued in Berlin as housekeeper and seamstress until 1927. In 1936 she went on mission to Chile, where she remained for the rest of her life. Her replacement in Berlin was Sister Friedberta Epple.

Walle, Sister Bonifatia
1889–1967
Assigned with Sister Pascalina to the nunciature in Munich for housekeeping and sewing in 1918. Sister Bonifatia returned to the motherhouse in 1920, and Sister Hilaria Wagner took her place.

Weber, Sister Theodosia
1892–1974
First in Munich nunciature and then in Berlin, Sister Theodosia served as cook until Sister Edgar Hettich replaced her in 1928.

Wendel, Josef
1901–1960
1943–1952 Bishop of Speyer; 1952 Archbishop of Munich and Freising; 1953 Cardinal.

INDEX